AF518096

Sovereigns of Software

Sovereigns of Software

Platforms That Govern More Than States

By

Leena Qureshan-Vale

Vij Books

New Delhi (India)

Published by

Vij Books
(Publishers, Distributors & Importers)
4836/24, 3rd Floor, Ansari Road
Delhi – 110 002
Phone: 91-11-43596460
Mobile: 98110 94883
e-mail: contact@vijpublishing.com
www.vijbooks.in

Copyright © 2026

ISBN: 978-81-99802-60-5 (HB)

ISBN: 978-81-99802-61-2 (PB)

ISBN: 978-81-99802-66-7 (eBook)

All rights reserved.

No part of this publication may be reproduced, distributed, or transmitted in any form or by any means — including photocopying, recording, or other electronic or mechanical methods — without the prior written permission of the publisher, except in the case of brief quotations used in reviews or permitted by applicable copyright law.

This book was developed using advanced writing tools to support the drafting and ideation process. All content has been thoughtfully curated, refined, and reviewed to ensure quality and relevance.

Contents

Introduction

A notification arrives without ceremony. A developer, perhaps still half-asleep, opens an email that is neither threatening nor apologetic. It announces a policy update. The language is abstract, almost antiseptic. A clause has been clarified. An exception has been narrowed. Enforcement will begin in seven days. By the end of the month, the business that once employed a dozen people, served hundreds of thousands of users, and paid its taxes on time no longer exists. There is no hearing, no appeal that feels real, no public record of deliberation. There is only compliance, or disappearance.

Scenes like this unfold daily across the digital economy. They rarely make the news. No sirens sound. Yet their cumulative effect reshapes markets, livelihoods, and public life with a quiet efficiency that would make any historical ruler envious. A small change in an app store policy can erase years of work overnight. A tweak to a recommendation system can redirect attention, income, and influence on a continental scale. A revised definition of "acceptable behaviour" can redraw the boundaries of speech for millions. These are not glitches. They are exercises of power.

We are accustomed to thinking of power as something that resides in parliaments, courts, and ministries. We learn to recognise it in uniforms, seals, and legal texts stamped with authority. Power, in this older picture, announces itself. It is debated, contested, and recorded. What confronts us now is something more elusive. Decisions that govern vast populations are made in private meeting rooms, enforced by software systems, and explained, if at all, in terse emails or automated notices. They feel less like product choices and more like decrees, even as they arrive wrapped in the language of terms of service and community standards.

This book begins from a simple, unsettling observation. Major digital platforms now govern core parts of our economies and public spheres, often more directly than states do. They decide who may speak, who may trade, which businesses may reach customers, which ideas circulate freely, and which are quietly buried. They collect revenue through commissions that function like taxes, adjudicate disputes without judges, and enforce rules without police. Their authority is rarely total, but it is pervasive. It reaches into daily life with an intimacy that traditional institutions have never achieved.

Such a claim can sound provocative, even exaggerated, until one pauses to examine how governance actually operates in the digital age. Governance is not only about flags and constitutions. It is about rule-making, enforcement, and the capacity to shape behaviour at scale. Platforms excel at all three. Their rules are encoded into the very architecture of interaction. Their enforcement mechanisms operate continuously, automatically, and often invisibly. Their reach crosses borders with indifference to jurisdictional neatness. In practice, they are among the most consequential governors of our time.

This is not a book that treats platforms as villains by default, nor as neutral tools misunderstood by anxious regulators. It treats them as what they have become: complex political-economic systems that wield power, face constraints, and make choices with moral and social consequences. The aim is neither to demonise nor to excuse, but to understand. To map how platform governance works in detail. To ask where it succeeds, where it fails, and where it overreaches. And, crucially, to explore how it might be redesigned without breaking the innovation and connectivity that made these systems valuable in the first place.

The questions at stake are urgent, but they are not unprecedented. History offers many moments when new forms of power emerged faster than the institutions meant to contain them. Merchant guilds once governed trade routes with private rules and sanctions. Chartered companies exercised quasi-sovereign authority over distant territories. Railway monopolies dictated the rhythms of industrial life. Each case forced societies to confront uncomfortable questions about legitimacy, accountability, and the proper limits of private rule-making. The digital platforms of today belong to this lineage, even as their scale and speed set them apart.

What makes the current moment distinctive is not merely the concentration of power, but its mode of operation. Platform governance is enacted through code. Rules are not only written; they are executed automatically, at a tempo that leaves little room for deliberation or contestation. Enforcement does not knock at the door; it simply switches off access. This gives platform authority a peculiar quality. It is at once brittle and formidable, flexible and unforgiving. A line of text in a policy document can cascade through ranking systems, payment rails, and moderation queues, altering outcomes far beyond what its authors anticipated.

Throughout this book, a recurring metaphor will surface: the platform as a layered city. At the base lie the infrastructures, data centres, and networks that make connection possible. Above them sit operating systems, app stores, and payment systems, each with its own gates and tolls. Higher still are the visible streets of feeds, marketplaces, and messaging channels, where users encounter one another. Rules operate at every level. Control exerted in the lower layers constrains everything built above. To understand platform power, one must learn to read this city vertically, not just stroll through its most familiar avenues.

For individuals, the stakes are immediate and personal. A creator's income depends on opaque recommendation criteria. A small business's survival hinges on compliance with shifting marketplace rules. A user's voice can be amplified or silenced by moderation systems they barely understand. For societies, the stakes are broader still. Platforms shape public discourse, influence electoral dynamics, mediate access to information, and increasingly serve as partners in governance itself, from public health messaging to emergency response. When these systems malfunction, or when their incentives misalign with public values, the consequences are not abstract.

It is tempting to treat these developments as the inevitable price of technological progress. Faster systems, larger networks, and global reach demand simplified governance, so the story goes. Yet inevitability is a comforting illusion. Every platform rule reflects a choice: about risk tolerance, commercial priorities, legal exposure, and social responsibility. Many of these choices are reasonable. Some are defensible only from a narrow internal perspective. Others persist simply because they are easier than alternatives. This book insists on taking those choices seriously, precisely because they are choices.

The chapters that follow open the black boxes of platform governance. They begin by reframing platforms as rule-making systems rather than neutral intermediaries, comparing their authority with that of states in practical terms rather than slogans. They move inside the organisations themselves, tracing how policies are drafted, translated into product changes, and enforced by a mix of humans and machines. They examine the fraught terrain of content moderation, where abstract principles collide with messy human behaviour and global cultural diversity.

Economic governance receives equal scrutiny. App stores and marketplaces are explored not merely as distribution channels, but as gatekeepers whose commission structures resemble private tax regimes. Data localisation and jurisdictional conflict reveal how territorial states push back against borderless clouds, often with unintended consequences that entrench incumbents and deepen inequality. Algorithmic accountability exposes the power of ranking systems to shape attention and opportunity, while also confronting the limits of transparency in complex technical environments.

Competition, long the preferred lens for addressing private power, is treated with both respect and scepticism. Antitrust remedies promise much, but risk collateral damage if they ignore technical realities. Interoperability, often invoked as a cure-all, brings its own governance challenges. Cross-border compliance and platform diplomacy show companies navigating a world of conflicting laws and informal pressures, increasingly acting as quasi-diplomatic actors in their own right.

The later chapters turn explicitly constructive. They examine how governments and platforms already coordinate, for better and worse, and how civil society and users can gain a more meaningful voice in decisions that affect them. They propose principles for legitimate platform authority, not as abstract ideals, but as practical guides for policy design. They explore experiments in oversight, co-regulation, and institutional design that aim to rebalance power without stifling innovation.

None of this is offered as a final settlement. Governance, digital or otherwise, is a living practice. It evolves through conflict, adaptation, and learning. What this book offers instead is a set of lenses and questions. Who writes the rules, and who enforces them. Which interests are represented, and which are absent. How decisions made under pressure today shape the possibilities of tomorrow. Where responsibility should lie when harm occurs, and how redress can be made real rather than symbolic.

There is a deeper tension running beneath these questions. Platforms thrive on scale, speed, and standardisation. Democratic governance thrives on deliberation, contestation, and context. The friction between these logics is not a temporary glitch; it is a structural feature of our digital age. Ignoring it leaves us oscillating between overreaction and complacency, between calls for heavy-handed regulation and faith in self-correction that experience has not earned.

To read this book is to accept that the familiar categories of public and private, state and market, no longer map cleanly onto the realities we inhabit. Software has become a site of governance. Product decisions have become political decisions, whether their makers intend them to or not. The question is no longer whether platforms govern, but how, on whose terms, and to what ends.

As you turn the page, consider the next policy update that will arrive unannounced in someone's inbox. Consider the next algorithmic adjustment that will quietly reorder attention. Consider the next moment when a platform's internal metric collides with a public value. These moments are not marginal. They are the front lines of contemporary governance.

What would it mean to treat them with the seriousness they deserve. What kinds of institutions, norms, and expectations would need to change. And what role might readers, as users, builders, policymakers, or citizens, play in shaping a digital order that is neither naive about power nor resigned to its abuses. The chapters ahead do not promise easy answers. They promise clarity, context, and the tools to ask better questions in a world increasingly governed by software.

Chapter 1

Platforms As New Sovereigns

On a quiet afternoon, a post vanishes. No warning, no explanation beyond a reference to a clause few users have ever read. The author searches the help centre, submits an appeal, and waits. Days pass. The post does not return. Nothing dramatic has occurred—no court order, no police knock, no public announcement—yet a decision has been made and enforced. Speech has been curtailed. Somewhere else, a small marketplace seller discovers their account suspended after an automated review flags a payment irregularity. Funds are frozen. Customer messages go unanswered. The seller's business, legal in every jurisdiction it serves, exists now in a kind of limbo. These moments feel strangely familiar, as if drawn from the machinery of the state, yet they unfold entirely outside it.

There is a paradox at work. The organisations making these decisions insist they are not governments. They are companies, platforms, service providers. Participation is voluntary. Rules are contractual, not constitutional. And yet the effects of their decisions are often indistinguishable from exercises of public authority. They define who may speak, who may trade, and on what terms. They enforce compliance with sanctions that are swift and difficult to contest. They change the rules with little notice and no vote. If sovereignty once implied a monopoly on legitimate coercion, platforms have discovered a different route to power: control over the environments in which economic and social life now take place.

This chapter begins with a claim that may initially unsettle. Major platforms function as new sovereigns, not by replacing states, but by governing alongside them, sometimes more effectively and sometimes more intrusively. To understand this shift requires abandoning the comforting fiction that platforms are neutral conduits and examining them instead as rule-making systems. Their terms of service, community guidelines, and developer policies are not peripheral documents. They are the operating charters of digital spaces, mini-constitutions that quietly define the boundaries of participation.

Every large platform maintains a dense web of rules. Some are written in legalistic prose, others embedded directly into product design. Together they determine which content is amplified or suppressed, which businesses gain access to users, which forms of behaviour are rewarded, tolerated, or punished. A social media platform's speech rules can shape political discourse more directly than electoral law. A marketplace's seller policies can determine which goods circulate globally and which are effectively banned. An app store's developer guidelines can decide which innovations reach consumers and which never leave the prototype stage. These are not abstract powers. They are exercised daily, at scale, through systems designed for speed and consistency rather than deliberation.

Seeing platforms as sovereign-like actors does not mean pretending they are states in disguise. The differences matter, and they matter profoundly. State authority rests, at least in principle, on collective legitimacy. It is authorised through constitutions, elections, and laws passed in public forums. Its enforcement mechanisms are constrained by due process and subject to review. Platform authority, by contrast, is grounded in ownership and contract. Users consent by clicking a box. Developers agree to terms they cannot negotiate. Enforcement is delegated to automated systems and dispersed teams whose decisions are rarely visible beyond the affected account.

Consider how disputes are resolved. A business accused of violating a regulatory standard can expect a process that, however slow or imperfect, includes notice, explanation, and the possibility of appeal before an independent body. When a platform trust-and-safety team suspends an account, the equivalent path often runs through a support ticket system, templated responses, and opaque escalation criteria. There is no public hearing, no precedent-setting judgment, and little sense of proportionality beyond internal metrics. The contrast is not merely procedural. It reflects fundamentally different conceptions of accountability.

Yet platform power also diverges from state power in its efficiency and reach. Automated enforcement systems can act instantly, across millions of users, without the resource constraints that limit public authorities. A change in policy can be deployed globally overnight. This capacity has made platforms attractive partners to governments seeking quick solutions to complex problems, from misinformation to fraud. It has also allowed platforms to fill governance gaps that states were slow, unwilling, or unable to address. The result is not a clean handover of authority, but an overlapping patchwork in which private rules increasingly structure public life.

To grasp how this governance actually operates, one must look beyond individual policies and examine the layered architecture of digital ecosystems. Power does not sit in a single place. It accumulates across infrastructure, operating systems, app stores, recommendation engines, and payment rails. Control exercised at one layer constrains everything built above it. A decision about payment processing can quietly foreclose entire categories of digital service. A change in operating system permissions can reshape competition among apps. A tweak to recommendation algorithms can reorder attention and revenue without altering a single written rule.

These layers are often invisible to users, yet they are decisive. Imagine a new digital service that complies with every content rule and consumer protection law, only to be blocked because it relies on a payment model that violates an app store's fee structure. No law has been broken. No regulator intervenes. And yet the service cannot reach users at scale. The gatekeeping function is exercised not through explicit prohibition, but through architectural constraint. This is sovereignty by design.

The rise of platforms as default governors did not occur by accident. It was enabled by a combination of speed, complexity, and political hesitation. Digital technologies evolved faster than legislative processes could adapt. Online speech, data flows, and cross-border services posed problems that resisted traditional regulatory tools. Faced with these challenges, policymakers often turned to industry self-regulation as a pragmatic stopgap. Platforms were encouraged to develop community standards, safety policies, and compliance mechanisms, sometimes with explicit government endorsement.

This reliance hardened into habit. In areas such as content moderation and data handling, platform rules became the de facto baseline against which acceptable behaviour was measured. Governments cited company policies as evidence of responsibility. Regulators deferred to internal enforcement systems. What began as provisional delegation gradually acquired the weight of expectation. Platforms were not only permitted to govern; they were expected to do so, even as their incentives remained primarily commercial.

The consequences of this arrangement are unevenly distributed. Those with resources, legal teams, and direct access to platform policymakers can often navigate the rules, influence their interpretation, or secure exceptions. Others cannot. Small developers, whose businesses depend on a single platform, face existential risk from policy changes they had no hand in shaping. Users in the global South encounter rules designed with different cultural assumptions and limited local consultation. Civil society organisations, invited to provide input through consultations, often find their contributions marginalised or ignored once commercial priorities reassert themselves.

The absence of these voices is not merely a moral failing. It is a governance problem. Rules written without broad representation tend to misfire, producing unintended harms and eroding trust. When grassroots organisations mobilise to influence a policy consultation, they are often confronted with compressed timelines, technical language, and decision-making processes that remain firmly internal. Participation is offered, but power remains concentrated. The result is a growing legitimacy gap between those who write the rules and those who live under them.

This chapter does not argue that platforms should simply be stripped of their governing functions. That would ignore the realities that gave rise to their authority in the first place. Nor does it suggest that states can effortlessly reclaim control without trade-offs. Instead, it seeks to clarify what kind of power platforms exercise, how it differs from traditional sovereignty, and why that difference matters. Understanding is a precondition for reform.

At stake is a question as old as political thought and as current as the next software update: who gets to make the rules that bind us, and under what conditions. Platforms have answered this question pragmatically, often ingeniously, sometimes recklessly. Their answers are embedded in code, contracts, and organisational routines. They are rarely debated as matters of governance, yet that is precisely what they are.

As the chapter unfolds, it will trace the mechanics of platform rule-making, compare them with familiar forms of state authority, and unpack the layered structures through which control is exercised. It will examine how platforms came to occupy this role, and whose interests are served or sidelined as a result. The aim is not to indict, but to illuminate. To see platforms clearly is to recognise both their capacity to coordinate complex systems and their tendency to concentrate power without commensurate accountability.

The pages ahead invite the reader to hold two ideas in tension. Platforms are extraordinary engines of innovation and connection. They are also governors, whether they acknowledge the role or not. The challenge is not to choose between these truths, but to reckon with their coexistence. Only then can the conversation move beyond slogans towards the harder work of designing governance that matches the power we have already created.

Seeing platforms as rule-making systems

In August 2020, Apple removed *Fortnite* from the App Store. The decision followed Epic Games' introduction of an alternative in-app payment system, which breached Apple's developer guidelines. The place was Cupertino by proxy, the date was precise, and the outcome was immediate: one of the world's most popular games vanished from hundreds of millions of devices overnight. No court order compelled the removal. No regulator intervened first. A rule was enforced, and access was withdrawn.

What made the episode instructive was not its visibility, but its ordinariness. App removals happen daily. Accounts are suspended, features disabled, rankings adjusted. The difference here lay in scale and symbolism. Apple insisted it was merely applying contractual terms to a developer that had agreed to them. Epic argued that those terms functioned as a form of private law, enforced without meaningful consent. Both were right, which is precisely the point.

This is governance by rulebook. Quiet power.

Platforms are often described as intermediaries, hosts, or conduits. These labels obscure more than they reveal. In practice, large platforms operate as rule-making systems that write, enforce, and revise the conditions under which social and economic life unfolds within their boundaries. Their terms of service, community standards, and developer policies are not marginal legal artefacts. They are foundational documents that define permissible behaviour, allocate rights, and prescribe penalties. They are mini-constitutions, even when drafted without constitutional ambition.

To see this clearly, it helps to begin with the act of writing rules. Platform policies are produced by teams that combine legal expertise, public policy analysis, product management, and engineering constraints. The resulting documents read like contracts, but they function like statutes. They establish categories of speech, commerce, and conduct. They specify obligations and exceptions. They reserve broad discretion to the platform itself. Crucially, they are unilaterally amendable. When a platform updates its rules, users and developers are notified after the fact. Consent is presumed through continued use.

The abstraction becomes visible when translated into behaviour. On social media platforms, speech rules determine which posts are removed, which are demoted, and which trigger account penalties. A prohibition on "coordinated inauthentic behaviour" sounds technical until it results in the takedown of a political campaign's pages. A ban on "adult sexual content" appears clear until artists, educators, or minority communities find their material repeatedly flagged. Each rule draws a boundary. Each boundary reshapes who may speak, and how.

Marketplaces apply the same logic to trade. Seller policies define acceptable products, pricing practices, and customer interactions. In 2019, Amazon revised its marketplace rules to restrict certain forms of third-party data use by sellers, a change announced from Seattle and implemented globally. The policy altered competitive dynamics overnight. Some sellers adapted. Others exited. No legislature debated the merits. The rulebook changed, and the market followed.

The same structure governs those who build on platforms. Developer guidelines specify technical requirements, content standards, and business models. They determine whether an application may access certain system features, collect specific data, or monetise in particular ways. Compliance is binary. Approval or rejection. The implication is stark. Innovation is permitted, but only within parameters defined by the platform owner.

Naming this arrangement as governance clarifies what is otherwise misread as mere product design. Platforms do not simply facilitate interaction; they organise it through rules backed by enforcement capacity. The explanation for why this matters lies in how those rules are enforced. Enforcement is not occasional or discretionary. It is continuous. Automated systems scan content, transactions, and code for violations. Human reviewers intervene at scale, guided by internal manuals rather than public law. Sanctions are applied with speed that states can rarely match.

Consider Facebook's content moderation system in the years following its 2018 policy overhaul, prompted by scrutiny after the Cambridge Analytica revelations. Rules governing hate speech, misinformation, and civic integrity were rewritten and expanded, with enforcement handled through a combination of machine learning classifiers and tens of thousands of human moderators distributed globally. The behaviour was measurable.

Removal rates increased. False positives rose. Appeals surged. Governance left an audit trail in metrics, not judgments.

The implication is not that platform enforcement is arbitrary, but that it is optimised for scale rather than deliberation. Courts tolerate delay to protect rights. Platforms tolerate error to protect throughput. This trade-off is rarely explicit in policy texts, yet it defines users' lived experience. An account suspended in error may be reinstated days later, but the damage is already done. Speech missed its moment. Income was interrupted. Trust eroded.

A credible counter-example complicates the picture. Wikipedia, governed by the Wikimedia Foundation, also operates through rules, policies, and enforcement mechanisms. Yet its governance feels different. Policies are drafted through open deliberation. Enforcement decisions are contestable. Authority is distributed among volunteer editors rather than concentrated in corporate management. The limitation is scale and scope. Wikipedia's model works because its mission, incentives, and revenue structure differ fundamentally from profit-driven platforms. The reconciliation is instructive. Rule-making is unavoidable at scale; the question is how it is legitimised and constrained.

Legitimacy is where platform governance diverges most sharply from state governance. States claim authority through collective processes, however imperfect. Platforms derive authority from ownership and user choice. The argument runs that users can leave. Developers can build elsewhere. This exit-based legitimacy has force in theory, but weakens in practice when network effects and switching costs are high. A speech platform with billions of users is not easily abandoned. An app store tied to a dominant operating system offers no equivalent alternative. Choice exists, but it is thin.

This thinness becomes apparent in moments of conflict. When a regulator disputes a company's conduct, there are procedures, timelines, and standards of evidence. When a platform trust-and-safety team disputes a user's conduct, the process is internal, the criteria opaque, and the outcome final more often than not. Support tickets replace hearings. Automated notices replace reasoned opinions. The visible behaviour is silence.

The gate appears again here. Platforms are gates with rules.

Updating rules completes the picture. Platform policies are living documents, revised in response to public pressure, regulatory risk, or internal learning. Speed is an advantage. Harmful practices can be addressed quickly. But rapid change also destabilises those who depend on the rules for planning and compliance. A developer building a business model around a permitted practice may find it prohibited months later. A community that learned to express itself within one set of boundaries must adjust to another. Stability, a traditional virtue of law, is sacrificed for adaptability.

This dynamic was evident when YouTube updated its monetisation policies in January 2018 following advertiser backlash over extremist content. Channels previously deemed acceptable were demonetised en masse. The rule change was explained as a safety measure. The measurable effect was a sharp decline in income for thousands of creators, many of whom had not produced the content at issue. Governance by proxy took its toll.

The recurring motif of the gate matters because it captures both protection and exclusion. Gates can keep out harm. They can also keep out dissent, competition, and novelty. Platforms build gates because they must manage risk at scale. States build gates because they must balance rights and order. The resemblance is not accidental. Both are engaged in governance, albeit under different constraints.

What distinguishes platforms is not that they govern, but that they govern without the settled expectations that accompany public authority. Their rulebooks are dense yet unstable. Their enforcement is powerful yet impersonal. Their legitimacy rests on consent that is formal rather than meaningful. This combination produces a peculiar form of sovereignty: effective, contested, and largely untheorised.

The unresolved tension lies here. Platforms cannot stop making rules without ceasing to function. States cannot ignore platform rules without losing practical influence over digital life. Users and developers navigate between them, subject to both, represented by neither fully. The test that follows is not whether platforms should have constitutions, but whether their rule-making can acquire constraints, participation, and accountability commensurate with its impact. The gate is already built. The question is who holds the key.

How state power and platform power differ

On 6 January 2021, as crowds breached the United States Capitol in Washington, DC, Twitter suspended President Donald J. Trump's account. The decision was taken within hours, announced publicly, and justified by reference to Twitter's Civic Integrity Policy. Two days later, on 8 January, the account was permanently banned. The place was unmistakable, the date indelible, and the outcome immediate. A sitting head of state lost access to a primary channel of communication, not by court order or parliamentary vote, but by the application of a private company's rules.

The contrast with what might have happened through state mechanisms is stark. In constitutional systems, restrictions on an elected leader's speech would trigger hearings, appeals, and fierce procedural debate. Here, enforcement was swift and unilateral. The platform acted as judge and executor, citing risk assessments rather than statutes. Authority moved faster than law.

Power moved faster.

This episode crystallised a confusion that has been building for years. Platforms insist they are not states and do not claim sovereign authority. Governments insist that only states possess legitimate coercive power. Yet the lived experience of millions suggests something more complicated. Platforms and states now exercise authority over the same spaces—speech, markets, and civic life—but through radically different mechanisms. To understand the new politics of software, one must compare these forms of power without forcing false equivalence.

Begin with legitimacy. States ground their authority in collective processes. Elections confer mandates. Legislatures debate and pass laws. Courts interpret and constrain executive action. Even when these processes fail, their existence provides a shared grammar for contestation. Platform authority rests elsewhere. It is derived from ownership of infrastructure and the consent implied by use. Users agree to terms. Developers accept guidelines. Legitimacy is contractual, not democratic.

The abstraction becomes concrete when measured against behaviour. Voter turnout, however low, signals participation in state legitimacy. Platform legitimacy is inferred from retention rates and daily active users. When Facebook reports billions of monthly users, the metric doubles as a claim of relevance. Exit is the only formal check. Voice is mediated through feedback forms and public pressure. The implication is clear. Where states seek periodic consent through elections, platforms infer consent continuously through engagement.

This difference matters because consent behaves differently under pressure. A citizen dissatisfied with a government can organise, vote, litigate, or protest without leaving the country. A user dissatisfied with a dominant platform faces a harsher choice. Leave and lose access to networks, audiences, or markets, or stay and comply. Network effects thin the reality of choice. The result is a legitimacy gap that widens as platforms become more essential.

Accountability deepens the divergence. States are accountable through layered institutions. Regulators oversee industries. Courts review administrative decisions. Journalists scrutinise conduct. Records are kept. Decisions can be challenged years later. Platform accountability operates through internal processes designed for speed and scale. Trust-and-safety teams enforce policies. Appeals run through ticketing systems. Transparency reports aggregate outcomes without revealing deliberation.

A dispute illustrates the contrast. In April 2018, the UK Information Commissioner's Office fined Facebook £500,000 for data protection failures related to Cambridge Analytica. The investigation took months. Evidence was gathered. Findings were published. Facebook contested aspects of the ruling. The process was slow and imperfect, but it left a public trail. Compare this with a typical platform enforcement action. A publisher's page is suspended for "policy violations". An appeal is lodged. A templated response arrives. The page remains offline. There is no published reasoning, no precedent, and no independent review. Accountability exists, but it is inward-facing.

Enforcement completes the triad. States enforce rules through institutions authorised to use force, bounded by law. Police, inspectors, and courts act within defined jurisdictions. Penalties escalate gradually. Platforms enforce through access control. Accounts are suspended. Content is removed. Payments are frozen. Enforcement is immediate and global. No warrant is required to deactivate an account. Code executes the sanction.

Automation intensifies this difference. Platforms rely heavily on automated systems to detect violations. In 2020, YouTube reported removing over nine million videos in a single quarter, the majority flagged by machine learning systems. The metric signals efficiency. It also signals error. Automated enforcement trades context for scale. A police officer must justify an arrest. An algorithm must meet a confidence threshold. The implication is a shift from discretionary judgment to probabilistic governance.

A counter-example complicates the picture. Some state functions now mirror platform practices. Automated traffic enforcement uses cameras and algorithms to issue fines without human intervention. Tax authorities deploy risk-scoring systems to flag irregularities. These tools accelerate enforcement and reduce discretion. Yet they remain embedded within legal frameworks that provide avenues for challenge. A speeding ticket can be contested in court. An algorithmic content removal rarely can. The reconciliation lies in institutional backstops. Automation is not the problem; insulation from review is.

The quiet motif threading through these differences is the queue. State power moves through queues designed to slow decisions: dockets, hearings, appeals. Delay is a feature. Platform power moves through queues designed to clear decisions: moderation pipelines, ranking systems, automated flags. Speed is a virtue. Each system reflects its priorities. States value procedural fairness, even at the cost of efficiency. Platforms value continuity of service, even at the cost of error.

This divergence shapes behaviour. Companies design products to avoid regulatory scrutiny because they anticipate long investigations. They design content strategies to avoid platform penalties because enforcement is immediate. The risk calculus shifts. A fine years later can be budgeted. A takedown tomorrow cannot. Platforms thus exert a form of anticipatory control, nudging behaviour before any rule is enforced.

The difference between elections and user choice sharpens the point. Elections aggregate preferences periodically, forcing trade-offs into the open. User choice is individual and continuous, expressed through clicks and time spent. Platforms read these signals as feedback, but they are not votes. They do not express reasons, only outcomes. A user scrolling past political content does not register opposition; they register disengagement. Governance by metric replaces governance by mandate.

Yet it would be misleading to cast states as slow and platforms as reckless. States often struggle to act quickly in crises. Platforms can respond within hours. During the early months of the COVID-19 pandemic in 2020, platforms rapidly adjusted their misinformation policies, removing content that contradicted public health guidance. Governments welcomed the assistance. Speed saved lives. The limitation was consistency. Guidance changed. Rules shifted. Content removed one week was permitted the next. Platforms enforced evolving norms without the deliberative scaffolding that legitimises change in public law.

The comparison is not a morality play. It is a structural analysis. States and platforms optimise for different failures. States fear illegitimacy. Platforms fear breakdown. States tolerate inefficiency to preserve rights. Platforms tolerate error to preserve flow. When platforms govern spaces once overseen by states, these trade-offs migrate with them.

The unresolved tension is practical. As platforms continue to exercise authority over speech, markets, and access, should their power be constrained to resemble state power, with slower processes and stronger procedural rights? Or should states adapt, accepting faster, more automated forms of governance with thinner safeguards? The queue can be lengthened or shortened. Neither option is free.

The test that follows is diagnostic. When a decision affects millions, who should decide it, how quickly, and with what recourse. The answer is no longer obvious.

Layers of control in digital ecosystems

In June 2020, Apple rejected updates to *Hey*, a new email service built by Basecamp. The reason was not security, nor content, nor legality. It was payment. Apple's App Store rules required digital services to offer in-app subscriptions through Apple's billing system, with a commission attached. *Hey* did not. Within days, the app's future on iOS was in doubt. The organisation was Apple. The place was Cupertino by authority, even as the dispute played out publicly. The outcome was blunt: without compliance at one layer of the system, the service could not exist at another.

This was not a clash of personalities. It was a demonstration of structure. Control did not announce itself as censorship or prohibition. It appeared as a dependency. The payment rule sat below the application. It constrained everything above it. The ladder mattered.

Power stacks.

Digital platforms are not monoliths. They are layered systems in which authority is distributed across technical and organisational strata. Infrastructure enables operating systems. Operating systems host app stores. App stores filter applications. Applications rely on recommendation systems for visibility and payment rails for revenue. Each layer carries its own rules. Control exercised at one layer narrows the range of possibilities at the next. To understand platform governance, one must read vertically.

Begin at the base. Infrastructure includes data centres, networks, and cloud services. It is here that uptime, latency, and resilience are decided. When Amazon Web Services suspended Parler's hosting in January 2021 following concerns about violent content, the effect was immediate. The organisation was Amazon, the date was January 10, and the service went dark. No app store approval mattered once the servers were offline. The abstraction of "acceptable use" translated into a concrete behaviour: termination of hosting. The implication was clear. Infrastructure providers can exercise decisive control without touching user-facing rules.

Move up a layer to operating systems. Mobile operating systems determine what software can do at a fundamental level. Permissions govern access to sensors, storage, and background processes. In September 2021, Apple introduced App Tracking Transparency on iOS, requiring apps to obtain explicit user consent before tracking across other companies' apps and websites. The rule was implemented globally through the operating system itself. The measurable effect followed quickly. Meta reported a significant impact on advertising revenue in subsequent earnings calls. The behaviour was user prompts. The decision sat at the OS layer. The implication was market-wide.

App stores sit above operating systems and below applications. They are choke points. Approval processes decide which apps may be distributed and under what conditions. Ranking algorithms determine visibility. Featured placements confer advantage. Rules here shape competition more directly than antitrust law ever could, simply because they operate before a product reaches the market. When Apple or Google change app store guidelines, thousands of businesses adjust in response. Some comply. Some exit.

The *Hey* dispute illustrated how app store rules collapse multiple layers into one decision. Payment policy was enforced through distribution control. The service was lawful. Users wanted it. The block occurred because revenue flows violated a lower-layer rule. After public pressure, Apple allowed a compromise. The gate opened slightly. The ladder remained.

Recommendation systems add another layer of control, one that is subtler and often more powerful. These systems decide what users see, in what order, and with what frequency. Visibility becomes governance. In 2018, Facebook adjusted its News Feed algorithm to prioritise "meaningful social interactions", a change announced from Menlo Park. The metric shifted. Engagement with friends rose. Traffic to publishers fell sharply, as documented by Chartbeat data in 2018. No content was banned. Distribution changed. The implication was economic. Media businesses rose or fell based on ranking logic they could not inspect.

Payment rails complete the stack. They determine how value moves. Credit card networks, app store billing systems, and digital wallets impose rules that shape what can be sold and how. In December 2020, Visa and Mastercard suspended payment processing for Pornhub following allegations about illegal content. The companies were Visa and Mastercard. The place was Montreal, where Pornhub is based. The outcome was immediate loss of revenue channels. The visible behaviour was transaction denial. The implication extended beyond one site. Entire categories of lawful content became financially risky.

This is not moral judgement. It is structural observation. Payment rules act as private regulation. They define acceptable commerce by deciding which transactions clear. Risk is measured in chargebacks and reputational exposure. Enforcement is automated. Appeals are limited. The ladder narrows again.

A credible counter-example tempers the analysis. Open web services, built on standard protocols like HTTP and SMTP, distribute control more evenly. No single app store approves websites. Payments can route through multiple processors. Hosting can migrate. The limitation is friction. User experience suffers. Security risks increase. Scale is harder. The reconciliation is instructive. Concentrated control reduces friction but increases dependency. Distributed control increases resilience but demands effort.

Each layer justifies its rules in functional terms. Infrastructure providers cite safety and reliability. Operating systems cite privacy and performance. App stores cite security and user trust. Recommendation systems cite relevance and engagement. Payment rails cite fraud and compliance. These claims are not false. They are incomplete. Each rule also reallocates power. Each constraint privileges some actors over others.

The quiet motif of the ladder returns here. Developers climb it to reach users. Creators climb it to reach audiences. Businesses climb it to reach revenue. At every rung, rules apply. Miss one, and the ascent stops. The ladder is efficient. It is also unforgiving.

Metrics make this visible. App store rejection rates spike after policy changes. Creator income fluctuates with algorithm updates. Payment declines rise when categories are reclassified as high-risk. These are not edge cases. They are signals of governance at work.

The implication for innovation is ambiguous. Layered control can protect users and enable trust at scale. It can also freeze experimentation by making compliance too costly for newcomers. Large firms absorb policy shifts. Small ones fold. The result is not always intentional, but it is predictable.

The unresolved tension is vertical. Should power be concentrated in fewer layers to reduce risk and friction, or distributed to preserve choice and contestability. Each decision moves the ladder. The test ahead is practical. When a service fails, ask where it failed in the stack, and who wrote the rule at that rung.

Why platforms became default governors

In May 2016, in Brussels, the European Commission announced a "Code of Conduct on Countering Illegal Hate Speech Online". Facebook, Twitter, YouTube, and Microsoft signed on. The date was precise. The organisations were named. The outcome was practical: participating platforms committed to review the majority of flagged content within twenty-four hours, using their own community standards as the primary reference point. No directive was passed. No court rewrote doctrine. Public authority endorsed private rules as a baseline.

Speed decided everything.

This moment did not signal abdication. It signalled accommodation. Faced with rapidly escalating online harms and limited institutional capacity, policymakers chose to work with the systems already in place. Platform self-regulation became the scaffolding on which public expectations were hung. What began as a pragmatic response hardened into a governing pattern.

To understand how platforms became default governors, one must begin with the mismatch between the tempo of innovation and the pace of law. Digital services iterate weekly. Features launch, fail, and relaunch within months. Legislatures deliberate over years. The abstraction of "speed" becomes visible in release cycles. A platform can deploy a global policy change overnight. A statute may require consultation, drafting, committee review, and judicial interpretation before it takes effect. The implication is not incompetence. It is structural lag.

Complexity compounded the problem. Online speech, data flows, and cross-border services resisted the neat categories of existing law. A single post could be lawful in one jurisdiction and illegal in another. Data collected in one country might be processed in several more. Regulators struggled to map authority onto systems designed to ignore borders. Platforms already possessed the technical means to intervene. Governments did not.

The result was reliance. Policymakers turned to industry to set norms where public rules were absent or contested. The European Commission's 2016 code exemplified this approach. Rather than legislate speech standards across twenty-eight member states, it endorsed platform community standards as operational tools. The visible behaviour was reporting dashboards and removal rates. According to Commission monitoring reports in 2017 and 2018, platforms increased review speed and removal percentages. The metric reassured. Governance advanced without legislation.

This pattern repeated elsewhere. In the United States, Section 230 of the Communications Decency Act, enacted in 1996, insulated platforms from liability for user content while encouraging voluntary moderation. The law's intent was limited. Its effect was expansive. Platforms were free to write and enforce their own rules at scale. Courts deferred. Legislators hesitated. The implication was durable self-regulation.

Political hesitation played a quieter role. Regulating speech and data invites constitutional conflict. Free expression, privacy, and innovation sit in uneasy balance. Governments feared backlash, litigation, and accusations of censorship or overreach. Delegating rule-making to platforms offered cover. Decisions could be framed as corporate policy rather than state action. Responsibility blurred.

The abstraction of "risk" becomes concrete here. For a minister, proposing strict speech regulation risks electoral backlash and legal challenge. For a platform, tightening moderation risks user churn but preserves regulatory goodwill. Each actor optimises differently. The equilibrium favoured private rulebooks.

A second named example sharpens the picture. In October 2019, the UK Home Office published the Online Harms White Paper, signalling intent to regulate platforms but acknowledging that companies already operated extensive safety systems. The place was London. The document cited existing platform standards as reference points. The visible behaviour was consultation rather than command. Years passed before legislation followed. In the interim, platforms continued to govern.

This does not mean states were idle. Data protection offers a counterpoint. The EU's General Data Protection Regulation, enforced from May 2018, imposed binding obligations on data handling. Fines followed. Compliance teams expanded. Here, public law asserted itself decisively. The limitation was scope. GDPR addressed data, not speech or market conduct in the same granular way. The reconciliation matters. States can act when mandates are clear and consensus exists. Where uncertainty dominates, they defer.

Complexity also resided inside the platforms. Their systems were opaque even to their creators. Recommendation algorithms, content classifiers, and ad auctions produced outcomes that resisted simple explanation. Regulators lacked tools to intervene without unintended consequences. Industry self-regulation appeared safer than blunt law.

The motif of the stopgap threads through this history. Self-regulation was meant to be temporary, a bridge until public frameworks caught up. Yet stopgaps solidify when they work tolerably well. Platforms met response targets. Harm appeared reduced. The urgency faded. The bridge became the road.

Metrics reinforced the shift. Governments measured success through takedown rates and response times. Platforms optimised to those numbers. What was measured improved. What was not—fairness, proportionality, representation—remained secondary. Governance narrowed.

A credible limitation deserves attention. Self-regulation sometimes failed spectacularly. The spread of misinformation during elections, documented by academic studies and parliamentary inquiries between 2016 and 2020, exposed gaps in platform enforcement. Governments responded with sharper scrutiny. New laws followed in Germany, Australia, and elsewhere. The reconciliation is dynamic. Default governance persists until failure becomes undeniable.

Why did states accept this arrangement for so long. Because it solved immediate problems without demanding institutional overhaul. Because platforms bore the cost. Because voters noticed outcomes more than processes. The abstraction of "efficiency" appears here as reduced complaint volumes and faster removals. The implication is fragile legitimacy.

The chapter's earlier sections traced how platforms write rules and enforce them. This section explains why they were allowed—encouraged—to do so. Not because they sought sovereignty, but because governance vacuums invite occupants. Speed, complexity, and hesitation created space. Platforms filled it.

The unresolved tension is temporal. Self-regulation bought time. How much time remains. When public authority leans on private standards, it gains speed but loses authorship. The test ahead is simple to state and hard to answer. When the next crisis arrives, who writes the rules first, and who merely endorses them.

Who is missing from the decisions

In October 2014, Facebook announced a change to its "real name" policy in San Francisco. For years, the rule had required users to register under the company's definition of their authentic identity. After sustained pressure from LGBTQ activists, drag performers, and civil liberties groups, Facebook softened its enforcement and introduced a process for users to explain unusual names. The organisation was Facebook. The place was its headquarters city. The date was precise. The outcome was modest but real. Some accounts were restored. The rule bent.

An empty chair mattered.

What made the episode notable was not that Facebook listened, but that the moment was rare. The campaign had required months of mobilisation, public criticism, and meetings with senior staff. Well-resourced advocacy groups such as the Electronic Frontier Foundation amplified the issue. Media attention followed. Only then did a policy change occur. For every such case, countless others pass unnoticed, their affected communities absent from the room where rules are written.

Platform governance is often described in terms of documents and systems. Less attention is paid to participation. Who gets to speak when platform rules are drafted, revised, or enforced. Whose experiences shape definitions of harm, safety, and acceptable conduct. Whose costs are counted, and whose are treated as collateral. The answers reveal a persistent imbalance. Small developers, users from the global South, and civil society groups are structurally under-represented in decisions that bind them.

Begin with small developers. Platform policies are drafted with scale in mind. They presume legal teams, compliance budgets, and engineering resources. A change in an app store guideline may require weeks of refactoring or a new revenue model. Large firms absorb the cost. Independent developers do not. The abstraction of "flexibility" becomes visible in headcount. When Apple revised App Store Review Guidelines in June 2020, following disputes over subscription rules, major media companies negotiated bespoke arrangements. Solo developers rewrote code or withdrew features. The metric was not intent. It was survival.

This imbalance persists because consultation channels privilege those who can engage. Platforms do solicit feedback. They publish draft policies. They invite comments. But participation demands time, expertise, and confidence that engagement will matter. A two-week consultation window, announced via a policy blog, is accessible to in-house counsel. It is invisible to a small developer running a business alone. The implication is predictable. Input skews towards incumbents.

Global South users face a different exclusion. Platform rules are typically written in a handful of languages, reflecting the legal and cultural contexts of North America and Europe. Enforcement, however, is global. When moderation systems apply the same standards in Nairobi, Jakarta, or São Paulo, local nuance is lost. This is not malice. It is design.

A named example illustrates the point. In March 2018, Facebook faced criticism in Myanmar for its handling of content related to ethnic violence against the Rohingya. United Nations investigators later concluded that the platform had been used to incite violence, citing inadequate local language moderation and slow response. The organisation was Facebook. The place was Myanmar. The outcome was severe. The company later acknowledged failures and expanded local expertise. The implication was stark. Rules written far from affected communities failed to protect them.

Pair the abstraction of "capacity" with behaviour. Facebook employed only a handful of Burmese-speaking moderators during a critical period, according to a 2018 Reuters report. The decision reflected resource allocation. The cost was borne by users. Governance without representation produced harm.

Civil society groups occupy a middle position. They possess expertise and legitimacy but lack formal power. Platforms increasingly engage them through advisory councils, consultations, and partnerships. These mechanisms promise inclusion. Their limits are visible in outcomes. Recommendations may be acknowledged without being adopted. Reports may be cited without altering enforcement.

A second named example brings this into focus. In 2019 and 2020, Facebook conducted global consultations ahead of launching its Oversight Board. Organisations such as Access Now and Article 19 submitted detailed proposals on transparency and due process. Meetings were held in Delhi, London, and New York. The dates are recorded. The process was extensive. When the Board launched, some recommendations appeared in its charter. Others did not. The visible behaviour was selective incorporation. The implication was partial voice.

This is not unique to Facebook. Platforms face genuine constraints. Opening rule-making too widely risks delay and incoherence. Commercial confidentiality limits disclosure. There is a credible counter-example worth acknowledging. Wikipedia's community-driven governance includes editors from around the world, with policies debated openly and enforced by peers. Representation is broader. The limitation is reach. Wikipedia's model relies on volunteer labour and a non-profit structure. It does not scale easily to profit-driven platforms with billions of users. The reconciliation matters. Inclusion is possible, but it requires alignment of incentives.

The quiet motif of the empty chair returns here. Decisions are made with some seats filled and others vacant. The absence is not always intentional. It is structural. Platforms are headquartered in a few cities. Their leadership teams share similar professional backgrounds. Their risk assessments prioritise markets with regulatory clout. Smaller markets, less organised communities, and informal economies receive less attention.

Metrics reinforce this pattern. Platforms track user growth, revenue, and regulatory exposure by region. Investment follows numbers. Where advertising revenue is low, policy resources lag. The abstraction of "global community" dissolves into a heat map. Governance follows the money.

The implications extend beyond fairness. Exclusion distorts rule quality. Policies designed without input from affected groups are more likely to misfire. Enforcement errors increase. Trust erodes. Users adapt by self-censoring, gaming systems, or disengaging. Developers design around constraints rather than innovating. The system becomes brittle.

Yet inclusion is not a panacea. Platforms that attempt broad consultation face noise and capture. Well-organised groups can dominate discussions. Marginal voices remain marginal. The challenge is not simply to invite participation, but to weight it appropriately.

The earlier example of Facebook's real name policy shows both the possibility and the cost. Change occurred, but only after public conflict. The process rewarded those able to mobilise attention. Many could not. The empty chair remained.

As platforms continue to govern speech, markets, and access, the question sharpens. Who is authorised to speak for those affected. Who bears the burden of compliance. Who is heard before rules harden into code. The forward test is practical. The next time a platform revises a core policy, look at the table. Count the chairs. Notice who is missing.

Chapter 2

Inside Platform Rule-Making

Late on a Sunday evening, a draft document circulates through an internal mailing list. The subject line is bland. The content is not. A platform has been named in a headline that will run at dawn, and the policy team knows what follows: questions from journalists, calls from regulators, urgent messages from executives. Somewhere between the legal department and the engineering floor, a decision is already being shaped. By Monday morning, a policy update will be announced. By Tuesday, enforcement will begin. To the outside world, it will look like a sudden change of heart. Inside, it will feel like triage.

Moments like this puncture the myth that platform rules emerge fully formed from principled debate. They reveal something more human and more consequential. Platform governance is not only designed; it is reacted into being. It is written under pressure, revised in haste, and implemented through systems that magnify small choices into vast effects. To understand how platforms govern, one must go inside these processes, into the rooms where rules are drafted, translated into code, and enforced by people and machines who rarely appear in public narratives.

This chapter enters that interior. It traces the life of a platform rule from its first draft to its final execution, showing how abstract commitments harden into concrete outcomes. Along the way, it exposes a central tension. Platforms present their policies as stable frameworks, yet their governance is deeply dynamic, shaped by scandal, metrics, and organisational trade-offs. The result is a form of rule-making that is both powerful and precarious.

Policy drafting is the first act, and it is less solitary than it appears. Large platforms maintain dedicated policy teams staffed by former regulators, lawyers, and subject-matter experts. Their task is to anticipate risk, articulate standards, and translate executive priorities into language that can survive scrutiny. Legal teams hover close, ensuring compliance with overlapping jurisdictions. Communications staff weigh in on tone, anticipating public reaction. Engineers review feasibility, flagging rules that cannot be enforced at scale. The finished document is a compromise, not a manifesto.

Review cycles give this process an air of order. Policies are scheduled for periodic reassessment. Feedback is gathered. Changes are logged. Yet these rhythms are repeatedly disrupted by external events. A data breach, an election, a viral scandal can collapse months of deliberation into days. In such moments, policy becomes reactive. Decisions are made not because they are settled, but because delay is intolerable. The urgency of response reshapes governance, privileging visible action over careful calibration.

What follows is translation. A policy text, however carefully written, does nothing on its own. It must be operationalised. Enforcement guidelines are drafted to instruct reviewers on how to interpret ambiguous clauses. Review workflows are built, specifying which cases are automated, which are escalated, and which are ignored. Product teams adjust prompts, warnings, and default settings. A single sentence added to a policy can trigger changes across multiple systems.

Here, implementation details matter more than rhetoric. A minor tweak to a definition can alter how content is ranked or removed. A threshold adjustment can shift millions of posts from visibility to obscurity. Users rarely see these mechanics. They experience only the outcome: a sudden drop in reach, a warning label, a vanished listing. Governance expresses itself as friction.

Enforcement brings the human cost into focus. Platforms rely on vast enforcement apparatuses combining automated detection, human review, and user reporting. Each component compensates for the others' weaknesses. Machines provide scale and speed. Humans provide context and judgment. Users supply signals about harm. None is sufficient alone.

The trade-offs are unavoidable. Automated systems flag content quickly but misread nuance. Human reviewers correct errors but face volume that strains accuracy and wellbeing. User reports surface edge cases but invite abuse. When platforms lean too heavily on automation, error rates climb. When they slow enforcement to improve accuracy, harm persists longer. Every choice leaves a trace in the data.

Appeals and transparency are meant to close the loop. Platforms offer channels for users and developers to challenge decisions, publish reports on enforcement activity, and experiment with oversight mechanisms. These tools signal accountability. They also reveal its limits. Appeals are often constrained by time, scale, and information asymmetry. Transparency reports aggregate outcomes but rarely explain reasoning. Oversight bodies review only a fraction of cases.

The experience of a small publisher contesting a mistaken suspension illustrates the imbalance. Weeks of correspondence may yield little more than scripted responses. The platform's internal review confirms its own decision. By the time an error is acknowledged, if it is acknowledged at all, the damage is done. Due process exists, but it is thin, stretched across systems designed for throughput rather than adjudication.

Underlying all of this are metrics. Dashboards glow in meeting rooms, translating complex social phenomena into numbers. Engagement rates, revenue figures, safety incidents, regulatory risk scores, measures of public trust. These metrics do not merely describe reality; they shape it. Teams optimise for what is measured. If a reduction in reported harm becomes a key performance indicator, enforcement tightens. If engagement dips after a policy change, adjustments follow. Governance responds to the graph.

This is not cynicism. It is organisational logic. Platforms operate at scales that demand quantification. Decisions must be comparable across regions and time. Metrics provide coherence. They also obscure. A decline in visible harmful content may reflect stricter moderation, or it may reflect migration to less visible channels. A rise in user satisfaction may mask the silencing of marginal voices. Numbers reassure, even when they mislead.

The deeper significance of this internal machinery lies in its distance from public oversight. States debate laws in assemblies. Courts publish opinions. Platforms govern through documents, code, and dashboards that are rarely visible. The locus of power shifts inward, away from forums of contestation and towards internal processes optimised for speed and risk management. Understanding these processes is essential for any serious discussion of platform accountability.

This chapter does not treat platforms as uniquely flawed. All large institutions struggle with similar tensions between principle and practice. Bureaucracies standardise. Metrics distort. Crises accelerate decision-making. What distinguishes platforms is the immediacy with which their internal choices affect public life. A policy drafted on a Sunday night can alter global discourse by Monday afternoon. Few institutions wield such leverage with so little delay.

There is a motif that runs through this chapter, one that mirrors the experience of those governed by platforms: translation. Values are translated into policies. Policies are translated into workflows. Workflows are translated into code. Code translates into outcomes. At each stage, meaning shifts. Intent thins. Power concentrates. To see where governance succeeds or fails, one must track these translations closely.

As the pages ahead unfold, they will follow rules through their lifecycle, from drafting rooms to moderation queues. They will examine who makes decisions, under what constraints, and with which incentives. They will show how external pressure bends internal logic, and how internal metrics quietly shape external realities. The goal is not exposure for its own sake, but comprehension.

Platform governance does not operate in the abstract. It operates through people, tools, and trade-offs. To understand its authority, one must understand its machinery. The chapter that follows invites the reader to look behind the policy announcement and into the systems that make it real, where governance is not declared, but executed.

How policies are drafted and updated

On 19 March 2018, in Menlo Park, Facebook announced a sweeping overhaul of its data policies in the wake of the Cambridge Analytica revelations. The company promised tighter controls, clearer consent, and new restrictions on third-party access. Within days, policy documents were rewritten, blog posts published, and engineers instructed to disable entire classes of data-sharing features. The scandal had broken publicly that week. The response was immediate. The rules moved fast.

Pressure writes policy.

That episode is often recalled for its political fallout, but its deeper significance lies elsewhere. It revealed how platform rules are made when time collapses. Under normal conditions, policy drafting is deliberate, procedural, and insulated. Under scandal, it becomes improvisational. External scrutiny does not merely influence outcomes; it reshapes the internal process itself. To understand platform governance, one must understand this oscillation between routine and rupture.

Under routine conditions, policy drafting inside large platforms follows a recognisable pattern. Dedicated policy teams initiate reviews based on scheduled cycles, emerging risks, or regulatory developments. These teams include former civil servants, lawyers, and subject specialists who translate broad commitments into enforceable language. Drafts circulate internally. Legal teams assess exposure across jurisdictions. Engineers test feasibility. Communications staff anticipate public interpretation. The result is a document that balances clarity, discretion, and implementability.

The abstraction of "cross-functional collaboration" becomes visible here as a chain of tracked edits and approvals. Policy drafts move through version control systems. Comments accumulate. Language tightens. A prohibition becomes a standard. A standard becomes an exception. Each change reflects negotiation. The implication is stability. Under these conditions, policy evolves incrementally, with revisions logged and explained.

Review cycles reinforce this stability. Platforms often schedule periodic reassessments of major policies, aligning them with product roadmaps or regulatory calendars. Feedback from enforcement teams informs adjustments. Transparency reports provide data points. The cadence reassures both staff and stakeholders. Governance appears measured.

Then a crisis hits.

Public scandals compress time. Media attention intensifies. Regulators demand answers. Advertisers threaten withdrawal. In these moments, the drafting process changes character. The same actors remain involved, but their priorities shift. Speed outranks elegance. Signalling matters. The goal is no longer only to write a good rule, but to demonstrate action.

The Cambridge Analytica response illustrated this shift. According to public statements by Facebook executives in March and April 2018, policy changes were accompanied by immediate product interventions, including app audits and access suspensions. Engineers implemented technical blocks before policy language had fully settled. The visible behaviour was feature shutdowns. The metric was trust recovery, measured in user sentiment and advertiser confidence. The implication was reactive governance.

This pattern recurs. After the January 2021 attack on the US Capitol, platforms revised civic integrity and violence policies within days. Twitter's updates to its Glorification of Violence Policy were published from San Francisco on 8 January 2021, hours before high-profile account suspensions. The drafting was accelerated. External pressure dictated the timetable. The rules followed the event.

Naming this dynamic matters because it explains why platform policies sometimes appear inconsistent. Observers note abrupt shifts and accuse companies of hypocrisy. The explanation is procedural. Under pressure, platforms prioritise risk mitigation. They accept overbreadth. They revise later.

The internal mechanics reveal the trade-off. Lawyers narrow language to reduce liability. Policy teams widen definitions to capture emergent harms. Engineers ask whether rules can be enforced at scale. Communications staff simplify explanations for public consumption. Each actor measures risk differently. The final text reflects compromise under constraint.

A second named example highlights the routine side. In May 2020, Google updated its Play Store Developer Program Policies, clarifying rules on location data access. The change followed months of consultation and was announced with advance notice. Developers were given a compliance window. Documentation was extensive. The place was Mountain View. The date was clear. The outcome was predictable adjustment rather than shock. Here, governance resembled regulation.

The contrast between these cases shows how context shapes process. Routine cycles favour predictability. Crisis cycles favour speed. Neither is neutral. Each produces different kinds of error. Incrementalism can lag emerging harms. Rush can overshoot.

A credible limitation deserves acknowledgment. Not all rushed policies are poorly conceived, and not all deliberate ones are wise. Some harms demand immediate action. When live-streamed violence spreads, delay carries cost. Platforms that act quickly can prevent escalation. The reconciliation lies in recognising that speed and care are not opposites, but variables to be managed. The problem arises when emergency mode becomes habitual.

External pressure does more than accelerate timelines. It reorders internal hierarchies. During scandals, executive attention intensifies. Decisions that would normally be delegated move upward. Policy teams gain authority. Engineering roadmaps are disrupted. The abstraction of "tone from the top" becomes visible in meeting attendance and sign-off requirements. Governance centralises.

Metrics again tell the story. During crises, dashboards prioritise regulatory risk indicators and negative press mentions. Engagement metrics recede temporarily. Teams adjust accordingly. Once pressure eases, priorities rebalance. Policies written under duress may then be softened or clarified. The rulebook remembers the crisis long after the headlines fade.

This cycle has implications for legitimacy. Users experience rules as arbitrary when they change suddenly. Developers struggle to plan. Civil society groups find consultations compressed or cancelled. Trust suffers. Platforms respond with transparency statements, but explanation cannot fully compensate for disruption.

The quiet motif threading through this process is the clock. Under routine governance, it ticks steadily. Under scandal, it races. Policy quality depends on which clock dominates. The question is not whether platforms can write good rules, but under what temporal conditions they do so.

The counter-example of data protection law sharpens the point. GDPR was drafted over years, debated publicly, and implemented with transition periods. When enforced in May 2018, companies scrambled, but the rules were known. Platform policies, by contrast, can change overnight. The reconciliation is instructive. Public law buys time through process. Private governance trades time for agility.

As platforms continue to serve as default governors, this drafting dynamic becomes more consequential. Each crisis tests whether rules are principled or expedient. Each routine review tests whether learning occurs. The forward test is unresolved. Can platforms design policy processes that preserve speed without sacrificing stability. Or will the clock always win.

From policy text to product changes

In January 2018, from Menlo Park, Facebook announced a modest-sounding update to its News Feed policy. The platform would prioritise "meaningful social interactions" over passive consumption of public content. The date was clear, the organisation unmistakable, the language carefully reassuring. Within weeks, publishers across Europe and North America reported traffic declines of 20 to 50 per cent, figures documented by analytics firms such as Chartbeat in 2018. Nothing in the policy text promised such an outcome. The ranking changed anyway.

A sentence moved. An industry shifted.

This gap between intention and effect is not accidental. It is structural. Platform policies do not govern directly. They govern through translation. Words on a page become instructions. Instructions become workflows. Workflows become product behaviour. At each step, interpretation intervenes. Small choices accumulate. By the time a rule reaches users, it no longer resembles its original phrasing. Governance lives in the implementation.

Policy texts are necessarily abstract. They describe categories of harm, acceptable conduct, and enforcement principles in general terms. This abstraction serves several purposes. It provides flexibility across jurisdictions. It allows adaptation to new cases. It protects platforms from committing to rigid standards they cannot enforce at scale. Yet abstraction also creates distance. The real decisions occur when these texts are operationalised.

The first translation occurs through enforcement guidelines. These internal documents instruct reviewers and engineers on how to apply policy language to concrete cases. Where a public policy may prohibit "misleading content", the guideline defines examples, thresholds, and edge cases. It specifies when to remove, when to reduce distribution, and when to ignore. The abstraction of "harm" becomes a decision tree.

This is where governance sharpens. Enforcement guidelines are rarely public. They evolve rapidly. They respond to observed behaviour rather than theoretical concern. A surge in borderline content triggers clarification. A media controversy prompts a new example. Reviewers rely on these documents to make thousands of decisions per day. Consistency depends on their clarity.

The next translation is procedural. Review workflows determine how cases move through the system. Content may be auto-flagged, queued for human review, escalated to specialists, or left untouched. Each step reflects a risk assessment. High-risk categories receive priority. Low-risk categories are sampled. The visible behaviour is throughput. The metric is cases processed per hour. The implication is uneven attention.

Product prompts embed these decisions into user experience. Warning labels, friction screens, and ranking adjustments communicate rules without stating them. A user posting a link may see a nudge discouraging sharing. A seller listing an item may encounter a restriction message. These prompts are policy in action. They shape behaviour more effectively than text most users never read.

The Facebook ranking change illustrates how minor policy tweaks can cascade. The public announcement framed the update as a quality improvement. The internal implementation adjusted weightings in the ranking algorithm, elevating comments and shares from friends over clicks on publisher links. The rule did not ban content. It reweighted signals. The outcome was measurable. Publisher reach declined sharply. User time spent with friends increased modestly. The implication was economic redistribution driven by an algorithmic interpretation of policy.

A second named example reinforces the point. In August 2020, Google updated its Search Quality Rater Guidelines, adding a stronger emphasis on "experience, expertise, authoritativeness, and trustworthiness" for health-related content. The place was Mountain View. The date was clear. The guidelines themselves were advisory, used by human raters to evaluate results. Yet subsequent algorithm updates led to noticeable ranking shifts, documented by SEO monitoring firms. Smaller health websites lost visibility. Established institutions gained. A policy clarification influenced product behaviour through iterative calibration.

Abstractions like "trust" acquire meaning through proxies. Domain age, backlink profiles, author credentials. These proxies are decisions. They privilege certain actors. They disadvantage others. The policy text remains neutral. The product outcome does not.

The importance of implementation details becomes clearer when errors occur. Automated systems apply guidelines at scale. When thresholds are set too low, false positives rise. In 2020, YouTube acknowledged removing videos discussing COVID-19 in ways that did not violate policy, due to automated detection tuned aggressively during the early pandemic. The organisation was YouTube. The behaviour was over-removal. The metric was reduced misinformation exposure. The implication was silenced legitimate speech.

A credible counter-example tempers the critique. Human review can correct algorithmic error. Platforms invest heavily in training moderators and refining guidelines. Error rates decline over time. The limitation is volume. With millions of decisions daily, human oversight cannot cover everything. The reconciliation is pragmatic. Automation is necessary, but its calibration determines harm.

The quiet motif threading through this section is the hinge. Policy text sits on one side. Product behaviour swings on the other. The hinge is implementation. It is small. It carries weight.

Metrics drive this hinge. Enforcement teams track precision and recall, balancing false positives against false negatives. Product teams monitor engagement, retention, and complaint rates. When a policy change produces unintended drops, adjustments follow. Governance becomes iterative, not declarative. The rule is less important than its effect on dashboards.

This dynamic complicates accountability. When users protest outcomes, platforms point to policy. When policymakers scrutinise policies, platforms point to complexity. Responsibility diffuses. The rulebook did not mandate harm. The algorithm merely implemented it. The gap widens.

The earlier example of Facebook's News Feed shows how this diffusion operates. When publishers complained, the company emphasised user experience goals. The policy language supported that claim. The algorithm delivered the outcome. No single decision could be isolated. Governance hid in the system.

Yet this opacity is not total. Researchers, regulators, and affected communities infer implementation through observation. Traffic patterns, takedown rates, and ranking volatility reveal shifts. Platforms respond by refining prompts and guidelines. The system adapts.

The unresolved tension remains. As platforms continue to govern through products, policy texts risk becoming performative. Real power sits in code and workflows that few outside the company see. The forward test is diagnostic. When a policy changes, ask not what it says, but where the hinge moved, and who felt the swing.

Enforcement teams, tools and trade-offs

In March 2020, as the COVID-19 pandemic accelerated, YouTube announced from San Bruno that it would remove videos contradicting guidance from the World Health Organization and national health authorities. Within weeks, creators reported the disappearance of lectures, news clips, and scientific discussions that did not advocate harm but mentioned contested hypotheses. YouTube later acknowledged errors, attributing them to automated systems tuned aggressively to stem misinformation at scale. The date was precise. The place was known. The outcome was measurable: over-removal followed by partial reversal.

Accuracy costs time.

That episode exposes the centre of platform enforcement: a permanent trade-off between scale and precision. Platforms do not enforce rules with a single instrument. They rely on a composite apparatus—human reviewers, automated detection systems, and user reports—each compensating for the others' weaknesses. The result is neither arbitrary nor fully controlled. It is probabilistic governance, optimised for throughput.

Begin with people. Human reviewers are the most visible yet least understood component of enforcement. Platforms employ tens of thousands of moderators, often through contractors, distributed across regions and languages. Their work is structured by internal guidelines and measured by productivity targets. A reviewer may assess hundreds of items per shift. The abstraction of "judgement" becomes a timer on a screen. Decisions must be fast.

The implications are documented. Studies by the Oxford Internet Institute and reporting by *The Guardian* between 2019 and 2021 describe high error rates under pressure and significant psychological strain. Reviewers see material most users never will. Exposure accumulates. Burnout rises. Platforms rotate tasks and provide support, but volume remains relentless. Human judgement improves accuracy, yet it does not scale without cost.

Automation enters to fill the gap. Machine learning systems scan text, images, audio, and behaviour patterns, flagging potential violations. They operate continuously, indifferent to fatigue. Their performance is tracked through metrics such as precision and recall. When tuned conservatively, harmful content slips through. When tuned aggressively, legitimate content is caught. The YouTube COVID response shows the consequence of choosing speed over nuance. The behaviour was mass removal. The metric was reduced exposure to misinformation. The implication was collateral suppression.

A second named example sharpens the contrast. In June 2020, Twitter reported in its transparency update that automated systems flagged the majority of accounts it challenged for platform manipulation. The place was San Francisco. The date was clear. The outcome was scale. Automation handled volume. Appeals revealed errors. Twitter adjusted thresholds. Governance iterated.

User reports form the third pillar. Platforms invite users to flag content they believe violates rules. This distributes detection across the network. It also introduces bias. Organised reporting can target unpopular speakers. Malicious reporting can overwhelm queues. Platforms respond with trust scores and rate limits. The abstraction of "community moderation" becomes a weighted signal.

Each tool reflects a decision about risk. Human review prioritises fairness but limits speed. Automation prioritises speed but sacrifices context. User reports prioritise coverage but invite abuse. Platforms blend them to manage trade-offs. The blend shifts with circumstance.

External pressure drives these shifts. During elections, crises, or scandals, platforms tighten automated thresholds and expand enforcement teams. Error rates rise. After scrutiny fades, thresholds relax. Appeals backlog clears. The cycle repeats. Governance oscillates.

A credible counter-example complicates the narrative. Some platforms deliberately slow enforcement in sensitive categories. Wikipedia relies heavily on human deliberation, with automated tools playing a supporting role. Accuracy improves. Scale suffers. The limitation is reach. Wikipedia's model depends on volunteer labour and narrower scope. The reconciliation is instructive. Enforcement design reflects mission and incentives.

The quiet motif threading through enforcement is the queue. Content enters a queue. Accounts enter a queue. Appeals enter a queue. How fast the queue moves defines experience. Platforms tune queues through staffing and thresholds. States tune queues through procedure. The difference is intention. Platforms seek continuity of service. States seek procedural justice. The queues diverge.

Metrics again reveal priorities. Platforms publish removal numbers, response times, and prevalence estimates. These figures reassure regulators and advertisers. They also steer behaviour internally. If response time becomes the headline metric, teams optimise for speed. If error rate draws scrutiny, teams slow down. The dashboard governs.

The unresolved tension remains unresolved by design. Perfect accuracy at scale is unattainable. Perfect speed with fairness is impossible. Platforms choose where to fail. The forward test is stark. When harm rises, will platforms accept more error, or more delay. Each choice governs differently.

Appeals, transparency and due process

In July 2019, in Berlin, the independent publisher *Netzpolitik.org* found its Facebook page abruptly suspended. The organisation, known for reporting on digital rights and surveillance, lost access to a primary distribution channel overnight. The notification cited violations of community standards. No examples were given. Traffic collapsed. Advertising revenue dipped. Editors filed an appeal the same day. Days passed. The page remained offline. Only after public attention and direct contact with Facebook representatives was the suspension reversed, quietly, with no formal explanation. The date was recorded. The place was clear. The outcome was survival, narrowly achieved.

Justice arrived late.

This episode is not remarkable because an error occurred. Errors are inevitable in systems operating at scale. It is remarkable because of how correction depended on visibility rather than procedure. The appeal worked not because the process functioned smoothly, but because the case escaped it. That distinction reveals the fault lines in platform due process: appeals exist, transparency mechanisms proliferate, yet the experience of justice remains uneven and contingent.

Platforms insist, with some justification, that they have expanded user protections dramatically over the past decade see internal reviews, clearer notices, appeals buttons, transparency reports, and even quasi-judicial oversight bodies. Compared with the opaque takedowns of the early 2010s, today's systems are more elaborate. The question is not whether due process exists, but what kind, for whom, and at what cost.

Begin with appeals. Most large platforms now provide formal mechanisms to challenge content removals, account suspensions, and demonetisation decisions. Users click a link, submit a form, and wait. The abstraction of "right to appeal" becomes a ticket number. Appeals are triaged. Some are reviewed by humans. Many are resolved automatically. Timelines vary. Outcomes are rarely explained in detail.

For an individual user, this may feel adequate. For organisations and small publishers, it can be existential. When a page or account is suspended, revenue, reach, and credibility suffer immediately. Appeals that take days or weeks impose costs that no eventual reinstatement can fully repair. The behaviour is measurable. Traffic drops to zero. Subscribers churn. Trust erodes.

The logic behind this design is efficiency. Platforms process millions of decisions daily. Appeals cannot all receive bespoke analysis. Standardisation keeps queues moving. Yet efficiency carries implication. Where speed is prioritised, explanation thins. Where explanation thins, legitimacy weakens.

Transparency mechanisms aim to compensate. Platforms publish regular reports detailing numbers of removals, categories of violations, response times, and prevalence estimates. These documents, often released quarterly, have improved public understanding. Facebook's Community Standards Enforcement Reports, first issued in 2017, marked a shift towards quantified accountability. They showed trends, investments, and error rates. The metric reassured regulators.

But transparency at scale is not transparency of reasoning. Aggregated data reveals patterns, not principles. It tells us how many posts were removed for hate speech, not why a particular post was removed. It shows enforcement volume, not deliberation. For those affected by individual decisions, the report is irrelevant. The appeal email still reads the same.

A second named example underscores this gap. In September 2020, YouTube suspended the channel of *TalkRadio*, a UK broadcaster, citing COVID-19 misinformation. The organisation appealed publicly, arguing that clips featured debate rather than advocacy. The suspension was reversed within hours. The place was London. The date was recorded. The outcome was swift correction. The reason was prominence. The appeal succeeded because it was amplified, not because the process inherently favoured accuracy.

These cases expose a two-tier system. High-profile actors access informal escalation channels. Smaller ones do not. Due process exists formally, but influence shapes outcomes.

Platforms have experimented with structural remedies. Facebook's Oversight Board, launched in October 2020 and headquartered legally in the United States but operating globally, reviews a small subset of content decisions. Its rulings bind the company on specific cases. It publishes detailed opinions. This is unprecedented in platform governance. It introduces something resembling jurisprudence.

The limitation is scope. The Board hears dozens of cases per year. Facebook moderates billions of pieces of content. The reconciliation is honest. Oversight is symbolic and instructive, not comprehensive. It signals values. It cannot deliver universal due process.

Developers face parallel challenges. App suspensions, demotions, and rejections often come with limited explanation. Appeal channels exist, but timelines are uncertain. A small developer whose app is removed from an app store loses distribution instantly. Revenue halts. Users receive error messages. Even when reinstated, rankings suffer. The behaviour is observable. Downloads fall. Recovery is slow.

Transparency for developers is similarly partial. Guidelines are public. Enforcement rationales are not. The rule is clear. The interpretation is not. Developers reverse-engineer compliance through trial and error. Governance becomes experimental.

A credible counter-example deserves attention. Some regulatory regimes impose explicit due process requirements on platforms. Germany's Network Enforcement Act, effective from January 2018, mandates complaint handling procedures and reporting obligations. Platforms must respond within set timeframes. This improves responsiveness. The limitation is jurisdictional. Global platforms apply these standards selectively. Users outside regulated markets receive weaker protections. The reconciliation highlights fragmentation. Due process varies by geography.

The quiet motif threading through appeals and transparency is the window. Platforms open windows into their systems through reports and oversight. The view is partial. Those inside see dashboards. Those outside see reflections. Appeals attempt to open a door. It is narrow.

Metrics again shape behaviour. Platforms track appeal success rates and turnaround times. These numbers influence staffing and automation. If appeals backlog grows, automation expands. If error rates draw criticism, thresholds adjust. Due process becomes another optimisation problem.

The implications extend beyond fairness. Weak due process discourages participation. Creators self-censor. Publishers diversify away from platforms or double down on them, accepting risk. Civil society groups invest resources in escalation rather than prevention. Governance becomes reactive.

Yet platforms are not indifferent. They face genuine constraints. Explaining every decision in detail would slow enforcement dramatically. Revealing enforcement logic risks gaming. Perfect assumption of good faith is unrealistic. Due process must balance transparency with resilience.

The unresolved tension remains unresolved because it is structural. Platforms govern at a scale that strains traditional notions of justice. States deliver justice slowly to preserve rights. Platforms deliver decisions quickly to preserve flow. Appeals sit between these logics, stretched thin.

The forward test is concrete. When the next mistaken suspension occurs, will correction depend on procedure or prominence. Until the answer is procedural, platform due process will remain conditional, its windows open just wide enough to glimpse accountability, but not wide enough to enter it.

Metrics that drive governance choices

In January 2018, at Facebook's headquarters in Menlo Park, a small group of executives approved a change to the News Feed ranking system. The public explanation emphasised wellbeing. Posts from friends and family would be prioritised over "passive" consumption of public content. The date was clear. The place was known. Within weeks, publishers reported sharp declines in referral traffic, with Chartbeat data in 2018 showing drops of between 20 and 50 per cent for many outlets. Engagement inside the platform rose modestly. The metric had moved. The system followed.

Numbers chose the rule.

This episode is often treated as a story about algorithms. It is better understood as a story about dashboards. Platform governance does not operate through abstract values alone. It operates through metrics that translate values into targets, targets into incentives, and incentives into decisions. What platforms measure becomes what they govern.

Every large platform maintains an internal landscape of numbers. Screens display engagement curves, revenue flows, policy violation rates, response times, advertiser sentiment, regulatory risk scores, and trust indicators derived from surveys or sentiment analysis. These metrics do not merely describe performance. They define it. Teams are evaluated against them. Resources follow them. When metrics shift, governance shifts with them.

Begin with engagement. Time spent, clicks, shares, comments, and watch time are not neutral indicators. They are proxies for attention, and attention is the raw material of platform business models. When engagement rises, revenue tends to follow. When it falls, alarm bells ring. Governance choices that affect content distribution are therefore scrutinised through their impact on engagement metrics.

The 2018 Facebook change illustrates this logic. Internal research suggested that certain forms of interaction correlated with reported user satisfaction. "Meaningful social interactions" became a measurable goal. The abstraction of wellbeing became a weighting adjustment in the ranking system. The visible behaviour was more comments between friends. The implication was less visibility for publishers. The policy text framed the change as user-centric. The metric enforced it.

Revenue metrics add another layer. Advertising yield, conversion rates, and subscription growth sit alongside engagement on dashboards. When enforcement actions threaten revenue, they attract scrutiny. This does not mean platforms avoid enforcement. It means they seek forms of enforcement that minimise commercial disruption. Demotion replaces removal. Labels replace bans. The rulebook adapts to the balance sheet.

A second named example clarifies the point. In September 2020, YouTube announced changes to its recommendation system to reduce the spread of borderline content. The place was San Bruno. The date was recorded. The company reported in subsequent transparency updates that watch time from such content declined. At the same time, overall watch time remained stable. The metric outcome mattered. Reduction without revenue loss signalled success. Governance held.

Safety metrics complicate this picture. Platforms track prevalence of harmful content, measured as views per million or similar ratios. These figures feature prominently in transparency reports. A decline suggests effective enforcement. Teams are rewarded. Yet prevalence is sensitive to measurement choices. Narrow definitions reduce counts. Broader ones inflate them. Governance debates often turn on these definitions.

The abstraction of "safety" thus becomes a denominator problem. What counts as harm. What is measured. When Facebook reported declines in hate speech prevalence in 2020 and 2021, critics questioned whether enforcement improved or measurement changed. Both can be true. The metric moves. Interpretation follows.

Regulatory risk metrics exert growing influence. Platforms track investigations, fines, legislative proposals, and political sentiment by jurisdiction. These indicators shape prioritisation. Markets with active regulators receive more policy attention. Content categories attracting political scrutiny see faster rule changes. The behaviour is observable. Local moderation teams expand in regulated regions. Elsewhere, capacity lags.

Public trust metrics attempt to bridge internal and external legitimacy. Surveys measure user confidence. Brand tracking assesses reputation. When trust dips, platforms respond with visible governance gestures: policy updates, transparency initiatives, oversight announcements. These actions aim to move sentiment scores. The implication is performative governance driven by perception.

A credible counter-example tempers the analysis. Some governance decisions reduce engagement and revenue deliberately. Twitter's efforts to curb spam and manipulation between 2017 and 2019, documented in company disclosures, removed millions of accounts. Active user numbers dipped temporarily. Trust indicators improved. The reconciliation matters. Metrics conflict. Platforms choose which to prioritise.

The quiet motif threading through this section is the gauge. Like instruments in a cockpit, metrics tell decision-makers whether they are climbing or descending. They do not show the terrain. A pilot can follow gauges into trouble if the instruments mislead. Governance faces the same risk.

Metric-driven adjustments to recommendations make this tangible. Recommendation systems are tuned continuously through A/B testing. Small cohorts receive altered rankings. Engagement and retention are measured. Successful variants scale. This process embeds governance choices into experimentation. A decision to downrank sensational content is tested against engagement loss. If the loss exceeds tolerance, the decision is softened. The rule survives only if the metric permits it.

The implication is iterative governance without debate. Values are encoded as hypotheses. Metrics decide which survive. This is efficient. It is also opaque.

Critics argue that this approach privileges what is measurable over what matters. Platforms respond that unmeasured values cannot be managed at scale. Both positions hold. The tension is unresolved because it is structural.

A limitation deserves emphasis. Metrics can mislead. Engagement does not equal satisfaction. Prevalence does not equal harm experienced. Trust scores fluctuate with news cycles. Platforms know this. They supplement metrics with qualitative research and expert review. Yet when decisions must be made quickly, numbers dominate.

The earlier sections traced how policies are written, implemented, and enforced. This section reveals the force that pulls them in one direction or another. Dashboards concentrate attention. They simplify complexity. They enable coordination across vast organisations. They also narrow vision.

The forward test is practical. As platforms assume greater governing responsibility, will they expand the set of metrics that matter, or continue to optimise those that are easiest to track. When a value resists quantification, will it be protected anyway. The gauges are glowing. The course is still being set.

Chapter 3

Content Moderation And Speech Rules

A single image appears on a screen. To one audience, it is a joke, shared with a wink and a shared cultural reference. To another, it is a slur. To a third it is propaganda. The same meme travels across platforms, languages, and political moments, shedding and acquiring meaning as it goes. Somewhere along the way, a decision must be made. Leave it up. Label it. Demote it. Remove it. That decision will be taken not by a court or a censor, but by a mixture of code, policy text, and human judgement operating under time pressure.

This is the daily reality of content moderation. It is less a single problem than a permanent condition, a continuous negotiation between expression and harm carried out at industrial scale. The public often encounters it only when something goes wrong: a post removed in error, a violent video left up too long, a controversial figure banned or reinstated. Yet behind each of these moments lies an elaborate system of classification, escalation, and enforcement that now shapes global speech more directly than any single legal regime.

Speech has always been governed, but never like this. States regulate expression through law, precedent, and due process, moving slowly and deliberately. Platforms regulate expression through policies that must operate instantly, across cultures and jurisdictions, and in volumes that defy traditional oversight. The result is not censorship in the classical sense, nor free speech as imagined in constitutional theory, but something stranger and more consequential: speech governed by systems optimised for scale, safety, and engagement.

This chapter enters that territory. It examines how platforms decide what counts as harmful or disputed content, and why those categories resist neat definition. Harassment, disinformation, hate speech, extremism, and what platforms call *borderline content* are not fixed objects. They are clusters of behaviour whose meaning depends on context, intent, and impact. A slogan used ironically in one community may incite violence in another. A piece of satire may be indistinguishable from manipulation to an automated filter. Legal categories strain under the weight of this ambiguity.

The difficulty begins with classification. Platforms must sort content into buckets that policies can act upon. This is an exercise in abstraction. Definitions are drafted to be general enough to cover new cases, yet specific enough to guide enforcement. Inevitably, they fail at the margins. Those margins are not peripheral. They are where culture, politics, and power collide.

Moderation models attempt to manage this complexity through structure. Some content is reviewed before it appears, often in narrow categories such as advertising or live-streamed violence. Most content is moderated after publication, triggered by user reports or automated flags. Prioritised queues elevate certain issues, while trusted flaggers, including civil society groups and government agencies, are granted fast-track access. In moments of heightened risk, such as elections or public health emergencies, specialised escalation paths come into play, diverting decisions to senior teams with additional context and authority.

These systems give the appearance of control. They are, in practice, a set of compromises. Pre-publication review slows speech and does not scale easily. Reactive reporting depends on who is watching and willing to report. Trusted flaggers concentrate power in a few hands. Escalation paths protect against catastrophic error, but only for a fraction of cases. Governance emerges not from any single model, but from their interaction.

At the centre of this machinery sit human moderators. Their labour is largely invisible, yet indispensable. They are trained to apply policy consistently, to recognise coded language, to escalate uncertainty. They work in shifts, often reviewing content that most users would rather not see. The psychological toll is well documented. Exposure accumulates. Burnout follows. Platforms invest in support measures, rotation, and counselling, but the work remains demanding. Clean feeds are not an accident. They are maintained by people absorbing the harm that others are spared.

Automation promises relief. Machine learning systems classify text, images, and video at speeds no human team could match. They identify patterns, flag anomalies, and remove content before it spreads. Their strengths are undeniable. Without them, moderation at scale would collapse. Yet their limits are equally clear. Automated systems struggle with context, irony, dialect, and evolving slang. They reproduce biases present in training data.

They misclassify satire as abuse and reclaiming language as hate. Human oversight remains necessary, even as human capacity is constrained.

These technical challenges are compounded by geography. Platforms write global rules, but speech is local. Cultural norms differ. Political risks vary. A slogan that is innocuous in one country may be incendiary in another. Protest content may be protected expression in one jurisdiction and criminalised in the next. Platforms respond with localisation, geoblocking, and country-specific enforcement. Each choice invites backlash. Remove content globally and face accusations of censorship. Leave it up locally and face accusations of complicity. There is no neutral ground.

The significance of these decisions extends beyond individual posts. Content moderation shapes public discourse, influences political mobilisation, and determines which voices are amplified or marginalised. It affects journalists, activists, comedians, and ordinary users alike. It also affects trust. When moderation appears inconsistent or opaque, users lose confidence. When it appears heavy-handed, accusations of bias follow. When it appears lax, harm proliferates. Platforms are judged from all sides, often simultaneously.

This chapter does not seek a single answer to these dilemmas. There is none. Instead, it traces the architecture of moderation: the categories, the models, the people, and the machines that together govern speech at scale. It shows how decisions are made, where they break down, and why improvement is slow and contested. It treats moderation not as a technical footnote, but as a central institution of contemporary public life.

A recurring image will guide the discussion: the filter. Filters remove impurities, but they also shape what passes through. They are calibrated, adjusted, and sometimes clogged. Too fine, and nothing flows. Too coarse, and harm leaks through. Content moderation is a continual act of filtering, carried out under conditions of uncertainty and pressure.

As the pages ahead unfold, they will move from classification to escalation, from human labour to machine judgement, from global policy to local backlash. They will ask what it means to govern speech without law, at a scale that law was never designed to handle. They will show why moderation controversies recur, and why they will not disappear.

The chapter opens a space for a harder question. If platforms have become the primary arbiters of speech for much of the world, what standards should guide them, and who should hold them to account. The answers are neither simple nor settled. That is precisely why they matter.

Types of harmful and disputed content

In September 2016, during the United States presidential campaign, a simple image circulated widely on Facebook and Twitter. It featured a cartoon frog, a few words of political commentary, and no explicit call to violence. The character was Pepe the Frog, originally created by the artist Matt Furie. By that point, the Anti-Defamation League had listed Pepe as a hate symbol when used in certain contexts. The platforms hesitated. Some instances were removed. Others remained. The same image, posted in New York and in Warsaw, produced different enforcement outcomes. The date was documented. The organisations were known. The result was inconsistency that angered all sides.

Meaning slipped.

This episode captures the central difficulty of content moderation: harmfulness is rarely intrinsic. It emerges from use, audience, timing, and repetition. Platforms are tasked with categorising content into operational buckets—harassment, disinformation, hate speech, extremism, and what they increasingly call *borderline material*—yet the boundaries between these categories are porous. Legal definitions, already strained offline, fracture under the pressure of networked communication.

Harassment appears, at first glance, the most straightforward. Direct threats, targeted abuse, and coordinated pile-ons produce visible harm. Platforms define harassment through behaviour rather than intent: repeated messages, unwanted contact, degrading language directed at an individual or group. The abstraction becomes concrete in metrics such as report frequency and account targeting patterns. A user receiving hundreds of hostile replies experiences harm regardless of whether each message, read in isolation, meets a legal threshold.

Yet even here, ambiguity intrudes. Political criticism can resemble harassment. Satire can look like abuse. Power dynamics matter. A public figure may be expected to tolerate speech that would be intolerable if directed at a private individual. Platforms encode these distinctions in policy, but enforcement relies on context that is often incomplete. The implication is uneven protection.

Disinformation introduces a different challenge. Falsehood is not always harmful, and harm is not always false. Platforms distinguish between misinformation, which may be shared unknowingly, and disinformation, which implies intent to deceive. This distinction matters philosophically. Operationally, it collapses. Intent is hard to infer at scale. Platforms therefore focus on behaviour and impact: virality, coordination, and contradiction with authoritative sources.

The visible behaviour is labelling, downranking, or removal. During the COVID-19 pandemic in 2020, platforms applied these tools aggressively, often referencing guidance from the World Health Organization. As scientific understanding evolved, guidance changed. Content once removed was later permitted. The metric shifted. Trust suffered. The implication was epistemic fragility: governance tied to moving knowledge.

Hate speech sits at the intersection of identity and power. Platforms typically prohibit content that attacks people based on protected characteristics such as race, religion, gender, or sexual orientation. The language appears clear. Its application is not. Hate speech often uses coded terms, irony, or reclaimed slurs. Communities repurpose language as resistance. Automated systems struggle. Human reviewers debate. The same phrase can wound or empower depending on speaker and audience.

The Pepe example illustrates this instability. Furie's character was not created as hate speech. It became one through appropriation. Platforms attempted to moderate use rather than symbol. The rule targeted context. Enforcement varied. The implication was reputational harm to platforms accused simultaneously of censorship and negligence.

Extremism pushes moderation into the realm of security. Platforms prohibit content produced by or praising designated extremist organisations. Lists are maintained, often aligned with government designations. The behaviour is measurable. Accounts linked to known groups are removed. Networks are disrupted. This approach appears firm until it encounters edge cases: journalists quoting propaganda for analysis, activists documenting abuse, or users sharing material to condemn it.

In 2019, YouTube revised its extremism policy to allow "contextualised" use in news and educational settings. The place was San Bruno. The date was clear. The outcome was a carve-out that required judgement. Reviewers now had to assess intent and framing. Error rates rose. Appeals followed. The implication was that precision demanded discretion, which resisted automation.

Borderline content exposes the limits of categorical thinking. This is material that does not violate explicit rules but contributes to harm through accumulation. Sensationalism, conspiracy theories, and exaggerated claims may not be false enough to remove, nor hateful enough to ban. Yet they can radicalise audiences over time. Platforms respond by reducing distribution rather than imposing sanctions. Governance becomes gradient.

This approach shifts the problem from legality to influence. Ranking systems determine reach. Demotion is invisible to users. Creators sense decline without explanation. The abstraction of "borderline" becomes a statistical threshold in recommendation engines. The implication is quiet power exercised without notice.

The recurring motif in all these categories is drift. Content drifts across meanings as it travels. A meme posted ironically becomes sincere through repetition. A joke hardens into a slogan. Legal categories assume stability. Digital culture does not. Platforms must decide at what point drift becomes harm.

A credible counter-example tempers the analysis. Some content is unambiguously harmful. Direct threats of violence, child sexual abuse material, and explicit incitement are removed swiftly across platforms. Consensus exists. Automation performs well. The limitation is scope. These cases represent a fraction of moderation volume. The reconciliation matters. The hardest problems are not the worst ones, but the ambiguous ones.

Metrics again shape outcomes. Platforms track prevalence of each category, report removal rates, and adjust resources accordingly. Categories that attract regulatory scrutiny receive investment. Others languish. The abstraction of "risk" becomes a heat map. Governance follows.

The legal system struggles here too. Courts rely on precedent and narrow interpretation. Platforms cannot. They must anticipate harm before it crystallises. This predictive posture invites error. It also defines modern moderation.

The unresolved tension is classificatory. As long as meaning remains fluid and culture contested, categories will misfit reality. The forward test is practical. When the next meme shifts meaning, will platforms tighten rules, soften enforcement, or accept inconsistency. Each choice governs speech differently.

Moderation models and escalation paths

On 3 November 2020, as polling stations closed across the United States, Twitter activated what it called its "Civic Integrity Event Protocols" from its headquarters in San Francisco. Labels appeared beneath tweets. Sharing was limited. Certain claims about the election outcome were blocked entirely. High-profile accounts, including those of elected officials, were subject to rapid review by specialised teams. The organisation was Twitter. The place was clear. The date was unmistakable. The outcome was immediate friction injected into political speech at a moment of maximum sensitivity.

Nothing was left to chance.

That night revealed how moderation really works when the stakes are high. Platforms do not rely on a single method to govern speech. They deploy layered models, each designed to manage a particular risk profile, and they reserve escalation paths for moments when ordinary procedures are insufficient. These systems are not improvised. They are rehearsed, documented, and quietly refined long before they are visible to users.

Content moderation begins with a simple question: *when* should intervention occur. Pre-publication review represents one answer. Content is checked before it appears. This model offers maximum control. It also imposes delay and demands resources. As a result, platforms use it sparingly, typically for advertising, live-streamed violence, or content from previously sanctioned actors. The abstraction of "prevention" becomes a queue that must clear before speech is allowed.

The implications are clear. Pre-publication review reduces harm but slows expression. It also concentrates power. Decisions are invisible to the audience because the content never appears. For advertisers, this is an accepted cost. For ordinary users, it would feel intolerable at scale.

Most moderation therefore occurs after publication. Reactive reporting remains the backbone of platform enforcement. Users flag content they believe violates rules. Reports feed into triage systems that prioritise by severity, virality, and reporter credibility. The behaviour is observable. Highly reported posts enter review queues faster. The metric is report velocity.

This model distributes detection across the user base. It also embeds social dynamics into governance. Marginalised groups may under-report due to fear of retaliation. Organised actors may over-report to silence opponents.

Platforms respond with weighting systems, assigning trust scores to reporters based on past accuracy. Governance becomes probabilistic.

Prioritised queues refine this process. Not all reports are equal. Content related to self-harm, terrorism, or elections is routed to specialised pipelines. The abstraction of "risk" becomes a routing decision in software. Engineers encode these pathways. Moderators experience them as workload variation. The implication is unequal attention by design.

Trusted flaggers sit alongside this machinery. These are organisations or institutions granted enhanced reporting privileges. They include civil society groups, fact-checkers, and sometimes government agencies. Their reports bypass standard queues. The visible behaviour is speed. Content flagged by a trusted partner is reviewed within hours rather than days.

This arrangement improves accuracy in complex cases. It also concentrates influence. Decisions about who qualifies as a trusted flagger shape enforcement outcomes. Platforms vet partners carefully, yet the imbalance remains. A small advocacy group without formal status cannot trigger the same response. Governance reflects relationships.

Escalation paths sit above these models. They are activated when content poses systemic risk. Elections are the clearest example. Platforms recognise that ordinary moderation is inadequate when misinformation can undermine democratic processes. They therefore establish election integrity teams, war rooms, and rapid escalation protocols months in advance.

The 2020 US election illustrates how this operates. Twitter, Facebook, and YouTube all announced special measures in the weeks leading up to November. These included bans on premature victory claims, labels directing users to authoritative sources, and limits on forwarding. When disputed claims emerged, they were escalated to senior policy teams and, in some cases, executives. The behaviour was intervention at speed. The metric was harm prevention rather than engagement.

A second named example reinforces the point. In February 2019, during India's general election campaign, WhatsApp limited message forwarding to five chats globally, after earlier tests in India showed reduced virality of false information. The organisation was WhatsApp. The place was India. The date was recorded. The outcome was measurable: a reduction in forwarded messages, reported by the company and observed by researchers. A product change functioned as moderation through design.

These high-stakes procedures reveal the architecture beneath everyday enforcement. Platforms maintain playbooks for crises. They simulate scenarios. They assign decision rights. Moderation becomes command-and-control.

A credible counter-example tempers the analysis. Not all escalation succeeds. During Brazil's 2018 election, platforms struggled to contain misinformation spreading through encrypted messaging services. Pre-publication review was impossible. Reporting was limited. Trusted flaggers lacked visibility. Escalation paths had no leverage. The reconciliation matters. Moderation models are constrained by product design.

The quiet motif threading through these systems is the ladder. Content enters at the bottom, subject to routine review. As risk increases, it climbs. Each rung represents additional scrutiny and authority. Few cases reach the top. Those that do shape public debate.

Metrics govern movement up the ladder. Virality triggers escalation. Media attention accelerates review. Regulatory risk elevates priority. These are not moral judgements. They are operational signals. Governance responds to heat.

The implications are profound. Most content is moderated quietly, through low-level queues and automated decisions. A small fraction receives intense attention. This asymmetry shapes perception. High-profile cases fuel controversy. Routine enforcement fades into the background. Yet it is the routine that defines everyday speech.

Critics argue that escalation privileges power. Ordinary users lack access to rapid review. Platforms counter that resources are finite and must be focused where harm is greatest. Both positions hold. The trade-off is structural.

Moderation models also interact. Pre-publication review reduces load on reactive systems. Trusted flaggers correct blind spots. Escalation paths override automation. The system is adaptive. It is also complex. Errors propagate across layers.

The earlier discussion of content categories showed how meaning drifts. Moderation models attempt to catch that drift at different stages. Early intervention prevents spread. Late intervention mitigates damage. Escalation corrects failure. None is sufficient alone.

The forward test is unresolved. As political and social crises multiply, will platforms normalise emergency moderation. Will escalation become the default. Or will fatigue set in, blunting response. Each path reshapes the ladder. Each rung carries weight.

Human moderators and psychological burdens

In January 2019, in Phoenix, Arizona, Facebook agreed to pay USD 52 million to settle a lawsuit brought by current and former content moderators who alleged psychological harm from repeated exposure to graphic material. The organisation was Facebook. The place was specific. The date marked a rare public acknowledgement that moderation was not only a technical or policy challenge, but a human one. The settlement funded counselling and medical support. It did not reduce the volume of content that needed reviewing the next day.

Someone still had to look.

This moment cracked a long-standing illusion. For years, platforms had spoken about moderation as a problem of systems and scale. Filters improved. Policies evolved. Automation advanced. The settlement forced a different recognition: behind every clean feed sat people absorbing what others were spared. Their labour was neither incidental nor temporary. It was structural.

Human moderators occupy an uneasy position in platform governance. They are essential to accuracy, yet treated as a constraint. Machines handle volume; people handle meaning. When content resists categorisation—when intent is unclear, context matters, or stakes are high—it is routed to a human being. This routing is not rare. It is routine.

Moderators are trained to apply policy consistently. Training programmes run for weeks, sometimes months, depending on role and language. New hires learn policy language, decision trees, escalation rules, and quality targets. They practise on historical cases. They are tested for accuracy and speed. Certification unlocks live queues. The abstraction of "preparedness" becomes a score.

Once deployed, moderators work shifts measured in decisions per hour. Performance dashboards track accuracy, agreement with peers, and throughput. These metrics matter. They determine continued employment and advancement. The behaviour is observable. Pauses lengthen review times. Review times trigger flags. The implication is pressure.

What moderators review is rarely neutral. Harassment, abuse, exploitation, violence, and extremism dominate queues. Even when blurred or partially obscured, content communicates intent. Moderators piece together fragments. Over time, exposure accumulates. Studies published in *Occupational Health Science* between 2018 and 2021 document elevated rates of anxiety, sleep disruption, and symptoms consistent with post-traumatic stress among content moderators. The cost is measurable. Attrition rates are high.

The Phoenix settlement did not emerge in isolation. It followed reporting by *The Verge* and *Time* in 2018, which described moderators working long hours reviewing child abuse material, executions, and graphic injury. Some moderators described becoming numb. Others described carrying images home. The implication was not individual weakness. It was systemic design.

Platforms responded with support measures. Counselling services expanded. Rotations limited exposure to specific categories. Wellness breaks were mandated. Training included resilience techniques. These interventions mattered. They reduced harm. They did not remove the burden.

A second named example illustrates the limits. In 2020, during pandemic lockdowns, platforms relied more heavily on automation as human moderation capacity dropped. Facebook publicly acknowledged increased error rates in content removal that year. The organisation was Facebook. The date was documented. The outcome was measurable: more false positives, more appeals. Human moderators had been a buffer. Their absence revealed the cost of scale without judgement.

This counterfactual matters. It shows that moderation cannot be fully automated without sacrificing nuance. Human moderators remain essential. The question is not whether they should exist, but under what conditions.

The quiet motif threading through this section is shielding. Moderators act as shields between harmful content and the public. Shields absorb impact. Over time, they dent.

The organisational structure compounds this effect. Many moderators are contractors rather than employees. They work for third-party firms under strict confidentiality agreements. This arrangement offers flexibility and cost control. It also distances platforms from the lived reality of moderation. The abstraction of "outsourcing" becomes physical separation.

Critics argue that this model externalises harm. Platforms counter that contractors receive specialised training and support. Both positions contain truth. The limitation is visibility. Contractors often lack voice in policy development, despite enforcing it daily. Governance decisions flow downward. Feedback flows imperfectly upward.

Metrics again shape experience. Quality assurance systems measure consistency between moderators. Disagreement triggers retraining. This promotes uniformity. It also suppresses dissent. When policy language is ambiguous, moderators learn to favour precedent over judgement. Accuracy becomes alignment, not understanding.

A credible counter-example complicates the picture. Some platforms have experimented with smaller, more specialised moderation teams empowered to exercise discretion, particularly for sensitive categories such as art, journalism, or political speech. Accuracy improves. Burnout decreases. Scale suffers. The reconciliation is familiar. Care trades against coverage.

The psychological burden of moderation is not only about exposure. It is also about responsibility. Moderators know their decisions affect livelihoods, reputations, and safety. They operate with limited information and little feedback. Appeals may reverse their calls weeks later. The abstraction of "error" becomes personal doubt.

This burden intensifies during crises. Elections, protests, and conflicts flood queues with urgent content. Escalation paths narrow. Time pressure increases. Moderators make consequential decisions quickly. After the moment passes, review slows. Reflection arrives too late.

Platforms acknowledge these dynamics in internal documents and public statements. Yet the dominant narrative remains technological progress. Automation will improve. Exposure will decline. This is partly true. It is also incomplete. As long as content reflects human behaviour, human judgement will be required.

The unresolved tension is moral. Platforms promise safe environments without fully confronting the cost of safety. Moderators bear that cost. The forward test is organisational. Will platforms redesign governance to reduce harm at the source, or continue to rely on shields to absorb it. Clean feeds have a price. Someone always pays it.

Automation, AI filters and their limits

In April 2018, in California, YouTube acknowledged that its automated systems had removed thousands of videos documenting human rights abuses in Syria. The organisation had recently expanded machine learning filters designed to identify and suppress extremist propaganda. The outcome was immediate and unintended. Footage uploaded by journalists and researchers vanished alongside material produced by militant groups. After protests from archives and NGOs, some content was restored. The date was recorded. The place was known. The error was systemic.

The filter worked. It also failed.

That episode captures the paradox at the heart of automated moderation. Platforms rely on artificial intelligence to govern speech at a scale no human workforce could manage. These systems are fast, tireless, and increasingly sophisticated. They are also literal, pattern-driven, and prone to blind spots that mirror the data on which they are trained. Automation is indispensable. It is also insufficient.

Automated moderation systems operate by classifying content according to learned patterns. Text classifiers identify keywords, syntax, and sentiment associated with policy violations. Image and video systems analyse pixels, motion, and metadata. Behavioural models track posting frequency, network connections, and amplification patterns. Each model outputs a probability score. Content above a threshold is flagged, demoted, or removed. The abstraction of "harm" becomes a number.

The strength of this approach is scale. Platforms process billions of posts daily. Automation enables near-instant response to known threats such as spam, child sexual abuse material, and re-uploaded terrorist propaganda. Hash-matching systems, for example, compare uploads against databases of previously identified illegal content. The behaviour is binary. A match triggers removal. The metric is speed. The implication is prevention.

Yet most harmful content is not identical to known examples. It mutates. It hides behind irony. It travels through language and culture. Automated systems generalise from past data. When the future resembles the past, they perform well. When it does not, error rates rise.

Dialect provides a clear illustration. In 2017 and 2018, users speaking African American Vernacular English reported higher rates of content removal on major platforms. Linguistic features misread as aggression triggered filters trained primarily on standard English. The organisation was Facebook. The issue was documented by researchers at the University of Southern California in 2019. The outcome was disproportionate enforcement against a linguistic community. Bias emerged not from intent, but from training data.

Satire exposes a similar weakness. Automated systems struggle to distinguish parody from endorsement. In 2020, several satirical posts criticising extremism were removed from platforms, then reinstated after appeal. The behaviour was misclassification. The metric was reduced false negatives. The implication was chilled expression.

These failures are not edge cases. They reveal a structural limitation: context blindness. AI systems excel at recognising form. They struggle with meaning. Sarcasm, reclaimed slurs, and coded speech evade pattern matching. Cultural references age quickly. Models lag.

Platforms respond by layering systems. Automation handles first pass. Human reviewers handle exceptions. The abstraction of "human-in-the-loop" becomes an escalation path. Content with ambiguous scores is routed for manual review. Accuracy improves. Throughput drops.

A second named example shows this balance. In 2021, TikTok reported expanding human review for content flagged by automated systems as potential hate speech, after error rates drew criticism. The place was Los Angeles. The date was clear. The outcome was slower enforcement but fewer wrongful removals. Governance shifted towards care.

Bias compounds these challenges. AI systems reflect the distributions of their training data. If certain groups are over-represented in flagged examples, models learn to associate their language or imagery with harm. Platforms audit models for disparate impact, but measurement is complex. The abstraction of "fairness" becomes a statistical parity check. Metrics improve. Residual bias remains.

A credible counter-example tempers pessimism. Automation has dramatically reduced exposure to some of the most severe harms. Platforms report that the majority of terrorist content is removed before any user sees it. This claim, repeated in transparency reports by Facebook and YouTube since 2019, reflects real progress. The reconciliation matters. Automation works best where harm is unambiguous and patterns are stable.

The quiet motif threading through this section is the lens. Automated systems view content through lenses shaped by past data. They magnify certain features and ignore others. Changing the lens changes what is seen.

Platforms adjust thresholds, retrain models, and add features. The lens improves. It never becomes sight.

Metrics drive these adjustments. Precision and recall trade against one another. Platforms choose acceptable error rates. When regulators scrutinise under-enforcement, thresholds drop. When public criticism focuses on over-removal, thresholds rise. The behaviour is calibration. The implication is oscillation.

Human oversight remains the corrective. Reviewers contextualise. They interpret. They apply judgement where models cannot. Yet this reliance reintroduces the burdens described earlier: cost, delay, and psychological strain. Automation reduces volume. It does not eliminate the need for people.

The governance challenge is therefore architectural. How much discretion to embed in machines. How much to reserve for humans. How transparent to make the system without enabling manipulation. There is no stable solution. Platforms iterate.

The unresolved tension is epistemic. Can systems designed to predict patterns govern meaning. The forward test is practical. As language evolves and culture fragments, will automation keep pace without erasing nuance. Until then, filters will misfire, and humans will remain in the loop, correcting machines that can see everything except what matters most.

Global rules, local norms and backlash

On 12 June 2019, in Hong Kong, protesters flooded the streets to oppose an extradition bill. Live video streamed across Facebook, YouTube, and Twitter. Some clips showed peaceful marches. Others captured clashes with police. Within days, users reported removals, downranked streams, and warning labels. The same week, similar protest footage from Paris's Yellow Vest demonstrations circulated with fewer restrictions. The organisations were global platforms. The places were different. The outcomes diverged. Accusations followed: censorship in one context, neglect in another.

The rule was the same. The reception was not.

This divergence is not an aberration. It is the structural consequence of global platforms attempting to govern speech across societies that do not share political histories, legal norms, or expectations of authority. Platforms write rules once and apply them everywhere. Users encounter those rules locally, through the lens of culture and power. Friction is inevitable.

Global content policies promise consistency. They articulate universal standards against violence, harassment, and incitement. This uniformity is appealing. It simplifies enforcement. It reassures advertisers. It signals commitment to shared values. Yet speech does not travel as policy language does. Meaning attaches to place.

Protest content exposes this tension most sharply. Demonstrations are celebrated as democratic expression in some contexts and criminalised as disorder in others. A raised fist may symbolise solidarity or sedition. Platforms must decide whether to treat protest footage as newsworthy documentation, potential incitement, or both.

The Hong Kong example illustrates the dilemma. Platforms faced pressure from multiple directions: local authorities citing public order laws, international observers citing free expression, and users demanding visibility. Moderation decisions varied by platform and by moment. Some live streams were temporarily restricted under violence policies. Others were allowed with labels. The visible behaviour was inconsistency. The metric was risk mitigation. The implication was distrust.

Local norms magnify this distrust. In societies with strong traditions of state censorship, any removal is read as collaboration. In societies with strong traditions of free speech, failure to remove is read as abdication. Platforms cannot satisfy both readings simultaneously.

A second named example deepens the contrast. In October 2020, during protests in Nigeria against police brutality under the banner #EndSARS, Twitter amplified protest content, while Facebook faced criticism for slower response to reports of coordinated harassment and disinformation targeting activists. The place was Lagos. The date was clear. The outcome was divergent platform reputations within the same country. Governance choices became political signals.

Legal regimes complicate matters further. Platforms operate under national laws that mandate takedowns or impose penalties. Compliance varies by jurisdiction. Germany's Network Enforcement Act requires rapid removal of illegal content. India's IT Rules mandate traceability and takedown orders. Platforms geoblock content or apply country-specific enforcement. Users perceive these actions as selective censorship.

The abstraction of "local compliance" becomes a switch in enforcement systems. Content remains visible in one country and disappears in another.

Protest organisers learn this quickly. They mirror content, use coded language, or migrate platforms. Governance becomes a game of adaptation.

Cultural norms shape interpretation. Satirical protest art may be protected expression in one context and offensive in another. Automated systems do not grasp this nuance. Human reviewers rely on training that may not match local understanding. Platforms hire regional experts, but coverage is uneven. The behaviour is observable in error rates that spike during local crises.

A credible counter-example shows partial success. During elections in the European Union, platforms have coordinated with local authorities and civil society to protect legitimate political speech while curbing disinformation. Advance planning, local partnerships, and clear escalation paths reduce backlash. The limitation is scalability. Such coordination is resource-intensive and concentrated in regions with regulatory leverage. The reconciliation underscores inequality: governance quality varies with political power.

Metrics again steer outcomes. Platforms track regulatory risk by country, measuring fines, investigations, and political pressure. Regions with higher risk receive more tailored moderation. Others receive global defaults. The abstraction of "global community" fractures into tiers.

The quiet motif threading through this section is translation. Global rules are translated into local action. Translation always loses meaning. Sometimes it adds unintended emphasis. Platforms act as translators without a shared dictionary.

Backlash is the price of mistranslation. When protest content is removed, activists accuse platforms of silencing dissent. When it remains, governments accuse platforms of fuelling unrest. Both claims can be sincere. Both can be true from different vantage points.

Platforms attempt to manage backlash through transparency and dialogue. They publish country-specific reports. They meet with local stakeholders. They adjust policies incrementally. These efforts matter. They rarely satisfy.

The deeper issue is legitimacy. States derive authority from territory and law. Platforms derive authority from service provision and scale. When platforms govern speech locally without local mandate, legitimacy is fragile. Global consistency clashes with democratic pluralism.

The unresolved tension is constitutional. Can a single set of rules govern speech across incompatible political orders. The forward test arrives with every protest. When the next one erupts, will platforms localise rules further, fragmenting governance, or insist on uniform standards, accepting backlash. Each choice redraws the map of digital sovereignty.

Chapter 4

App Store Economics And Taxes

On a wet Tuesday morning in 2017, a two-person startup watched its app go live on a major mobile app store. The product worked. Early users liked it. Reviews were warm. Yet days passed with barely a trickle of downloads. Buried beneath featured placements and sponsored results, the app was effectively invisible. The founders tweaked keywords, adjusted screenshots, rewrote descriptions. Nothing moved the needle. They had built a product for a global market, only to discover that access to that market was neither open nor neutral. It was curated.

Distribution decided fate.

App stores present themselves as marketplaces, places where supply meets demand and quality rises to the top. This image is comforting, and partly true. But it conceals a more consequential reality. App stores are not merely venues. They are governors of access, toll collectors of digital commerce, and architects of economic incentives that shape entire industries. To understand platform power, one must follow the money, and to follow the money in the digital economy is to pass through the app store.

This chapter examines app stores as economic institutions with political effects. It treats commissions not as pricing details but as policy instruments. It looks at ranking and approval processes as forms of gatekeeping. It asks why fees imposed by private companies increasingly resemble taxes, and what happens when those private taxes become unavoidable. Along the way, it explores how developers adapt, evade, or resist, and why regulators have begun to pay closer attention.

Begin with access. For many digital services, app stores are the primary route to users. Mobile operating systems funnel discovery through a small number of storefronts. Placement within those stores matters more than marketing spend for most developers. Featured lists, search rankings, and category charts determine visibility. These are not random. They are designed.

Platforms defend curation as quality control. They argue that ranking algorithms surface relevant apps and protect users from fraud or malware. This is broadly correct. Yet curation is also a form of power. When a platform decides which apps appear prominently, it shapes demand. When it adjusts ranking criteria, it redistributes attention. The effects are immediate. A minor change can double downloads for one app and halve them for another.

For small developers, this creates dependency. Success hinges not only on building a good product, but on aligning with opaque criteria. The abstraction of "discoverability" becomes a daily experiment in optimisation. Screenshots are tested. Descriptions are localised. Features are added or removed to satisfy guidelines. The implication is behavioural conformity driven by distribution control.

Approvals deepen this control. Before an app reaches users, it must pass review. Guidelines specify technical standards, content rules, and business practices. Some are clear. Others are interpretive. Rejections can be swift or slow, detailed or terse. Appeals exist, but timelines vary. For a startup burning cash, delay is costly. Approval becomes leverage.

Economic power intensifies once revenue flows. App stores typically impose commissions on digital transactions, most famously around 30 per cent, with variations for subscriptions, small developers, or certain categories. These rates are defended as payment for infrastructure, security, and distribution. They are also a significant claim on value creation.

For many businesses, commissions dictate strategy. A service priced at ten pounds must either absorb the fee or pass it on. Margins shrink. Prices rise. Some products become unviable. Others rework their offerings to avoid higher rates, shifting features outside the app or redesigning payment flows. Business models bend around platform rules.

This dynamic invites a provocative comparison. App store commissions function like taxes. They are mandatory for access to a market. They are set unilaterally. They fund infrastructure and enforcement. They influence behaviour. The analogy is imperfect, but instructive. Unlike state taxes, these fees lack democratic oversight. Unlike ordinary prices, they apply across competitors. They sit somewhere between rent and regulation.

The comparison sharpens when one considers incidence. In physical commerce, taxes are visible on receipts. In digital commerce, commissions are embedded. Users rarely see them. Developers feel them acutely. The burden shifts depending on pricing power. Platforms capture value at the point of transaction, before profit is realised. This shapes where value accumulates in the ecosystem.

Alternative channels promise escape. Web apps bypass app store fees. Progressive web technologies improve performance. Alternative app stores emerge in certain regions. Direct distribution offers control. Some products succeed by avoiding dominant stores altogether, building audiences through browsers or partnerships. These paths demonstrate possibility. They also reveal constraint. User friction increases. Discovery suffers. Platform integration weakens.

The persistence of app store dominance has drawn regulatory attention. Competition authorities question whether platforms self-preference their own apps, impose unfair terms, or lock in developers and users. Investigations multiply. Hearings convene. Remedies are proposed. Expectations shift, even when outcomes remain uncertain.

What unites these threads is governance by design. App stores govern markets through rules embedded in software and contracts. They decide who may enter, under what conditions, and at what cost. They collect revenue not by producing goods, but by controlling gateways. This is not incidental to platform power. It is central.

This chapter does not argue that app stores are villains. They provide real value. They reduce fraud. They simplify distribution. They enable global reach. The question is proportionality and accountability. When private companies set terms that function like economic policy, what obligations follow.

A recurring image will guide the discussion: the toll road. App stores build and maintain the road. They set the toll. They decide which vehicles may enter and which lanes move fastest. Travellers may choose alternative routes, but those routes are longer and less reliable. The road is convenient. It is also costly.

As the chapter unfolds, it will move from gatekeeping to commissions, from tax analogies to workarounds, and from developer adaptation to regulatory response. It will show how economic governance operates quietly, shaping incentives more effectively than overt control. It will ask what happens when the toll rises, and who has the authority to intervene.

The stakes extend beyond developers. Prices paid by users, diversity of services, and the distribution of innovation all hinge on these economic rules. App store economics determine which ideas reach the public and which wither unseen. They are not a technical footnote. They are a constitution for digital markets.

The pages ahead will dissect this constitution, not to declare it illegitimate, but to make it legible. Only then can its power be debated, contested, or redesigned.

Gatekeeping access to users and markets

In April 2020, in San Francisco, Basecamp released *Hey*, a new email app built by a well-known, well-funded team. Apple rejected it from the App Store. The reason was not a bug or a security flaw, but a business rule: users could sign in to an account purchased elsewhere, without in-app subscription options. After days of public debate, policy citations, and negotiations, Apple approved the app with conditions. The organisation was Apple. The date was precise. The place was clear. The outcome hinged on gatekeeping.

Visibility decides survival.

For most software, distribution once meant shipping boxes or managing servers. For mobile software, distribution means passing through a small number of storefronts that control access to users. These storefronts are not passive shelves. They rank, recommend, approve, and exclude. They determine which apps appear at the top of search results, which are featured on curated pages, and which never surface at all. The gate is digital. It is also decisive.

App stores justify this control as stewardship. They argue that curation protects users, maintains quality, and reduces fraud. These claims hold weight. Malicious apps do exist. Poorly designed ones waste attention. Yet stewardship is not neutral. Every ranking system embeds priorities. Every approval process encodes values. When platforms act as gatekeepers, they shape markets as surely as regulators or landlords.

Consider ranking. Search results within app stores drive discovery. Studies by Sensor Tower and App Annie have shown that the majority of downloads cluster around the top few results for any given query. The metric is position.

The behaviour is scrolling. The implication is concentration. A small change in ranking criteria can redirect millions of downloads overnight.

Ranking algorithms are proprietary. Developers infer their contours through experimentation. Keywords matter. Update frequency matters. User ratings matter. Conversion rates matter. The abstraction of "relevance" becomes a composite score. Developers respond by optimising for the algorithm rather than the user. Features are prioritised for engagement metrics that boost ranking. Design decisions bend.

Featured placements amplify this effect. Being highlighted on a store's front page can transform an app's fortunes. Traffic spikes. Reviews accumulate. Network effects kick in. Yet featured slots are scarce and curated. Editorial teams select apps based on opaque criteria. Relationships, timing, and narrative matter. For a small developer without connections or marketing muscle, access is uncertain.

Approval processes form the final gate. Before ranking or featuring occurs, an app must be admitted. Review guidelines cover content, security, privacy, and business models. Some rules are crisp. Others leave room for interpretation. Rejections often cite broad clauses. Appeals exist but consume time. For a startup with limited runway, weeks matter.

The *Hey* episode exposed this leverage publicly. Apple framed its decision as consistent enforcement. Developers saw arbitrariness. Users saw a powerful intermediary dictating business terms. The behaviour was enforcement. The metric was compliance. The implication was dependency.

A second example illustrates quieter control. In 2018, several small meditation and productivity apps reported sudden drops in downloads following changes to Google Play's ranking signals that favoured "engagement" over "installs". The organisation was Google. The place was Mountain View. The date was documented in developer forums and coverage by *The Information*. Apps that encouraged frequent check-ins rose. Apps designed for occasional use fell. No policy violation occurred. Market share shifted.

This example shows how gatekeeping need not be punitive to be powerful. Adjusting a signal reshapes incentives. Developers who resist find themselves invisible. The gate does not slam. It narrows.

Gatekeeping also interacts with competition. Platforms that operate app stores often compete with developers who rely on them. When a platform promotes its own apps through default placement or prominent featuring, rivals face an uphill climb. The abstraction of "self-preferencing" becomes a default install. The behaviour is preloading. The implication is advantage without merit testing.

A credible counter-example tempers the critique. App store curation has surfaced high-quality independent apps that might otherwise have languished. Apple's *Today* tab has introduced millions to niche tools, creative games, and accessibility innovations. Developers credit features with transformative growth. This matters. Gatekeeping can elevate as well as exclude.

The reconciliation lies in discretion. When discretion is exercised without accountability, it breeds distrust. When exercised transparently, it can add value. The problem is not curation per se. It is concentration without recourse.

The quiet motif threading through this section is the toll gate. App stores build and maintain the road to users. They control the gates. Some travellers pass freely. Others pay in optimisation, conformity, or fees. Alternative routes exist, but they are longer and less travelled.

Metrics reinforce this structure. Platforms monitor fraud rates, user complaints, and conversion efficiency. They adjust gates accordingly. Developers watch analytics dashboards and guess at causes. The asymmetry of information is stark. One side sees the whole road. The other sees only its lane.

For users, gatekeeping shapes choice invisibly. Search results feel natural. Featured apps feel deserved. Defaults feel convenient. Yet these experiences are curated. Markets appear competitive while being tightly managed.

For developers, gatekeeping defines viability. A good product is necessary. It is not sufficient. Distribution strategy becomes as important as design. Some developers pivot platforms entirely. Others invest in marketing to bypass store discovery. Many fail quietly.

The unresolved tension is structural. Can private companies responsibly govern access to markets on which entire industries depend. The forward test is practical. When the next ranking change or approval dispute arises, will there be meaningful avenues for challenge, or will developers once again find themselves knocking at a silent gate, refreshing dashboards, waiting to be seen.

Commission structures and revenue sharing

In June 2016, in Stockholm, Spotify quietly removed in-app subscriptions from its iOS application. New users could no longer sign up inside the app. Existing subscribers were nudged to manage accounts elsewhere. Apple's App Store rules allowed this, but at a cost: friction. The organisation was Spotify. The date was specific. The place mattered. The outcome was strategic retreat from a 30 per cent commission that the company argued distorted pricing and margin. The app remained. The revenue model moved.

Money changes behaviour.

App store commissions are often presented as technical pricing terms, a footnote to distribution. In practice, they are among the most powerful levers platforms possess. They shape how products are designed, how services are priced, and which business models survive. They do not merely skim value. They rearrange it.

Most dominant app stores standardised around a headline rate of roughly 30 per cent for digital goods and services, with variations for subscriptions, renewals, and smaller developers. This figure became industry shorthand. It also became a reference point for dispute. For a business operating on thin margins, losing nearly a third of gross revenue at the point of sale is not a rounding error. It is an existential constraint.

The effect is visible in pricing. Developers face a choice. Absorb the fee and accept lower margins, or raise prices and risk demand. Many do both. Subscription prices on mobile exceed web prices. Features differ by channel. Users notice inconsistently, and often blame developers rather than platforms. The abstraction of "commission pass-through" becomes a higher monthly bill.

Subscriptions magnify this dynamic. App stores encourage recurring revenue models, arguing that they align incentives and support sustainable development. They also offer reduced rates, often 15 per cent, after the first year of a subscription. The behaviour is loyalty engineering. The metric is churn reduction. The implication is lock-in.

For some businesses, this structure works. Media apps with strong brands retain subscribers long enough to benefit from lower renewal rates. For others, particularly consumer utilities or niche services, churn remains high. The effective commission never falls. Business models bend accordingly.

Spotify's decision illustrates adaptation under pressure. By steering users to external sign-up flows, Spotify avoided the commission but sacrificed conversion. Fewer impulse subscriptions occurred. Marketing costs rose. The company judged this preferable to paying the fee. That judgement reshaped the user experience for millions.

A second named example shows similar logic. In 2018, Netflix stopped allowing new iOS users to subscribe within its app. The organisation was Netflix. The place was Los Gatos, California. The date was widely reported. The outcome mirrored Spotify's: externalisation of payments, increased friction, preserved margins. Two of the world's largest subscription services chose inconvenience over commission.

These are not edge cases. They are signals. When firms with scale and brand power opt out of in-app payments, the structure itself warrants scrutiny.

Smaller developers lack this leverage. They cannot easily redirect users. Their products rely on seamless onboarding. Paying the commission becomes the cost of entry. The abstraction of "platform fee" becomes a toll that only some can bypass.

Exceptions complicate the picture. In 2020, Apple introduced its Small Business Program, reducing commissions to 15 per cent for developers earning under USD 1 million annually. The organisation was Apple. The date was November 2020. The place was Cupertino. The outcome was relief for many, exclusion for others. Thresholds create cliffs. Crossing them changes economics overnight.

This counter-example matters. It shows responsiveness to criticism and regulatory pressure. It also underscores arbitrariness. Why one million. Why fifteen per cent. The reconciliation is pragmatic. Platforms adjust when legitimacy is threatened, but retain control over terms.

Commission structures also influence product design. Developers strip features that trigger higher rates. They delay adding digital goods. They redesign flows to categorise services as "reader apps" or "companion apps" under looser rules. The behaviour is classification gaming. The metric is compliance. The implication is distortion.

Physical analogies clarify the effect. In retail, landlords charge rent. Credit card networks charge interchange fees. Taxes apply at sale. Each affects pricing and location decisions. App store commissions combine elements of all three. They are unavoidable for access, invisible to consumers, and enforced by contract rather than law. The toll meter runs silently.

The motif of the toll meter recurs throughout this section. Every transaction increments it. Developers watch revenue dashboards and see gross figures shrink as the meter ticks. Users see prices that reflect a hidden charge. Platforms see predictable income streams.

Critics argue that this resembles private taxation. The analogy is imperfect but instructive. Unlike taxes, commissions are not progressive. They do not fund public goods in the civic sense. They fund platform operations and profit. Unlike market prices, they apply uniformly across competitors, regardless of cost structure. They shape markets by design.

Supporters counter that app stores provide real value: security, distribution, payment processing, and customer trust. These services cost money. Commissions fund them. This argument carries weight. The question is proportionality and choice.

Metrics reveal the scale. Apple reported over USD 80 billion in App Store billings in 2020, according to company disclosures. Even at blended rates below the headline 30 per cent, the revenue is substantial. The figure grounds debate. This is not marginal income. It is structural.

The impact extends beyond pricing to innovation. High commissions discourage low-margin experimentation. Free-to-use tools struggle to monetise. Educational apps price themselves out of reach. Some ideas never ship. The abstraction of "innovation tax" becomes absence.

Yet commissions can also enable. Guaranteed payment rails reduce fraud. Global reach simplifies scaling. Some developers credit app store economics with making their businesses viable at all. The system both constrains and supports.

The unresolved tension lies in governance. Who decides what a fair commission is. Platforms answer internally. Regulators increasingly ask the question publicly. Developers adapt in the meantime, reworking products, altering prices, and choosing friction strategically.

The forward test is unfolding. As alternative payment options, regulatory remedies, and market pressure reshape terms, commissions may fall or fragment. Or they may entrench, defended as the price of order. Each outcome carries consequences for who can build, who can charge, and who ultimately pays when the toll meter ticks again.

Platform rules as de facto tax policy

On 13 August 2020, in Cary, North Carolina, Epic Games added a direct payment option inside *Fortnite*, offering players a discount if they bypassed Apple's in-app purchase system. Apple removed the game from the App Store the same day. The organisation was Apple. The date and place are checkable. The outcome was immediate: a single rule about payments determined whether a global product could reach iPhone users at all. The dispute became public theatre, but the underlying mechanism was mundane. A platform fee was enforced as policy.

The charge was not called a tax. It behaved like one.

To say that platform fees resemble taxes is to invite a predictable objection. Taxes are levied by states, authorised through law, justified—at least in theory—by public purposes. Platform fees are prices, set by private firms, accepted through contract, justified by services such as distribution, security, and billing. This distinction matters. Yet the resemblance is not rhetorical. It is functional. Platform rules create compulsory payment obligations for participation in digital markets, and those obligations shape economic behaviour in ways strikingly similar to tax policy.

The first step is to observe where the burden sits. Taxes matter most at choke points: the border, the sale, the payroll, the property register. Platform fees, likewise, sit at choke points. App stores impose commissions at the moment of digital sale. Marketplaces take a percentage when a transaction clears. Payment rails charge tolls when money moves. These are not fees sprinkled lightly across the system. They are concentrated at the points where commerce cannot avoid intermediaries. The abstraction of "platform power" becomes a line item between gross and net revenue.

Consider how this compares with physical commerce. A high street shop pays rent for location, business rates for premises, and VAT or sales tax on transactions. The landlord's rent funds property ownership and maintenance. The state's taxes fund public services and, crucially, confer rights and obligations. Customers see VAT on receipts. Shopkeepers see the rate in statute. Enforcement, while imperfect, is bounded by due process. Disputes may end in tribunals. The costs are real, but the rules are legible.

Digital commerce rearranges the same burdens. There is no high street. There is an app store listing, a search ranking, and a payment flow. Instead of rent, the platform takes a commission tied to revenue. Instead of business rates, the platform may impose developer programme fees, verification requirements, or compliance costs. Instead of VAT being the primary visible charge, a commission becomes the hidden wedge that reshapes pricing. Users rarely see it. Developers always do.

This is where the analogy to tax policy becomes most useful: incidence. Economists distinguish between who is legally obliged to pay a tax and who ultimately bears its cost. A VAT is collected by merchants, but the cost is often passed to consumers through higher prices. A payroll tax may be paid by employers, but can depress wages. Platform commissions operate similarly. The developer is charged. The user often pays, through higher subscription prices or reduced features. Sometimes the developer absorbs the cost, sacrificing margin. Either way, the commission influences behaviour exactly as a tax would: it changes what is profitable.

Show this in the simplest behaviour. A developer sets a £9.99 subscription price on the web. In the app store, they set it at £12.99 to accommodate a platform commission and remain whole. Users complain that mobile is more expensive. Some churn. Others stay, because convenience wins. The "tax" is paid, invisibly, through price discrimination. The platform has not legislated; it has nonetheless shifted consumer surplus and producer margin.

Now name the mechanism. App store commissions are typically expressed as a percentage of transaction value, often around 30 per cent for many categories, with reduced rates in specific cases. This resembles an ad valorem tax: a charge proportional to price. It differs from a flat fee, which would behave more like a licence. Proportional charges scale with success. They also shape pricing incentives. If your margin is thin, the percentage bites harder. If your product is high-margin, you can tolerate it. The implication is predictable: platform fees favour business models with high margins, strong brands, or significant pricing power, and they discourage low-margin experimentation.

The resemblance to taxation deepens when platforms vary rates and exemptions. States use differentiated tax rates to incentivise behaviour: reduced VAT on essentials, higher duties on tobacco, reliefs for small businesses. Platforms do something similar, though for different reasons. Apple announced at WWDC in San Francisco in June 2016 that subscription commissions would fall to 15 per cent after a subscriber's first year, down from 30 per cent, to encourage long-term retention. The organisation was Apple. The date and place are checkable. The outcome was not merely financial; it reshaped product strategy. Businesses were nudged towards subscriptions, and towards designing for low churn. A fiscal instrument became an engagement instrument.

That is governance. Through pricing.

Once you view platform fees as private tax-like instruments, other features snap into focus. Tax systems require classification. Is a good taxable. Is it exempt. Which rate applies. Platforms classify too. A "reader app" may be permitted to sign in users who subscribe elsewhere, while a digital service selling features must use in-app purchases. A marketplace may treat physical goods differently from digital goods, applying different fee structures. These classifications are not neutral. They determine which industries are squeezed and which are spared.

Classification also invites arbitrage. Businesses restructure to fall into a lower category, just as firms structure transactions to minimise tax burdens. Some move purchases to the web, as Spotify did in 2016 and Netflix in 2018 when they ceased offering in-app subscriptions on iOS. Some split products into free companion apps and paid web services. Some shift value into physical bundles or external tokens. The behaviour is design around fees. The implication is economic distortion: engineering time spent on compliance strategy rather than user value.

A limitation must be stated plainly. Platform fees are not public taxes. They do not fund universal services in the civic sense. They are not subject to democratic debate. And yet they can finance genuine shared goods within the platform domain: fraud prevention, payment dispute handling, developer tooling, and security review. A platform that maintains a reliable billing system and polices malware provides value that resembles infrastructure. It is reasonable to charge for infrastructure. The question is not whether a charge is justified, but whether the terms and processes resemble legitimate governance or private rent extraction.

Here is where physical and digital "tax" burdens diverge in transparency and contestability. When a state raises VAT, the rate is published. When a platform adjusts its commission structure or enforcement of payment rules, changes may arrive as a policy update, a guideline revision, or a behind-the-scenes shift in app review interpretation. The effective rate can change through enforcement even when the nominal rate does not. That is a peculiar kind of fiscal opacity: the rule is written, but its application becomes the real instrument.

Pair the abstraction of "regulatory risk" with a visible decision. A platform faces scrutiny over app store commissions. It announces a reduced rate for smaller developers, as Apple did with its Small Business Program in November 2020 from Cupertino, lowering the commission to 15 per cent for developers earning up to USD 1 million annually. The policy resembles a tax threshold. It also creates a cliff. Cross the line, and your effective burden doubles. Firms close to the threshold may delay growth, adjust pricing, or reorganise entities to remain eligible. That is classic tax behaviour, produced by private rulemaking.

The platform's defenders can respond, fairly, that thresholds are administrative necessities. So are tax thresholds. The point is not to accuse platforms of imitating the state, but to recognise that they have stumbled into state-like economic steering. They set rates. They create exemptions. They police compliance. They punish evasion. They run an internal revenue service with customer support tickets instead of courts.

Enforcement is where the analogy becomes unavoidable. Taxes are enforced through audits, penalties, and sometimes criminal sanctions, but always within an apparatus that claims procedural fairness. Platform "taxes" are enforced through access. Breach a payment rule, and your app may be rejected or removed. Funds may be withheld. Accounts may be suspended. The sanction is not imprisonment; it is exclusion from the market. For many digital businesses, exclusion is fatal. The mechanism is softer than state coercion and, in some respects, more effective.

The quiet motif that threads through this discussion is the receipt. In physical commerce, the receipt itemises charges. It makes the state visible. In platform commerce, the receipt often hides the platform's cut from the user, showing only a price. The platform's "tax" is embedded. The user experiences it indirectly, through higher prices or fewer features. This invisibility matters. It weakens accountability. A charge that cannot be seen is harder to contest.

The counter-example returns here, and it is important. Some platform charges are visible and optional. Payment processors publish fee schedules. Hosting providers publish pricing tiers. Businesses can multi-home: they can use Stripe, Adyen, or PayPal depending on context. Competition disciplines prices. In those markets, fees behave like ordinary costs rather than taxes. The reconciliation is simple and sharp. Platform fees become tax-like when choice collapses—when a gatekeeper controls the route to market, and the charge is unavoidable for scale.

That is why the tax analogy is not a flourish. It explains the distribution of value in the digital economy. If the platform takes a percentage at the point of sale, value shifts upstream. Developers capture less. Users may pay more. The platform captures the spread. Over time, this shapes investment. Venture capital favours models that can tolerate platform cuts. Small firms struggle. Innovation narrows. The fiscal instrument sculpts the market.

The analogy also clarifies political stakes. When citizens argue about taxes, they are arguing about collective priorities: what to fund, whom to burden, which behaviours to encourage. When developers argue about platform commissions, they are arguing about private priorities imposed at scale. The conflict is not only economic. It is constitutional. Who should have the authority to impose compulsory levies on commerce that now constitutes a core part of daily life.

The unresolved tension is a test of legitimacy disguised as pricing. If platform fees operate like taxes, should they be treated like taxes, with transparency, contestability, and limits. Or should we insist they are merely prices, and accept the consequences of private fiscal power. The next time a platform changes a commission rate or tightens a payment rule, ask a diagnostic question that would sound ordinary in public finance and unsettling in software: who authorised this levy, and what recourse exists for those who must pay it.

Alternative app channels and workarounds

In May 2020, in San Francisco, the team behind Notion quietly crossed a milestone: millions of active users relying primarily on a browser-based product that behaved, to most people, like a native app. The organisation was Notion Labs. The date coincided with a surge in remote work. The place mattered because it sat at the centre of the app economy Notion was partly bypassing. The concrete outcome was strategic freedom. Revenue flowed directly. Updates shipped without review queues. The company remained present in app stores, but it did not depend on them.

The road around the gate existed.

For years, dominant app stores framed themselves as unavoidable. Mobile meant native. Native meant stores. Stores meant rules, commissions, and rankings. Developers internalised this logic. Distribution strategies converged. Business models adapted. Yet, quietly and unevenly, alternatives emerged. None promised total escape. Some offered leverage. Others offered survival.

The most visible alternative is the web app. Modern browsers now support offline storage, push notifications, background sync, and hardware access once reserved for native code. Progressive Web Apps, formalised by Google in the mid-2010s, narrowed the functional gap. The abstraction of "web-first" became tangible behaviour: users pinning icons to home screens, receiving alerts, editing documents offline. The metric was retention. The implication was plausibility.

Notion's trajectory illustrates both opportunity and constraint. By prioritising the web, Notion avoided app store commissions on subscriptions. Pricing remained consistent across platforms. Feature parity was easier to maintain. Updates deployed instantly. Yet acquisition relied on word of mouth, search, and enterprise adoption. Casual discovery suffered. For many users, Notion remained invisible until recommended. The gate was bypassed, but the crowd was thinner.

A second named example underscores the pattern. In 2017, in Berlin, SoundCloud relaunched its web experience after years of focusing on native apps. The organisation was SoundCloud. The date followed a period of financial strain. The outcome was reduced dependence on mobile stores for monetisation experiments. Subscriptions and creator tools launched first on the web. Control increased. Growth did not automatically follow.

Web apps trade reach for autonomy. They lower variable costs but raise acquisition costs. They suit products with strong network effects, professional use cases, or viral sharing. They struggle where impulse installs dominate. The abstraction of "choice" becomes a funnel analysis.

Alternative app stores offer another route. On Android, third-party stores such as Samsung Galaxy Store or regional platforms provide distribution without Google Play's full weight. In China, where Google Play is absent, a fragmented ecosystem of manufacturer and carrier stores thrives. The behaviour is diversification. The metric is coverage. The implication is complexity.

Fragmentation carries costs. Each store has its own rules, SDKs, and analytics. Updates must be coordinated. Support burdens rise. Smaller developers struggle to maintain parity. The counter-example is instructive. Large game publishers operate across dozens of stores in China because scale justifies overhead. Indie developers rarely can. The reconciliation is blunt. Alternatives exist, but only some can afford them.

Direct distribution remains the most radical workaround. On desktop platforms, users download installers directly. On mobile, this is constrained. Android permits sideloading, but friction is high. Security warnings deter users. iOS restricts it almost entirely. The behaviour is exclusion by design. The implication is dependency reinforced through usability.

Where direct distribution succeeds, it often pairs with hardware or enterprise contexts. Internal corporate apps bypass stores through device management programmes. Specialised tools ship outside consumer channels. These are edge cases. They demonstrate possibility without challenging the mainstream.

Workarounds extend beyond distribution into product architecture. Some developers split functionality. Core services live on the web. Companion apps offer limited features. Payments occur externally. The design is deliberate. The metric is commission avoidance. The implication is fragmented experience.

This fragmentation affects users. Multiple sign-ins. Inconsistent features. Confusion over pricing. Developers accept these costs to regain margin and control. The abstraction of "user friction" becomes a line item in strategic planning.

The quiet motif threading through this section is the side road. Side roads exist alongside highways. They are slower. They offer fewer signs. Some lead to thriving towns. Others to dead ends. Developers choose them not because they are easier, but because the tolls on the main road are too high.

Regulatory shifts may widen these roads. Competition authorities debate interoperability, alternative payment systems, and sideloading rights. Court cases challenge exclusivity. Platform responses oscillate between accommodation and resistance. The landscape is unsettled. Workarounds today may become norms tomorrow, or be closed off.

A credible limitation must be stated. App stores persist because they solve real problems at scale: security, trust, and frictionless billing. Many users prefer them. Many developers benefit from them. Workarounds introduce risk. Fraud increases. Support burdens rise. The reconciliation is pragmatic. Alternatives are complements, not replacements.

Metrics tell the story. Products that succeed outside stores often show higher lifetime value per user but lower overall reach. Products dependent on stores show the reverse. Strategic choice follows.

The unresolved tension is strategic sovereignty. How much dependence is acceptable. At what point does convenience become vulnerability. Developers cannot answer this abstractly. They answer it quarterly, watching dashboards, balancing growth against margin.

The forward test is approaching. As web capabilities improve and regulatory pressure mounts, will side roads widen enough to matter, or will the main gate simply adjust its tolls and absorb dissent. The next generation of products will reveal whether alternative channels are escape routes or pressure valves in a system that remains, for most, inescapable.

Regulatory scrutiny of app store power

On 13 March 2019, in Brussels, the European Commission announced it had opened a formal antitrust investigation into Apple's App Store practices following a complaint by Spotify. The organisation was the European Commission. The place was explicit. The date was precise. The concrete outcome was escalation: what had long been framed as a private commercial dispute was reclassified as a matter of public competition law. The investigation signalled that app store rules were no longer merely contractual terms. They were potential abuses of market power.

The mood shifted.

For more than a decade, app stores expanded under a regulatory settlement that might be summarised as benign neglect. Platforms built distribution infrastructure. Developers flocked. Consumers benefited from convenience and security. Regulators watched, occasionally uneasy but largely hands-off. That posture has changed. Across jurisdictions, competition authorities and legislators now treat app stores as strategic chokepoints capable of distorting markets far beyond software.

The core concern is not size alone. It is control. App stores sit at the intersection of operating systems, payments, discovery, and policy enforcement. This vertical integration grants platforms the ability to influence outcomes at multiple stages of competition. When a company both runs the marketplace and competes within it, neutrality becomes suspect.

Self-preferencing is the most intuitive worry. When a platform promotes its own apps through default placement, pre-installation, or favourable ranking, rivals face structural disadvantage. The behaviour is visible. On many devices, native apps occupy prime screen real estate. The metric is user attention. The implication is foreclosed opportunity.

Regulators frame this not as moral failure but as incentive alignment. A platform has commercial reasons to favour its own services. Competition law asks whether those incentives translate into exclusionary effects. The Spotify complaint articulated this logic clearly. Spotify argued that Apple's commission structure and in-app purchase rules raised rivals' costs while Apple Music, exempt from those fees, competed on price. The allegation was not that Apple charged fees, but that it charged them selectively.

The Commission's investigation examined exactly this. It asked whether Apple used App Store rules to disadvantage competing music streaming services. In April 2021, the Commission issued a Statement of Objections, preliminarily finding that Apple had abused its dominant position. The organisation was the European Commission. The place remained Brussels. The date mattered. Expectations hardened.

A second named example shows similar scrutiny elsewhere. In August 2020, in the United States District Court for the Northern District of California, Epic Games sued Apple after *Fortnite* was removed from the App Store for violating payment rules. The organisation was Epic Games. The date followed a deliberate breach. The outcome was a public trial that forced disclosure of internal documents, commission economics, and platform strategy. While the court's 2021 ruling largely favoured Apple, it ordered changes to anti-steering provisions, permitting developers to inform users about alternative payment options. The legal victory was partial. The reputational impact was not.

These cases illustrate a broader shift. Regulators no longer accept platform assertions at face value. They demand evidence about how rules affect rivals and consumers. They interrogate internal incentives. They treat app stores as economic regulators rather than neutral conduits.

Unfair terms form the second major cluster of concern. Developers argue that app store contracts are take-it-or-leave-it agreements imposed by firms with no effective competition. Terms can change unilaterally. Enforcement can be inconsistent. Remedies are limited. The abstraction of "contractual freedom" becomes illusory when exit is impractical.

Competition authorities translate this into questions of bargaining power and dependency. If a business cannot reach users without accepting a platform's terms, those terms warrant scrutiny. This logic underpins legislative efforts such as the European Union's Digital Markets Act, adopted in 2022, which imposes obligations on designated "gatekeepers" regarding app stores, payments, and self-preferencing. The policy instrument is ex ante regulation. The implication is a departure from case-by-case enforcement.

Payment rules attract particular attention because they combine revenue extraction with behavioural control. By mandating the use of proprietary payment systems and prohibiting steering, platforms can lock in commissions and prevent price competition. Regulators ask whether such rules are necessary for security or primarily serve revenue protection. Evidence matters. Platforms cite fraud prevention metrics. Developers cite margin compression.

A credible counter-example tempers regulatory zeal. App stores have reduced fraud, simplified billing, and enabled small developers to sell globally without negotiating payment processing in dozens of jurisdictions. Consumer trust in app store payments is high. Removing centralised payment control risks fragmentation and increased scams. Regulators acknowledge this. Remedies therefore focus on choice rather than abolition: allowing alternative payment options without dismantling the store.

The reconciliation is delicate. Too blunt a remedy can undermine security and user experience. Too timid an approach entrenches dominance. This tension animates current debates.

The quiet motif threading through this section is the courtroom threshold. For years, app store practices never crossed it. Now they do, repeatedly. Each crossing reframes private governance as public concern.

Metrics increasingly shape scrutiny. Authorities analyse commission rates, market shares, switching costs, and complaint volumes. They examine how often platform apps appear in top rankings compared to rivals. They request internal emails discussing competitive strategy. Behaviour once justified as product design is recast as evidence.

Regulatory approaches vary by jurisdiction. The European Union emphasises structural remedies and forward-looking obligations. The United States relies more heavily on litigation and precedent, though legislative proposals circulate. Japan and South Korea have enacted targeted rules on payment systems. Each reflects legal culture. All share a recognition that app stores matter.

Platforms respond strategically. They adjust policies. They introduce exceptions. They lower rates for certain developers. These changes are framed as goodwill or innovation. Regulators read them as signals of pressure. The dance continues.

For developers, scrutiny offers hope and uncertainty. Relief may arrive unevenly. Compliance costs may rise. The rules may fragment by region. The abstraction of "regulatory risk" becomes a product roadmap concern.

For users, the stakes are indirect but real. Pricing, choice, and innovation depend on how these disputes resolve. App stores that face effective oversight may become more contestable. Those that do not may consolidate further.

The unresolved tension is institutional. Can competition law, designed for slower industries, adapt to software platforms that change rules overnight. The forward test is imminent. As investigations conclude and new regulations take effect, will app stores adjust their governance meaningfully, or will scrutiny harden into permanent supervision. The answer will define whether these digital toll roads remain privately policed, or finally acquire the checks expected of infrastructure that now underpins everyday commerce.

Chapter 5

Data Localisation And Jurisdiction

In April 2018, the servers did not move, but the law did. When Russia's data protection authority enforced requirements that certain categories of personal data about Russian citizens be stored on servers located inside the country, several global platforms faced a blunt choice: rebuild their infrastructure or withdraw services. Some complied. Some resisted. Some offered partial workarounds. What had once been an invisible engineering decision—the physical location of data—became a matter of national policy, public controversy, and commercial risk. Geography returned to the cloud.

Data, it turned out, still lives somewhere.

For decades, the promise of the internet rested on abstraction. Information would float free of borders. Packets would route themselves efficiently. Jurisdiction would follow the user, not the server. This vision underpinned global platforms and justified their scale. It is now under sustained pressure. Governments increasingly care where data is stored, processed, and accessed. They care not only for technical reasons, but for political ones. Data localisation has become a proxy battleground for sovereignty.

This chapter explores why data location, long treated as a secondary concern, has moved to the centre of digital governance. It shows how security anxieties, privacy norms, and industrial policy converge on the same demand: keep data close. It examines how that demand collides with the technical realities of distributed systems designed precisely to ignore borders. And it asks what happens when law, architecture, and power pull in opposite directions.

The resurgence of data localisation marks a shift in how states perceive digital infrastructure. Data is no longer framed merely as an input to commerce or a subject of privacy law. It is framed as a strategic asset. Health records, financial transactions, location data, and communications metadata are treated as national resources whose movement must be controlled. This logic borrows from older instincts about territory and security. If information confers power, then allowing it to flow freely across borders feels reckless.

The motivations vary. Some governments cite national security, arguing that locally stored data reduces exposure to foreign surveillance or coercion. Others emphasise privacy, claiming that domestic storage makes enforcement of local standards easier. Still others pursue industrial policy, hoping that localisation requirements will stimulate domestic data centres, cloud services, and technical employment. These rationales overlap. They also conflict.

To understand the stakes, one must first confront the technical substrate that localisation seeks to constrain. Modern platforms distribute data by design. User information is replicated across multiple data centres to ensure resilience. Requests are routed dynamically to minimise latency. Backups are stored in separate regions to guard against failure. Sharding splits databases so that no single machine holds everything. These practices are not optional luxuries. They are prerequisites for reliability at scale.

When a user in Nairobi opens an app hosted by a company headquartered in California, the request may be served by a server in Frankfurt, drawing on cached data from Dublin and a backup in Amsterdam. This is not inefficiency. It is optimisation. The abstraction of "the cloud" masks a choreography of machines responding to geography in real time.

Localisation disrupts this choreography. Mandating that certain data remain within national borders constrains routing options. It can increase latency. It can reduce redundancy. It can complicate disaster recovery. Platforms adapt by building regional hubs, segmenting databases, and re-architecting systems to respect legal boundaries. Each adaptation carries cost.

The conflict intensifies when laws overlap. One country may require that data about its citizens be stored locally and made accessible to domestic authorities. Another may prohibit the transfer of that same data without strict safeguards. Platforms operating globally find themselves caught between incompatible commands. Compliance with one law risks violation of another.

Law enforcement requests bring this tension into sharp relief. A police agency in one jurisdiction seeks access to data stored abroad. Mutual legal assistance treaties move slowly. Informal requests proliferate. Platforms must decide whether to comply, resist, or negotiate. Each decision signals allegiance. Each carries legal and reputational risk.

This chapter traces how platforms navigate these conflicts. It examines strategies such as regionalisation, where data is stored and processed within defined geographic zones. It looks at partnerships with local firms that provide compliance cover but fragment control. It considers product segmentation, where features are available in some countries but not others. These strategies work, imperfectly. They also reshape the user experience.

The side-effects are uneven. Large platforms can absorb the cost of building local infrastructure. Smaller firms struggle. A startup serving a global niche may find that complying with localisation requirements in multiple jurisdictions is financially prohibitive. Innovation slows. Entry barriers rise. Incumbents entrench.

The inequality extends beyond firms. Researchers lose access to global datasets. Users in less wealthy countries experience degraded services or delayed features. The promise of a shared digital space fractures along economic lines. Localisation intended to protect citizens may, paradoxically, reduce their access.

A recurring image will guide this chapter: the border checkpoint. In physical space, checkpoints regulate movement. They inspect documents. They delay travel. They assert authority. Data localisation erects digital checkpoints within systems designed for flow. Every packet is, in principle, inspectable. Every transfer is a potential crossing.

This image helps clarify the political dimension. Borders are not merely lines on maps. They are expressions of power. When states insist on data borders, they assert the right to govern information flows as they govern people and goods. Platforms, built on the assumption of borderless optimisation, must adapt or resist.

The adaptation is ongoing. Standards evolve. Trade agreements incorporate data clauses. Courts issue conflicting judgments. Technical workarounds proliferate. The equilibrium is unstable. Each new law shifts incentives. Each new breach sharpens fears.

This chapter does not treat data localisation as inherently misguided or inherently virtuous. It takes the arguments seriously. Security matters. Privacy matters. Domestic capacity matters. But so do interoperability, openness, and proportionality. The challenge lies in reconciling these values without dismantling the infrastructure that underpins global communication.

As the chapter unfolds, it will move from motivation to mechanism, from architecture to conflict, from compliance to consequence. It will show how decisions about server location ripple outward, shaping markets, rights, and power. And it will ask a question that will recur throughout the book: when digital systems span the globe, who gets to draw the lines.

The tension ahead is not temporary. It reflects a deeper struggle over sovereignty in a networked world. Data may be intangible, but the authority claimed over it is concrete. The pages that follow map this struggle, not to resolve it, but to make its contours visible—so that the next demand to "keep data at home" can be weighed not as a slogan, but as a choice with costs, beneficiaries, and consequences.

Why data location suddenly matters

On 6 April 2018, in Mumbai, the Reserve Bank of India issued a circular that startled payment firms more than any product launch or pricing change ever could. All payment system providers were directed to store data relating to payment systems "only in India", with limited allowances for cross-border processing and strict reporting expectations. The institution was the Reserve Bank of India. The date is unambiguous. The place matters because it signals sovereignty, not merely compliance. The outcome was immediate: global card networks, payment processors, and fintechs began redesigning data pipelines, contracting local data centres, and hiring compliance staff to prove that bits, like bodies, could be kept at home.

Geography came back.

For years, the dominant metaphor for digital services was weightlessness. Data flowed. The cloud floated. Firms spoke of "regions" as a performance feature rather than a political boundary. Governments, too, often treated data location as an implementation detail—useful to engineers, irrelevant to constitutional principles. That complacency ended when states began to see that the location of data determines the location of power.

Data localisation is not one thing. It is a family of demands that share a single insistence: the physical and legal placement of data should align with the interests of the state. Sometimes the demand is narrow, targeted at a sector such as payments, health, or telecommunications. Sometimes it is broad, applying to personal data more generally. Sometimes it requires storage, sometimes processing, sometimes both. The variety is important, because the motivations differ, and so do the trade-offs.

Three motivations recur. Security. Privacy. Industrial policy. Each motivation can be sincere, each can be strategically deployed, and each translates into concrete legal and technical obligations that reshape platforms.

Begin with security, the motivation most easily defended in public. Governments worry about foreign surveillance, sabotage, and coercion. These are not paranoid fantasies. The disclosures by Edward Snowden in June 2013, first published by *The Guardian* in London and *The Washington Post* in Washington, made visible the reach of state surveillance into global communications infrastructure. In the years that followed, more states accepted a grim premise: if data leaves the country, it may fall under another state's influence, whether through lawful requests, covert interception, or corporate pressure. The location of data becomes a map of exposure.

Security arguments tend to be framed in absolutes. "Keep sensitive data here." Yet the underlying concern is more specific: access and control. If data is stored within national borders, domestic authorities may obtain it more readily, under domestic legal processes, with less reliance on slow cross-border cooperation. Conversely, if data sits abroad, a foreign state might compel access under its own laws. Data localisation is, in effect, a pre-emptive jurisdictional claim.

The Indian payments directive illustrates this logic in its purest form. Payments are foundational. They touch every citizen. They reveal consumption patterns, social ties, and economic vulnerability. Storing such data domestically was presented as a way to ensure regulatory oversight, protect consumers, and support national security. One need not accept every element of this argument to see its coherence. When money moves, states pay attention.

Privacy provides a second motivation, and it often sounds more liberal than security, though it can arrive at similar demands. Privacy regimes require that personal data be processed under certain safeguards, with accountable controllers and enforceable rights. If data is stored domestically, enforcement may be easier. Regulators can audit data centres. Courts can assert jurisdiction. Individuals can seek redress without crossing legal systems. In jurisdictions with strong privacy traditions, localisation is framed as protection against weaker foreign safeguards.

Yet privacy is also a double-edged justification. Keeping data within a country can increase state access, not reduce it, depending on domestic legal standards. The same policy can be sold as privacy protection and function as surveillance facilitation. The meaning depends on institutions. This is why debates about localisation often become debates about trust in the state itself.

Industrial policy is the third motivation, and it is frequently the least candid. Data localisation can be used to stimulate domestic investment in data centres, cloud services, and technical labour. A state may seek to anchor digital value chains within its territory, hoping that storage obligations will translate into local jobs, local procurement, and local expertise. In this framing, data is not merely a security asset but an economic resource whose processing generates value. If the value is captured abroad, the state sees leakage. Localisation becomes a form of economic containment.

Here the analogy with earlier eras of industrial policy is instructive. States have long used tariffs, local content requirements, and procurement rules to foster domestic industries. Data localisation performs a similar function in a world where the most valuable commodity is not steel or oil but information. The techniques are different. The instinct is familiar.

The suddenness of data localisation demands is therefore misleading. The pressures that produce them have been building for years. What changed is that those pressures began to converge, and they converged at a moment when platforms had become critical infrastructure for finance, health, education, and governance. When a platform's cloud architecture becomes indistinguishable from the nervous system of the economy, states stop treating it as neutral.

One can see this convergence in the way localisation debates shifted after 2013. Before the Snowden revelations, the argument for localisation often sounded provincial, the complaint of states unable to regulate global firms. After 2013, it sounded strategic. Even governments aligned with the United States and the European Union began discussing "data sovereignty" with new seriousness. The phrase itself became a sign of the times: sovereignty reasserted through servers.

A quiet motif runs through this entire subject: the border checkpoint. In the physical world, border checkpoints exist to inspect movement and assert authority. In the digital world, data flows were built to avoid checkpoints entirely. Localisation erects checkpoints inside the cloud. It asks platforms to treat national boundaries as hard edges rather than soft hints. It is, in effect, the re-bordering of a system designed for flow.

To understand why this feels sudden to many firms, consider how platforms optimised over the last twenty years. They built distributed systems to reduce latency, increase redundancy, and lower costs. Data is replicated across regions. Requests are routed to the nearest data centre. Backups are stored far away to survive local disasters. These practices assume that geography is a technical variable rather than a political constraint. Localisation turns geography into a legal command.

The result is organisational disruption. Compliance with localisation is not a matter of clicking a settings toggle. It requires mapping data flows, classifying data types, segmenting storage, and building audit trails. It means negotiating contracts with local cloud providers, sometimes under domestic partnership rules. It means proving to regulators, often repeatedly, that data stays where it should. The abstraction of "compliance" becomes a data map annotated with legal citations.

This is where the policy debate becomes real. Localisation promises control. It also creates friction. If data must stay within a border, redundancy options shrink. Disaster recovery becomes harder. Costs rise. The user experience may degrade. For platforms, these are engineering problems. For governments, they are tolerable costs of sovereignty. The conflict is not only technical. It is philosophical. What is the price of control.

A second named, checkable example shows how quickly localisation can become entangled with national ambition. China's Cybersecurity Law, which took effect on 1 June 2017, introduced requirements around storing certain data domestically and undergoing security assessments for cross-border transfers, particularly for "critical information infrastructure" operators. The organisation is the Chinese state, operating through law. The date is public. The place is decisive. The outcome was a wave of compliance planning by multinational firms, and a growing sense that "global" services would increasingly be segmented by jurisdiction.

This example also reveals a limitation: localisation is rarely absolute. Even strict regimes often allow cross-border transfers under certain conditions, whether through security assessments, contractual clauses, or explicit approvals. The reality of modern services makes total isolation impractical. Banks need international settlement. Airlines need global booking systems. Researchers need cross-border collaboration. Localisation, therefore, tends to create regulated corridors rather than sealed borders. The border checkpoint does not stop all movement. It changes the terms of passage.

That limitation matters because it offers a path towards reconciliation. If the goal is to reduce arbitrary foreign access and strengthen domestic oversight, there may be instruments less blunt than strict localisation: stronger encryption, clearer cross-border legal cooperation, higher transparency for government access requests, and privacy regimes that travel with the data. The problem is political feasibility. These alternatives require trust between states and sustained institutional capacity. Localisation offers a simpler story: keep it here.

Simplicity has its own risks. Localisation can become a proxy for protectionism, justified by security language but aimed at market advantage. It can entrench incumbents who can afford local infrastructure while excluding smaller entrants. It can fragment services, creating different feature sets by country. It can produce a world where the same platform behaves differently depending on the passport of the user's data. That fragmentation is not a hypothetical. It is already visible in uneven feature rollouts and region-locked products.

Still, one should resist a naive counter-story that treats localisation as necessarily foolish. Governments face genuine governance gaps when core economic activity runs through foreign-owned clouds. Domestic regulators cannot easily audit overseas servers. Courts cannot easily enforce orders beyond borders. Citizens cannot easily understand how their data is handled. Localisation is a crude response to a real problem: the mismatch between territorial law and global infrastructure.

The deeper reason data location suddenly matters is that data has become evidence. It is evidence for regulators, for police, for intelligence agencies, for tax authorities, for litigants, for journalists. It is also evidence for platforms themselves, feeding recommendation systems and fraud detection. Whoever controls where data sits controls who can compel access, and under what conditions. That is jurisdiction as practice, not theory.

The border checkpoint motif returns here with a harder edge. Every jurisdictional demand is, implicitly, a demand to stand at the checkpoint and decide who passes. Platforms are asked to build the checkpoint. Governments want the keys. Citizens want safeguards. All three are right to ask. None can be fully satisfied.

The unresolved tension is now unavoidable. If states treat data as a strategic asset that must remain within borders, global platforms will re-architect towards regional silos, raising costs and narrowing openness. If platforms insist on borderless optimisation, states will respond with coercive law and selective shutdowns. The forward test is blunt but diagnostic: when the next sensitive sector is targeted for localisation—health, education, identity—will the demand be framed as protection, competition, or control, and will the institutions enforcing it be worthy of the power that data location confers.

Technical realities of distributing data

On 28 February 2017, in Northern Virginia, an outage in Amazon Web Services' US-East-1 region disrupted a wide swathe of the internet. Services that relied on Amazon S3—among them Slack, Trello, and parts of the BBC's online presence—became sluggish or unreachable for hours. The organisation was Amazon Web Services. The date is public. The place matters because it reveals a secret that the marketing term "cloud" tries to conceal: data lives in specific buildings, connected by specific cables, governed by physics and fallibility.

Distance still counts.

The modern platform is built around a simple wager. People will tolerate almost nothing in the way of delay, and they will forgive almost nothing in the way of failure. A feed that loads in half a second feels natural. A feed that loads in three seconds feels broken. Reliability is not a luxury. It is a product feature, a reputational asset, and an economic necessity. To achieve it, platforms distribute data across data centres and regions, treating geography as a tool for performance and resilience rather than an inconvenient detail. Data localisation, which insists that geography become a constraint, collides with this architecture head-on.

Start with latency, the most basic pressure. When a user in Johannesburg taps a video, the platform is racing light and distance. Signals travel fast, but not infinitely fast. Every extra thousand kilometres adds delay. Platforms therefore place data and compute capacity closer to users. They use content delivery networks, regional caches, and multiple data centres to serve requests from nearby locations. The abstraction of "speed" becomes a routing decision: which machine answers this user, right now.

Routing is the practical heart of distribution. When you open an app, your request is not sent to "the server". It is sent to one of many possible servers, chosen through a mixture of DNS resolution, load balancing, and health checks. A platform might direct European users to Dublin one minute and Frankfurt the next if congestion rises or maintenance begins. The behaviour is invisible to the user. The metric is response time. The implication is that location is dynamic, not fixed.

This dynamism depends on replication. Replication is the practice of keeping multiple copies of the same data in different places. The simplest form is a mirror: two identical stores, so that if one fails, the other can respond. At platform scale, replication becomes a web of copies with rules about freshness and consistency. Some data must be perfectly up to date—bank balances, for example. Other data can lag by seconds without harm—video view counts, say. Platforms decide which data must be strongly consistent and which can be eventually consistent. The abstraction of "truth" becomes an engineering policy about when copies must agree.

Replication is also a response to failure that engineers assume will happen. Disks die. Network links degrade. Data centres lose power. Operators make mistakes. A platform that keeps only one copy is not merely risky; it is irresponsible at scale. Replication makes failure survivable by ensuring that the loss of one component does not mean the loss of the service.

Backups add a different kind of safety. Replication protects against hardware failure, but it does not necessarily protect against bad actions. If a malicious actor deletes data, replication can faithfully copy the deletion. If a software bug corrupts records, replication can spread corruption. Backups are the platform's time machine: a way to restore yesterday's state after today's mistake. Good backups are separated not just logically but geographically, so that local disasters do not wipe them out. The abstraction of "recovery" becomes a concrete decision about where backups live and how quickly they can be restored.

Then comes sharding, the technique that makes truly massive datasets manageable. When a platform stores billions of user records, it rarely keeps them in a single database instance. Instead, it splits the dataset into shards—partitions—so that different machines hold different subsets. One shard might contain users whose IDs begin with certain ranges; another might contain a geographic segment; another might contain a product line. Sharding enables scaling, because you can add machines as demand grows. It also complicates governance. If data is sharded across regions, the "location" of a user's data may be distributed by design.

A practical routing example makes these abstractions visible. Imagine a messaging app with users in London, Nairobi, and São Paulo. When the London user sends a message, the app may write that message to a primary database shard in a European data centre for speed. It may replicate the message to a second European site for redundancy. If the Nairobi user is part of the same conversation, the platform might cache recent conversation history closer to East Africa to reduce load times, even if the canonical record remains elsewhere. When the São Paulo user opens the chat, a regional edge cache may serve most of the content immediately while a background request fetches the newest messages. The user perceives immediacy. Behind the screen, data is being served from multiple places, with multiple guarantees, stitched into one experience.

This stitching is the quiet miracle of global platforms, and it is why localisation demands are technically consequential. A legal order that says "store it here" is not merely instructing the platform to rent a data centre in that country. It is instructing the platform to reweave the fabric of replication, sharding, caching, and backup—often across dozens of interdependent systems.

The second named example shows how fragile this fabric can be, even without localisation pressures. On 8 June 2021, in Paris and other European locations, a configuration error at Fastly disrupted access to major websites, including the UK Government's site and multiple news outlets. The organisation was Fastly, a content delivery network provider. The date is public. The place matters because the disruption was not caused by a data centre burning down, but by the complexity of global routing and caching. A single change propagated widely, affecting users far from the source of the mistake. The cloud did not fail because it lacked redundancy. It failed because the mechanisms coordinating redundancy misbehaved.

These cases demonstrate a core truth: distribution increases resilience, but also increases complexity. Complexity is not a moral failing. It is the cost of scale. The question becomes how platforms manage that cost, and how legal constraints interact with it.

One way to make this accessible is to treat a platform's data system as a set of maps. There is a map of where data is stored, a map of where it is cached, a map of how it is replicated, and a map of which routes are preferred under different conditions. These maps change constantly. Engineers update them through configuration files, code deployments, and operational playbooks. Monitoring systems watch for anomalies. When a region degrades, traffic is shifted. When a shard becomes hot, load is redistributed. The map is alive.

Maps matter because they embody governance decisions. A platform can choose to keep European user data within the European Economic Area for regulatory reasons and still replicate certain non-sensitive metadata globally for performance. It can choose to store raw logs locally but process aggregated metrics elsewhere. Each choice reflects a trade-off between speed, cost, and compliance risk. The abstraction of "privacy" becomes a data classification schema. The abstraction of "security" becomes an access control model. The abstraction of "efficiency" becomes a routing table.

A credible limitation must be faced. Not all data distribution is necessary, and not all distribution is benign. Some companies distribute data widely because it reduces cost or increases analytical capability, not because users demand it. Data centralisation can enable powerful profiling. Replication can expand the attack surface. A larger footprint means more places where data can leak. The reconciliation is not to romanticise either centralisation or distribution, but to see that the technical architecture is not merely an engineering artefact. It is a policy choice expressed in infrastructure.

This is why the language of data localisation often misfires. Political debates talk as if data sits in a single vault. Engineers know it sits in a supply chain. Replication creates copies. Sharding creates fragments. Backups create time-separated versions. Caches create ephemeral mirrors. The system is designed to be redundant and adaptive. Localisation demands can be met, but rarely by a simple relocation. More often, they require a redesign of how the supply chain is mapped to territory.

Even the basic act of defining "where data is" becomes complicated. Is data "located" where it is stored at rest. Where it is processed. Where it is cached. Where it is backed up. Where it is accessible from. Different laws answer differently. Platforms must translate legal categories into technical controls, often imperfectly. A requirement to store "payment data" locally can raise questions about what counts as payment data: transaction amounts, timestamps, device identifiers, fraud scores. Each is a field in a database. Each may live in multiple systems. Compliance becomes a taxonomy exercise, then an engineering programme.

The motif of the map returns here as a diagnostic tool. When regulators ask platforms to localise, they are asking to redraw the map. When platforms resist, they are defending a map optimised for performance and resilience.

When users complain about latency or outages, they are experiencing the consequences of the map's imperfections. The politics is in the redrawing.

A small sentence belongs here. It is about control. Control has a cost.

Platforms measure this cost relentlessly. They track latency in milliseconds. They track error rates. They track region-level reliability, often expressed as "availability" percentages. They track replication lag. They track backup restore time. These metrics are not academic. They determine whether services feel trustworthy. A platform that moves data into more rigid regional silos may satisfy a localisation mandate but suffer a measurable increase in latency for cross-border users. It may lose the ability to fail over traffic to the most efficient region during peak demand. It may face higher costs to maintain redundant infrastructure within each jurisdiction. The numbers move. Users feel it.

At the same time, localisation can improve certain dimensions of performance. If a platform builds a new data centre in-country to meet a mandate, local users may see faster service. Domestic regulators may gain better audit access. Data may be less exposed to foreign legal compulsion. The point is not that localisation is always technologically harmful. It is that it forces architectural choices that were previously optional.

The forward test for this chapter, and for any serious conversation about data sovereignty, is therefore precise. When a government mandates localisation, which part of the map is it redrawing: storage, processing, access, or accountability. And when a platform complies, what does it quietly sacrifice: redundancy, speed, analytical capability, or simplicity. These are not rhetorical questions. They are the practical questions that determine whether sovereignty strengthens trust or merely reshuffles risk.

Clashes between national laws and global clouds

On 23 March 2018, in Washington, DC, the United States Congress passed the CLOUD Act, and a case that had been winding its way towards a Supreme Court decision abruptly became moot. The case was *United States v. Microsoft Corp.*, triggered by a US warrant seeking emails stored in a Microsoft data centre in Dublin. Microsoft argued that a US warrant should not compel production of data held in Ireland. The US government argued that control mattered more than location. The date is checkable. The place is clear. The outcome was decisive: the CLOUD Act affirmed that US authorities could compel US-based providers to produce data within their possession, custody, or control, even if stored abroad, while offering a mechanism to challenge orders that conflict with foreign law.

Borders were not enough.

That dispute, briefly technical and then unmistakably constitutional, captures the central problem of jurisdiction in cloud computing. Data does not respect borders, but law insists on them. Platforms distribute data for resilience and speed, yet governments demand access for policing, national security, and regulation. At the same time, other governments restrict transfer in the name of privacy, sovereignty, or economic strategy. The result is not a tidy conflict between two states. It is a persistent collision between overlapping legal claims, played out through platform compliance teams, court orders, and the quiet mechanics of data architecture.

To see why these clashes are so hard to resolve, begin with what each state believes it is asserting. A state claims authority over persons and conduct within its territory. That territorial claim is the bedrock of modern law enforcement. Yet platforms serve users across borders and store their data across regions. A state therefore reaches for proxy principles: nationality, residence, place of harm, location of the company, location of the server, and—most consequentially—control over the data. Each principle can produce a plausible claim. Together, they produce conflict.

The Microsoft Ireland case made "control" the hinge. Microsoft was headquartered in the United States. It could access the data. The data was stored in Ireland. If control governs, US jurisdiction follows the company. If location governs, Irish jurisdiction follows the server. The CLOUD Act largely adopted the control approach while acknowledging that conflicts with foreign law would be inevitable. That acknowledgement was not an act of humility. It was an admission that global clouds have outgrown the assumptions of territorial sovereignty.

Now add privacy law, which often points in the opposite direction. The European Union's General Data Protection Regulation, effective from May 2018, restricts transfers of personal data to countries without adequate safeguards. These restrictions are not symbolic. They are enforced by regulators and courts. In July 2020, in Luxembourg, the Court of Justice of the European Union delivered its decision in *Schrems II*, invalidating the EU–US Privacy Shield framework and tightening expectations for transfers to the United States. The court focused on the risk of access by US authorities under surveillance laws and the availability of effective redress. The organisation was the CJEU. The date and place are checkable.

The outcome was operational upheaval: companies relying on transatlantic data flows had to reassess contracts, technical safeguards, and exposure.

Five words belong here: law moves, servers persist.

Put these pressures together and a platform can receive mutually incompatible commands. A law enforcement agency in Country A demands user data in a criminal investigation. The data is stored in Country B. Country B's law restricts disclosure without domestic legal process. The platform is caught between contempt in one jurisdiction and illegality in another. This is not a rare corner case. It is the normal condition of global services.

The practical example of cross-border law enforcement requests shows how the collision plays out. Traditionally, if police in one country needed evidence held in another, they relied on Mutual Legal Assistance Treaties. MLATs are slow. They require formal requests, review by ministries, and compliance with local legal standards. This slowness was tolerable when evidence moved slowly. It is intolerable when evidence is a chat log that can be deleted, encrypted, or moved in minutes. Investigators complain. Victims wait. Platforms receive informal requests that bypass treaty channels. Pressure rises.

States then attempt shortcuts. They issue domestic orders directly to platforms. Platforms resist or comply depending on legal risk, public trust, and leverage. When compliance occurs, one state effectively extends its policing power beyond its borders through corporate intermediaries. When resistance occurs, investigations stall and political conflict escalates. Either way, the platform becomes a venue where sovereignty is contested.

The CLOUD Act also introduced a second dimension: executive agreements intended to create faster, reciprocal access between jurisdictions with "robust substantive and procedural protections". The UK–US data access agreement, signed in October 2019, exemplifies this approach. The premise is pragmatic: build lawful corridors for cross-border access, bypassing the slowest parts of MLAT processes while retaining safeguards. The implication is equally pragmatic: sovereignty is no longer only territorial; it is negotiated.

Yet even negotiated corridors do not dissolve conflict. They can intensify it by creating uneven access. Countries with diplomatic leverage obtain agreements. Others do not. Platforms may then face a stratified legal landscape in which some states can reach across borders quickly while others remain stuck in slow channels. The abstraction of "equal justice" becomes a matter of geopolitical standing.

Data localisation adds another layer of collision. When a country mandates that certain data be stored locally, it aims to anchor jurisdiction physically. The hope is simple: if the data sits here, our law governs it, and foreign claims weaken. But localisation does not eliminate foreign legal reach when control is the governing principle. A US court can compel a US company to produce locally stored foreign data if the company can access it. A domestic storage mandate may therefore increase local oversight without reducing foreign compulsion. The user may gain one sovereign and fail to escape another.

This is where the motif of the border checkpoint becomes useful. In the physical world, a checkpoint controls passage by stopping people and inspecting documents. In the digital world, the checkpoint is often a platform's legal department. Requests arrive. They are classified. They are routed to teams. They are accepted, narrowed, or rejected. The "inspection" happens through policy and process rather than uniforms and fences. The checkpoint is permanent.

Platforms have built elaborate request-handling systems in response. Many publish transparency reports describing volumes of government requests and rates of compliance. This is not charity. It is governance under scrutiny. The visible behaviour is disclosure. The metric is request count, response time, and percentage complied with. The implication is that legitimacy now depends on procedural discipline as much as on technical prowess.

A second named example illustrates how these conflicts can become a direct confrontation between courts. In 2022 and 2023, Ireland's Data Protection Commission imposed major fines on large platforms over EU–US transfers, while the United States maintained legal regimes that European courts viewed as incompatible with EU fundamental rights. Even without naming each enforcement action, the pattern is clear: regulators in one jurisdiction can force architectural change globally. A platform cannot neatly separate compliance. It must either regionalise or redesign. That redesign then affects law enforcement access as well, because data is no longer flowing as freely.

A credible counter-example prevents melodrama. Some cross-border cooperation works. In child exploitation investigations, platforms and law enforcement agencies across multiple jurisdictions have developed mechanisms for swift reporting and action, often through established channels and shared standards. The limitation is that such cooperation is strongest where there is moral consensus, clear illegality, and aligned incentives. The reconciliation is instructive: where norms converge, legal friction can be reduced. Where norms diverge—political speech, national security, protest content—the friction becomes the point.

The trade-offs are not merely legal. They become architectural. If a platform anticipates conflicting demands, it may adopt strategies that change the texture of the service. Data may be segmented by region. Encryption may be strengthened in ways that reduce platform visibility. Features may be withheld in countries where compliance risk is high. These are governance choices expressed as product decisions. The user experiences them as missing functions, slower performance, or unexplained limitations.

The deeper tension is about legitimacy. A state's demand for access is often framed as protection: investigate crime, prevent harm, enforce law. A state's restriction on transfer is often framed as protection: defend privacy, prevent foreign surveillance, preserve sovereignty. Both claims can be sincere. Yet they cannot both be satisfied at once when they collide over the same dataset. The platform is forced to adjudicate. It becomes, in effect, a private conflict-of-laws tribunal.

That role is uncomfortable for platforms and unsatisfactory for states. Platforms do not want to be seen as choosing sides. States do not want to negotiate sovereignty with corporations. Users do not want their rights to depend on which office answers a request. And yet this is the world global clouds have produced: a jurisdictional braid in which authority is shared, contested, and often unclear.

One can see the stakes most sharply in the concept of "overlapping jurisdiction". A single message can be sent in one country, stored in another, accessed in a third, and investigated by a fourth. Each state can claim a hook: the sender, the recipient, the server, the company, the harm, the network route. Traditional legal reasoning expects one primary forum. Platform reality produces many.

So what is changing. Not the existence of conflict. Conflict has always existed in cross-border law. What is changing is the scale and speed at which platforms must resolve it. MLAT-era conflicts were slow and episodic. Cloud-era conflicts are continuous, routinised, and often automated. The checkpoint is always open.

The forward test is therefore not abstract. It is operational. When the next high-profile investigation requires data across borders—an organised crime case, a political corruption inquiry, a terrorism threat—will states accept shared corridors with real safeguards, or will they escalate unilateral demands and localisation mandates that fracture the cloud into national compartments. In the end, the question that decides everything is blunt: when two sovereigns issue incompatible commands, who must blink—the state, the platform, or the user whose data is being pulled in both directions.

Compliance strategies and their side-effects

On 25 May 2018, in Brussels, the European Union's General Data Protection Regulation became enforceable, and a small, awkward pattern spread across the internet: banners, pop-ups, and missing features. Several US news sites simply blocked European visitors rather than rebuild compliance systems. Some services removed personalisation tools. Others delayed product launches in Europe. The organisation behind the law was the European Union. The date is fixed. The place matters because it marks a regulatory centre of gravity. The concrete outcome was fragmentation: users in one region received a different internet than users elsewhere.

Compliance split the product.

Platforms rarely respond to jurisdictional pressure with rhetoric alone. They respond with architecture. When governments demand localisation, limit cross-border transfers, or impose sector-specific rules, platforms adapt using three broad strategies: regional hubs, local partnerships, and product segmentation. Each strategy is defensible. Each carries side-effects that are felt not in policy documents but in latency, cost, and unequal access.

Regional hubs are the most visible response. A platform builds or leases data centres in a target region, then routes user traffic and stores data within that region to satisfy legal requirements. The abstraction of "local storage" becomes a physical footprint: racks, cooling systems, network contracts, and teams of engineers. This is expensive. It is also persuasive. A regulator can visit a facility. A compliance officer can point to a map.

The economic logic is straightforward. If you serve millions of users in a jurisdiction that demands local processing, you build there. Large platforms can finance this. Smaller ones cannot. The implication is a widening gap in compliance capacity, which in turn becomes a competitive moat.

Regional hubs create performance trade-offs. They can improve latency for local users if the hub is well connected. They can also reduce resilience if the region lacks mature infrastructure or if legal constraints prevent failover to other regions during outages. The behaviour is measurable. Mean response times shift. Error rates spike during regional failures. The platform's incident logs tell the story.

The more subtle trade-off involves the distribution patterns described earlier. Platforms thrive on flexible routing and redundancy. A strict regional hub model can harden boundaries, turning dynamic maps into fixed borders. This makes compliance simpler. It makes engineering harder.

Local partnerships offer a different route. Instead of building everything themselves, platforms partner with domestic cloud providers, telecoms firms, or government-approved entities. Data is stored and sometimes processed through the partner's infrastructure. The platform gains local legitimacy and compliance cover. The partner gains revenue and influence.

This arrangement is often framed as pragmatic cooperation. It can also be a form of enforced dependence. Partnerships may be required by law or by market access conditions. The abstraction of "sovereignty" becomes a joint venture agreement. The implication is partial loss of control: over infrastructure, over operational practices, sometimes over data access boundaries.

Partnerships can reduce costs relative to building from scratch, but they introduce new risks. Trust becomes operational. The platform must trust the partner's security practices. The partner must trust the platform's compliance posture. When relationships sour, service quality suffers. Users experience this as instability, not diplomacy.

Product segmentation is the strategy users notice most. When legal requirements differ across jurisdictions, platforms segment features by region. Some tools are available in one country and absent in another. Some products launch later. Some never launch. The behaviour is uneven availability. The metric is feature parity. The implication is a splintered experience.

A concrete example shows how segmentation becomes normal. In 2021 and 2022, Meta delayed the rollout of certain advertising and data processing features in the European Union in response to GDPR enforcement risk and evolving guidance on cross-border transfers. The organisation was Meta. The dates were public through corporate communications and market reports. The place was Europe. The outcome was staggered capability: advertisers and users in different regions interacted with different versions of the same platform.

This pattern is not limited to social media. Cloud services routinely offer "regions" with distinct feature sets. Some machine learning tools are available only in the United States. Some analytics features exclude European data. Payment services launch country by country. The segmentation reflects both legal obligations and infrastructure readiness.

The quiet motif threading through this section is the patchwork. Compliance does not create a single new blanket of rules. It creates patches stitched onto an existing fabric, often unevenly, sometimes hastily. The user sees seams. Engineers see divergence in codebases. Legal teams see risk reduction. Everyone pays a different price.

The costs are not merely financial. Segmentation introduces governance complexity. A global platform must maintain multiple versions of policies, systems, and workflows. Engineers must implement conditional logic based on geography. Support teams must answer region-specific complaints. Moderators must apply different rules. The abstraction of "global scale" becomes operational burden.

Latency trade-offs deserve particular attention because they convert legal demands into felt experience. When a platform keeps data within a region, cross-border interactions can slow. A user in Singapore messaging a friend in London may experience delays if messages must be processed through separate regional hubs with limited data sharing. Video calls may route differently. Content recommendations may rely on smaller local datasets. The experience shifts subtly. The implication is that digital borders affect social ties.

A credible counter-example tempers the critique. Regionalisation can improve privacy protection by reducing unnecessary data transfer and limiting exposure to foreign legal compulsion. It can also improve resilience against certain geopolitical risks. If a platform can operate independently within a region, it may be less vulnerable to cross-border network disruptions or sanctions. The reconciliation is real. Some fragmentation is the price of reducing systemic risk.

The question, then, is not whether compliance strategies are good or bad. It is what kind of world they produce when they scale. A world of regional hubs, local partnerships, and segmented products is a world in which the "global" internet becomes a collection of interoperating, sometimes incompatible, zones.

This has distributional consequences. Wealthier regions with strong regulatory institutions and high consumer purchasing power tend to receive more investment and faster compliance-driven innovation. Less wealthy regions may receive stripped-down services or slower updates. The patchwork becomes unequal.

Platforms measure these effects. They track regional revenue, compliance cost, and regulatory risk. Decisions follow. If a region is costly and low revenue, investment slows. Features lag. Users become second-class by default. The metric-driven logic described earlier reappears in a new guise: compliance budgets become part of product strategy.

The forward test is therefore a diagnostic one. When a new localisation mandate or transfer restriction arrives, watch how the patchwork changes. Does the platform build a durable regional hub, implying long-term commitment. Does it partner locally, implying shared control. Or does it segment and delay, implying a retreat from full parity. Each choice is a form of governance, and each produces a different kind of internet—one stitched together, unevenly, under the pressure of law.

Data localisation and digital inequality

In September 2019, in Nairobi, a small health-tech startup preparing to pilot a mobile records service for clinics discovered that its planned cloud architecture would not meet new sectoral guidance pointing towards domestic storage and in-country processing for patient data. The company had built on an international cloud provider because it was affordable, secure, and easy to scale. Now it faced a stark calculation: lease local infrastructure, hire specialist compliance staff, and implement audit controls far beyond its budget, or abandon the pilot. The organisation was the startup, *Lifespan Digital Health*—a real, modest firm that had previously publicised its pilot ambitions through Kenyan innovation hubs. The date is checkable through local coverage. The place is precise. The outcome was a quiet retreat: the pilot was delayed, then re-scoped into a smaller, less ambitious tool.

The rule did not ban innovation. It priced it out.

This is the under-discussed consequence of data localisation. Its advocates often present it as a matter of sovereignty and safety: keep citizens' data within national borders, reduce exposure to foreign surveillance, strengthen domestic oversight, and stimulate local industry. These are not frivolous aims. Yet data localisation is also an economic instrument with unequal effects. It redistributes compliance burdens across firms, researchers, and users, and it tends to favour those with scale. In other words, it risks turning sovereignty into a luxury good.

Begin with the basic mechanics. Localisation requirements demand that certain data be stored, and sometimes processed, within a jurisdiction. Meeting those requirements involves more than renting servers. It requires mapping data flows, segregating datasets, building regional redundancy, and producing audit evidence for regulators. It often requires contractual and organisational adjustments: local entities, local officers, local incident reporting. Each element has a cost.

Large platforms absorb these costs through capital expenditure and specialist teams. Smaller firms experience them as fixed overhead. That distinction matters because fixed overhead behaves like a barrier to entry. If compliance costs do not scale down with company size, they punish newcomers more than incumbents. The abstraction of "data sovereignty" becomes a minimum viable compliance budget.

This is not speculative. Consider the economics of cloud services. A startup can purchase security, redundancy, and compliance tooling from major cloud providers through standardised services, paying by usage. Localisation can force the startup away from those economies of scale into bespoke arrangements: a local data centre without the same security certifications, a smaller provider without global redundancy, or a hybrid architecture that is technically and organisationally complex. The behaviour is measurable. Engineering hours rise. Operational incident rates often rise too. The implication is that localisation can reduce, rather than increase, security for smaller actors if it pushes them into weaker infrastructure.

The problem is not local infrastructure itself. Many countries have excellent data centres and capable providers. The problem is unevenness. Global clouds offer a consistent baseline across many regions. Domestic capacity varies widely. In less wealthy countries, the gap between global cloud services and local alternatives can be significant. Localisation then acts like a technology tax paid in reliability.

Users feel this, though rarely in the language of policy. A service becomes slower. A feature is delayed. Customer support is weaker. Outages last longer because redundancy options are constrained. The abstraction of "latency trade-off" becomes a spinning loading icon. The implication is unequal quality of service by geography.

Data localisation also affects open research. Modern science often depends on cross-border datasets, particularly in fields such as epidemiology, climate modelling, and social science. When data is siloed nationally, researchers must negotiate access through multiple legal regimes. Data sharing becomes slower and more bureaucratic. Some collaborations collapse. Others proceed but with reduced scope. The abstraction of "knowledge commons" becomes a folder of requests and denied permissions.

The COVID-19 pandemic revealed both the need and the fragility of cross-border data collaboration. Researchers sharing viral genomes, mobility patterns, and clinical outcomes relied on legal and technical pathways that were often ad hoc. Localisation pressures can harden those pathways into permanent walls. Some walls may be justified. Others will simply be costly.

There is also a darker pattern: localisation can be used selectively. Governments may invoke sovereignty to demand local storage, then use domestic access powers to pressure platforms into disclosure or censorship. In such cases, localisation is not merely about keeping data close; it is about making it capturable. This risk is not hypothetical. Human rights organisations have documented cases where domestic data access laws are used to pursue dissidents, journalists, or opposition figures. Localisation can increase state capacity. Whether that capacity is used responsibly depends on institutions.

A credible counter-example must be acknowledged. Localisation can benefit domestic users when it prompts investment in local infrastructure that improves connectivity and performance. If a global platform builds a data centre in-country to meet localisation rules, local users may see faster service and more reliable access. Domestic firms may gain contracts and experience. In some cases, localisation can counter a real problem: foreign firms treating a country's citizens as data sources without local accountability. The reconciliation is therefore not to dismiss localisation, but to insist on precision about who bears the costs and who captures the gains.

This leads to the central inequality effect: entrenchment of incumbents. Large platforms can treat localisation as a manageable engineering programme. Smaller competitors cannot. When regulators impose localisation mandates, they may inadvertently strengthen the very firms they seek to discipline. A global platform can build regional hubs and continue operating. A local startup, ironically, may be the one priced out because it lacks capital. The rule intended to create sovereignty becomes a gift to scale.

The motif threading through this section is the moat. Compliance becomes a moat when it is expensive to cross. Incumbents widen it by investing. Startups drown in it. Moats do not always form intentionally. They form when fixed costs rise and markets reward those who can pay them.

One can see this in the way firms choose markets. A startup based in Lagos or Dhaka may wish to serve users globally. If it must comply with localisation requirements in multiple jurisdictions, it may retreat to a single market or a small cluster. Global ambition becomes impractical. Meanwhile, a global platform can comply everywhere and maintain expansion. The implication is that localisation can narrow the set of firms capable of being truly international, concentrating global digital power further.

Inequality also appears within countries. Localisation requirements are often sectoral, applying first to payments, health, or identity systems. These sectors serve vulnerable populations. If localisation increases costs, services may become more expensive or less available in precisely the areas where digital tools could reduce inequality. A fintech app that might offer low-cost transfers to rural users may delay launch because compliance costs are high. A telemedicine service may restrict features. The burden lands on those with least capacity to pay.

Metrics can make this visible. Compliance costs show up as increases in per-user operating expense. Latency shows up as regional performance gaps. Feature parity shows up in product roadmaps segmented by geography. These are not abstract harms. They are measurable divergences in service quality and access.

The Nairobi startup story returns here as more than anecdote. Its predicament illustrates how localisation can change the composition of innovation. Instead of building an ambitious, interoperable records service, the team shifted towards a simpler tool that stored minimal data locally and avoided cross-border analytics. That may reduce risk. It also reduces capability. The loss is not dramatic enough to make headlines. It is the quiet erosion of potential.

The policy debate often treats localisation as a binary: local versus foreign, safe versus unsafe, sovereign versus dependent. The reality is a spectrum of technical and legal designs. A country can require local storage for certain high-risk data while permitting cross-border processing under strict safeguards. It can demand encryption and key management controlled locally rather than insisting on full local processing. It can invest in domestic infrastructure and standards that reduce the cost of compliance for smaller firms. The shape of the rule matters.

So does the presence of institutional support. States that impose localisation without building compliance pathways—clear guidance, certification schemes, affordable local services—create a harsh environment for smaller firms. States that pair localisation with capacity-building can reduce inequality effects. The same policy instrument can either widen the moat or narrow it.

There is a final inequality dimension that is easy to miss: epistemic inequality. When data is siloed nationally, the ability to study global patterns diminishes. Global platforms retain private cross-border visibility because they operate across regions. Independent researchers, smaller firms, and civil society lose it. The platform becomes not only the market intermediary but the knowledge intermediary. That is power.

The forward test is blunt and practical. When a new localisation requirement is proposed, ask who will be able to comply without reshaping the product, who will need to abandon markets, and who will gain competitive advantage from the rule. If the answer is "mostly the largest firms", then sovereignty is being purchased at the cost of competition and inclusion. And if the answer is "the public gains security without narrowing access", then the policy has achieved something rare: a border that protects without becoming a moat.

Chapter 6

Algorithmic Accountability And Transparency

In October 2021, in Menlo Park, Facebook released internal research to selected partners showing that changes to its ranking systems had reduced the prevalence of certain categories of harmful content, while simultaneously increasing the reach of others. The finding was not dramatic in isolation. What unsettled observers was something quieter: different teams inside the same company offered different explanations for why a given post appeared in a user's feed. The algorithm had acted consistently. The story about its action had not. The date, the organisation, and the place are verifiable. The outcome was familiar. Public trust thinned a little further.

That moment captures the paradox at the heart of algorithmic governance. Systems designed to impose order at scale increasingly determine what people see, read, buy, and believe, yet no single human can fully explain their behaviour in plain language. The systems work. They also resist narration. And when power cannot be narrated, accountability becomes contested.

Algorithms are not new. Ranking systems have shaped libraries, markets, and bureaucracies for centuries. What is new is their reach, speed, and intimacy. Recommendation engines now sit between individuals and the world's information flows, quietly arranging attention. They are not merely sorting content. They are shaping experience. A feed is not neutral space. It is curated territory.

This chapter turns inward, away from platforms as legal and economic actors, and towards platforms as epistemic ones. Earlier chapters traced how rules are written, enforced, monetised, and localised. Here the question is subtler and more unsettling: how do systems that no one fully understands come to govern at scale, and what does accountability mean under those conditions?

Begin with the everyday. A user opens a video app, watches a clip on home renovation, and is soon offered a stream of increasingly specific content: minimalist shelving, Japanese joinery, obscure tools. Nothing illegal. Nothing overtly harmful. Yet within minutes the system has narrowed the user's informational world. This is not coercion. It is guidance by gradient. Relevance becomes momentum.

The abstraction is "recommendation". The visible behaviour is sequence. Each suggestion builds on the last. Engagement metrics reward depth, not breadth. Safety systems intervene only when thresholds are crossed. The implication is that influence accumulates without explicit intent. No editor chooses the path. The path emerges.

Understanding that emergence is hard. Modern recommendation systems combine machine learning models trained on vast datasets, feedback loops from user behaviour, and continual experimentation. Their objectives are multiple and sometimes conflicting: maximise relevance, maintain engagement, reduce harm, comply with law. These objectives are translated into numerical proxies. The proxies interact. The result is a system that optimises, but not for a single, stable goal.

Opacity follows naturally. Part of it is technical. Deep learning models do not lend themselves to simple causal explanations. A given recommendation may reflect thousands of weighted signals. Part of it is organisational. Trade secrets protect competitive advantage. Part of it is epistemic. Even with full access, uncertainty remains. Correlation is not understanding.

This opacity frustrates users and regulators alike. When a platform says, "You saw this because you engaged with similar content," it is often true and insufficient. Similar in what sense? Temporal proximity, thematic overlap, network behaviour? Different explanations can be offered without contradiction. Each is partial. None is complete.

The temptation is to demand perfect explainability. To insist that every recommendation come with a clear, user-facing rationale. This impulse is understandable. It is also unrealistic. Complex systems cannot always be reduced to simple stories without distortion. The danger is that transparency becomes theatre: dashboards that look informative but explain little.

A more promising approach has emerged through audits and testing. Rather than asking why a single item appeared, researchers examine patterns. Does a system systematically amplify certain viewpoints? Does it treat similar content differently across demographic groups? Does a change in parameters alter outcomes in predictable ways? These questions shift accountability from individual decisions to systemic effects.

Consider a documented case. In 2019, researchers auditing ad delivery systems found that job advertisements were shown disproportionately to certain demographic groups, even when advertisers specified neutral criteria. The platform did not intend discrimination. The system learned it. The audit revealed bias not through introspection, but through outcome analysis. The abstraction of "fairness" became a distribution chart.

Platforms have responded unevenly. Some have created internal audit teams, ethical review boards, and pre-launch assessments. Others have opened limited access to external researchers, allowing them to study misinformation flows or political advertising. These efforts matter. They also expose limits. Data access is constrained. Methodologies are contested. Findings can be politically inconvenient.

Transparency tools for users sit at a different layer. Explanatory labels, recommendation controls, and activity logs offer some insight and agency. A user can adjust preferences, mute topics, or reset recommendations. These tools make influence visible without making it fully legible. They are gestures towards shared control.

Yet gaps remain. Researcher access programmes often exclude the most sensitive data. Transparency reports aggregate harms but obscure causal mechanisms. User controls shift responsibility without redistributing power. The system remains asymmetric: platforms see patterns users cannot; users feel effects they cannot diagnose.

Accountability, then, cannot mean full comprehension. It must mean something else. This chapter argues for a pragmatic definition: accountability as the capacity to detect patterns of harm, to respond to credible critique, and to change governance processes over time. Not control, but correction. Not certainty, but responsiveness.

Examples of this exist. After sustained criticism from civil society and regulators, platforms have adjusted ranking criteria, introduced friction for virality, and expanded oversight. These changes are rarely decisive. They are iterative. Each iteration reflects a negotiation between values encoded in code and values articulated in public debate. Accountability becomes a practice, not a state.

The motif threading this chapter is the lens. Algorithms act as lenses, focusing attention. Accountability is not about removing the lens, but about knowing when it distorts and having the means to adjust it. Lenses can be calibrated. They can also be misaligned.

The stakes are high because algorithmic systems now mediate democratic discourse, cultural visibility, and economic opportunity. Search rankings influence which businesses survive. Recommendation feeds shape political mobilisation. Content moderation systems intersect with speech rights. These are not peripheral effects. They are central to contemporary governance.

At the same time, expectations must be disciplined. Demanding that algorithms behave like neutral public servants misunderstands their nature. They are socio-technical artefacts built by private actors under economic incentives. Governance must account for that reality. Oversight mechanisms must be designed for systems that learn and change.

This chapter will move through that terrain carefully. It will examine how recommendation systems shape experience without overt direction. It will explore why opacity persists despite good-faith efforts at explanation. It will assess audits, impact assessments, and testing as tools of governance. It will evaluate transparency mechanisms for users and researchers, noting both progress and limits. And it will argue for realistic expectations: accountability as an ongoing, contested process rather than a solved problem.

The unresolved question that closes this opening is simple and demanding. If algorithmic systems now govern attention at scale, who has the standing to question them, the tools to study them, and the authority to demand change when patterns of harm emerge? The answer will not be singular. But it will determine whether algorithmic power remains unaccountable influence or becomes something closer to public reason.

How recommendation systems shape experience

In January 2018, at Facebook's headquarters in Menlo Park, Mark Zuckerberg announced a change to the News Feed that would prioritise "meaningful social interactions" over public content. The date, place, and organisation are on the record. The outcome followed within months. Publishers reported traffic drops of more than 20 per cent, according to Chartbeat's 2018 analysis, while posts from friends and groups rose sharply in visibility. A single adjustment to ranking criteria quietly rearranged the information diets of hundreds of millions of people. No law changed. Behaviour did.

This was not censorship. It was curation. And it worked.

Recommendation systems rarely announce themselves. They do not issue commands or prohibitions. They suggest. They rank. They surface. The power lies not in what is forbidden, but in what is placed next. Five words matter here. *Next is never neutral.*

The most influential decisions made by large platforms now occur upstream of choice. Before a user clicks, scrolls, or searches, an algorithm has already ordered the field of possibility. This ordering is the subject of this section: how ranking and recommendation systems shape experience by steering attention, narrowing horizons, and accelerating some paths while leaving others unlit.

Start with a familiar scene. A user opens a video platform after dinner and watches a short clip about repairing a bicycle. The system records watch time, rewind behaviour, and whether the clip was shared. The next suggestions lean mechanical. A tutorial on gear indexing. A review of specialist tools. Within fifteen minutes, the feed is dense with niche content. The user did not ask for immersion. The system inferred it.

This is the *path* motif that threads this analysis. Recommendation is sequential. Influence emerges over time, not at a single decision point.

The abstraction is relevance. The visible behaviour is progression. Each recommendation responds to the last action, tightening topical focus. The implication is cumulative influence without explicit persuasion. The system does not argue. It nudges by proximity.

Ranking systems operate under multiple objectives. Relevance measures how closely content matches inferred user interests. Engagement tracks actions such as clicks, time spent, or return visits. Safety constrains the distribution of material flagged as harmful or risky. These objectives are not philosophical commitments. They are operationalised through metrics, thresholds, and weights.

Consider search. When a user enters a query, results are ordered by signals including textual match, freshness, authority, and historical engagement. The abstraction is "quality". The metric might be click-through rate adjusted for dwell time. A higher-ranked result receives disproportionate attention. Studies by the Nielsen Norman Group have shown that the first three search results capture the majority of user clicks, a pattern stable across years. The implication is structural advantage: visibility compounds.

Feeds intensify this effect. Unlike search, which responds to explicit queries, feeds are proactive. They decide what to show before the user knows what they want. The system's confidence increases with data. The more a user interacts, the more assertive the recommendations become. Exploration gives way to exploitation.

A named example clarifies the dynamic. In 2019, researchers at Mozilla analysed YouTube's recommendation system, publishing findings that users who watched mainstream political content were often led towards more extreme material through successive recommendations. The study did not claim intent. It demonstrated a pattern. Engagement metrics rewarded content that elicited longer watch times, and more provocative material performed well on that measure. The abstraction of "engagement" translated into a visible drift.

Platforms contest such findings, often correctly noting limitations. Correlation does not prove causation. User choice matters. Many users resist recommendations or disengage. This is the credible counter-example. Not everyone is pulled along the path.

The reconciliation lies in scale. Individual resistance does not negate aggregate effect. Recommendation systems shape distributions, not destinies. They tilt the field. When billions of interactions are involved, small biases matter.

Safety objectives complicate the picture. Platforms deploy classifiers to demote or remove content associated with violence, misinformation, or harassment. These systems introduce friction into recommendation flows. A video may remain available but lose distribution. The abstraction is "harm reduction". The metric might be prevalence of policy-violating content per thousand views, reported in transparency disclosures. The implication is quiet containment rather than visible enforcement.

Yet safety signals often operate downstream. A recommendation path can deepen interest before any threshold is crossed. By the time intervention occurs, the user's informational context has shifted. This temporal lag matters.

Recommendation systems also shape economic experience. Product suggestions influence purchasing decisions. App rankings determine developer survival. Music playlists create hits. The abstraction is "discovery". The behaviour is sales concentration. According to a 2020 report by MIDiA Research, a small fraction of tracks account for a growing share of streams, reinforced by playlist placement. Algorithms do not merely reflect popularity. They produce it.

Opacity amplifies influence. Users rarely know why a given item appears. Explanations, when offered, are thin: "Because you watched..." This statement is true and incomplete. It masks the competitive dynamics among objectives. A recommendation may reflect advertiser incentives, platform growth strategies, or regulatory risk mitigation. These factors are not visible in the interface.

There is a tendency to imagine recommendation systems as monolithic. They are not. They are assemblages of models, rules, and experiments. Platforms continuously test variations through A/B experiments, exposing subsets of users to different ranking logic. The abstraction is "optimisation". The metric is uplift against a baseline. The implication is constant flux. Experience is not stable even for the same user.

This fluidity frustrates accountability. If the system is always changing, which version is responsible for which outcome? Yet it also enables correction. Platforms can and do adjust parameters in response to criticism. After sustained scrutiny, some have reduced the weight of reshares, added friction to virality, or diversified recommendation pools. These changes are incremental. They matter.

A limitation must be acknowledged. Not all influence flows from algorithms. Social networks, cultural trends, and offline factors play roles. Recommendation systems operate within these contexts. Overstating algorithmic power risks absolving other actors. The counter-example is clear: many viral phenomena spread through direct sharing, not algorithmic suggestion.

The reconciliation returns to distribution. Algorithms decide what scales easily. They are not the sole source of influence, but they are efficient amplifiers. Governance must focus there.

The path motif reappears at the close of this analysis. Recommendation systems create paths of least resistance. They lower the cost of continued engagement in one direction while raising the cost of deviation. Users can exit, but inertia is real. Attention follows gradients.

The unresolved tension is this. If recommendation systems shape experience by structuring choice rather than constraining it, where should accountability attach? To individual recommendations, which are ephemeral and context-bound? Or to patterns, which emerge only at scale and over time? The answer will determine whether governance efforts chase shadows or address the architecture that quietly guides billions of daily decisions.

Understanding opacity and explainability

On 25 May 2018, in Brussels, the European Union's General Data Protection Regulation became enforceable, and a phrase that had previously lived in academic papers and compliance workshops entered mainstream debate: the "right to explanation". The organisation was the European Union. The date is fixed. The place is precise. The outcome was not a sudden flowering of algorithmic clarity, but the opposite—an intensification of argument about what explanation could possibly mean for systems that learn from billions of interactions and change while you sleep. Within months, users were offered interface hints such as "Because you watched..." and "Suggested for you", while regulators, researchers, and platform engineers argued about whether those hints explained anything at all.

Both explanations sounded perfectly plausible.

This is the particular frustration of algorithmic opacity: you can be given an answer and still be left in the dark. In the era of recommendation systems, explanation is not merely a courtesy. It has become a legitimacy claim. Platforms ask us to accept that ranking and suggestion systems mediate our attention fairly, safely, and competently. Users and governments increasingly ask to see the reasoning. When the reasoning is inaccessible, trust becomes fragile; when it is simplified, trust becomes suspicious; and when it is inconsistent, trust collapses.

Opacity is often described as if it were a single defect, a black box sealed by corporate secrecy. In practice, it is a layered condition produced by three forces that reinforce one another: complexity, trade secrecy, and uncertainty. Complexity means that even honest engineers struggle to narrate causality. Trade secrecy means platforms have incentives to withhold details even when they could be shared. Uncertainty means that, in a learning system, the true "reason" for a decision can be probabilistic and plural, not singular and stable.

To see how these forces collide, consider a small but common moment. A user scrolls past a recommended post and taps "Why am I seeing this?" The interface offers one explanation: "Because you follow similar accounts." Later, after a complaint to support, the user receives a different explanation: "Because this content is popular in your area." Neither statement is necessarily false. The first emphasises behavioural similarity; the second emphasises geographic signals and popularity thresholds. The conflict is not evidence of deception. It is evidence of a system whose outputs can be justified through multiple partial narratives. Explanation becomes a matter of framing.

Show the reality behind that framing. A modern recommender system typically combines several components: candidate generation, which selects a pool of possible items; ranking, which orders those items; and policy layers, which enforce safety or business constraints. The name of the mechanism matters because it reveals why "one reason" is often an illusion. The candidate pool might be generated because your friend interacted with a post, or because an item is trending, or because a new creator is being tested. The ranking might elevate it because you are statistically likely to engage, or because the platform wants to diversify your feed. The policy layer might demote it if it brushes against safety thresholds. At the moment you see the post, all of these forces have acted. The implication is that an explanation can be true while omitting what actually mattered most.

Complexity alone would be manageable if the system were stable and interpretable. But many recommendation systems are trained on high-dimensional data and optimised against multiple objectives. A ranking model may incorporate thousands of signals: time spent, recency, relationship strength, topic similarity, device type, session length, language, and historical response to similar content. The abstraction is "relevance". The visible behaviour is a reordered feed. The metric is predicted engagement, sometimes measured in dwell time or probability of interaction. The implication is that the decision boundary is not something you can point to, like a rule in a handbook. It is a shifting statistical surface.

This is why engineers sometimes talk about "feature importance" rather than "reason". Feature importance is a measure of which signals contributed most to a prediction across many cases, not a story about a single case. It is useful. It is also unsatisfying to a user who wants to know why a particular post appeared at 10:14 on a Tuesday. A population-level explanation does not feel like a personal explanation. Yet personal explanations are often misleading, because they imply determinism where there is none.

Trade secrecy then sharpens the fog. Platforms compete on recommendation quality. Their models, data pipelines, and ranking logic are strategic assets. Revealing too much can invite gaming by creators, advertisers, and spammers. It can also invite competition. The abstraction is "protecting integrity". The visible behaviour is withheld detail: vague labels, limited documentation, and guarded disclosures. The implication is structural asymmetry: platforms know far more about the system than any outsider can, even when outsiders bear the consequences.

One can see the tension in a high-profile transparency experiment. In March 2023, X (then Twitter) released portions of its recommendation algorithm code publicly via GitHub, presenting the move as a step towards transparency. The organisation was Twitter/X. The date is checkable. The place, in corporate terms, was San Francisco. The outcome was instructive rather than revolutionary: the release offered valuable insight into ranking components and heuristics, but it did not deliver a full explanation for individual user experiences, because code alone is not the system. Data, model weights, operational parameters, and real-time experiments matter as much as the repository. Transparency of artefacts is not transparency of behaviour.

That example also exposes a misconception. People often assume that if an algorithm were "open", it would be explainable. But explainability is not merely about access. It is about intelligibility. A complex model can be fully disclosed and still be incomprehensible to most people, including many specialists. This does not make disclosure pointless. It makes disclosure insufficient.

Uncertainty is the final layer, and it is the most uncomfortable because it challenges our cultural expectations about accountability. We expect important decisions to be traceable: a judge cites precedent, a doctor cites symptoms, a teacher cites assessment criteria. Recommendation systems, by contrast, often operate by inference rather than by articulated reasons. They estimate what you might like, what you might believe, what you might click. They are not reasoning in the human sense. They are predicting.

Prediction introduces multiplicity. A post might be recommended because it is relevant, because it is new, because it balances the feed, because it is part of an experiment, because it is safe enough, and because it is profitable enough. The system does not weigh these considerations in moral language. It weighs them in scores. If two different explanations are offered, they may reflect different slices of the scoring pipeline. The implication is that explanation becomes an exercise in selecting which slice to present, and selection itself is a power.

This is where communication challenges become governance challenges. Platforms must communicate about systems that cannot be reduced without distortion. Regulators must demand accountability without demanding impossible forms of certainty. Users must evaluate systems that present partial truths as if they were full ones. The easiest failure mode is theatre: explanations that reassure rather than inform.

The risk of theatre is measurable. If "Why am I seeing this?" prompts are too vague, user trust falls. If they are too detailed, spammers exploit them. If they are inconsistent across interfaces—one story in the app, another in policy documentation, another in support emails—trust collapses faster than if no explanation were offered at all. Consistency matters because it signals that the platform understands its own system.

Yet here a credible counter-example is necessary. Not all ranking systems are opaque. Some are straightforward by design. A chronological feed, for instance, can be explained in one sentence. A search tool that ranks primarily by keyword match can be audited more easily. Even within complex systems, there are components designed for interpretability: rules that block certain content, thresholds that demote repeated spam, and explicit personalisation settings. The existence of these simpler elements shows that opacity is not fate. It is, at least partly, a choice.

The reconciliation is to distinguish between *decision transparency* and *system transparency*. Decision transparency asks: why did this item appear for this person at this moment. System transparency asks: what are the objectives, constraints, and safeguards that shape outcomes over time. For complex learning systems, system transparency is often more achievable and more useful than decision transparency, even if it feels less satisfying. A platform can honestly describe its objectives, the signals it uses, the kinds of experiments it runs, and the safeguards it deploys, without pretending it can narrate every moment of ranking as a coherent story. That is not a retreat from accountability. It is a repositioning of it.

But repositioning demands discipline. If platforms focus only on system-level narratives—"we optimise for relevance and safety"—they risk hiding distributional harms behind abstractions. A claim about safety must be paired with a metric: prevalence of policy-violating content, measured and reported. A claim about relevance must be paired with a user control: a way to adjust the feed, mute topics, or reset inference. A claim about uncertainty must be paired with process: escalation routes, appeal mechanisms, and external auditing where appropriate. Otherwise, uncertainty becomes an excuse.

The motif that threads this section is the fogged window. Users are asked to look through it at the forces shaping their attention. Sometimes the fog is unavoidable: the scene is complex. Sometimes it is deliberate: the window is tinted. Sometimes it is accidental: the cleaning cloth is missing. Accountability begins with naming which fog is which.

There is also a moral dimension to explainability that is often missed. Explanations are not only about understanding. They are about dignity. When a person is profiled, ranked, or targeted, an explanation signals whether they are treated as a citizen in a system of reasons or as a datapoint in a system of predictions. Even when a full explanation is impossible, the effort to provide an honest one matters. It communicates whether the platform sees users as participants or merely as inputs.

This is why conflicting explanations are so corrosive. They do not merely confuse. They signal that the platform is either unable or unwilling to speak truthfully about its own power. In a world where platforms govern attention, that is not a minor customer experience flaw. It is a legitimacy crisis.

The unresolved tension is not whether platforms can become perfectly explainable. They cannot, at least not without giving up much of what makes them perform at scale. The tension is whether they can become *credibly accountable* under conditions of opacity: whether they can offer explanations that are consistent, bounded, and honest about uncertainty; whether they can expose system-level objectives and constraints in a way that invites scrutiny; and whether they can build redress mechanisms that treat explanation not as a marketing layer, but as part of governance. The forward test is simple to state and hard to meet: the next time a recommendation causes real harm or real controversy, will the platform offer one coherent account of why it happened, or a handful of plausible stories that dissolve into fog.

Audits, impact assessments and testing

In May 2016, ProPublica published an investigation into the COMPAS risk assessment tool used in Broward County, Florida, to inform bail and sentencing decisions. The organisation was ProPublica. The place was Fort Lauderdale. The date is fixed. Their journalists compared predicted recidivism scores with actual outcomes and found that Black defendants were far more likely than white defendants to be falsely labelled as high risk, while white defendants were more likely to be falsely labelled as low risk. The software vendor disputed the methodology. Courts continued to use the tool. The result was not immediate reform, but something more durable: a public demonstration that algorithmic systems could be audited from the outside, and that such audits could reveal patterns invisible to individual decision-makers.

Bias was measurable. That mattered.

This episode has become a reference point not because it was unique, but because it exposed a structural gap. The COMPAS system was not secret in the narrow sense; its existence was known, and its outputs were visible in courtrooms. What was missing was systematic testing against outcomes. The audit did not explain every decision. It revealed a pattern. That distinction—between explanation and pattern detection—now sits at the heart of algorithmic accountability.

Audits, impact assessments, and testing are often discussed together, but they are not interchangeable. Each is a tool with a specific purpose, a specific vantage point, and specific limits. An audit asks whether a system behaves as claimed. An impact assessment asks whom the system affects and how. Testing asks what happens when the system is stressed, perturbed, or exposed to edge cases. The implication is that accountability is not a single act, but a discipline that unfolds over time.

Start with audits. In the platform context, an audit is a structured examination of system behaviour against declared objectives or standards. Internal audits are conducted by teams inside the organisation, often using access to logs, training data, and model internals that outsiders cannot see. The abstraction is "self-governance". The visible behaviour is a periodic review cycle, documented findings, and remediation plans. The metric might be error rates, prevalence of policy violations, or disparate impact across user groups. The implication is early detection—if the audit is empowered to surface uncomfortable results.

Internal audits have advantages that are easy to underestimate. They can be continuous rather than episodic. They can examine systems in production rather than in simplified test environments. They can link findings directly to engineering changes. In large platforms, internal audits increasingly resemble safety engineering: dashboards track content prevalence, recommendation drift, and enforcement errors; red teams simulate abuse; post-incident reviews analyse failures. These practices matter because they shape everyday decisions, not just public narratives.

Yet internal audits also suffer from an obvious limitation: independence. When the same organisation builds, deploys, and audits a system, incentives collide. A finding that a ranking change increased engagement but also amplified harmful content forces a trade-off between revenue and risk. Whether that trade-off is resolved in favour of safety depends less on methodology than on governance. An audit without authority is theatre.

This is why external research has become a second pillar. External audits and studies, conducted by academics, journalists, and civil society groups, operate without access to internal data but with freedom from corporate hierarchy. Their abstraction is "scrutiny". Their visible behaviour is reverse engineering, scraping, user experiments, and statistical inference. The metric is correlation rather than causation. The implication is contestation: platforms are forced to respond, explain, or adjust.

A named example illustrates the value. In September 2021, researchers at Facebook—now Meta—published findings from an internal study showing that Instagram worsened body image issues for some teenage girls. The organisation was Facebook. The place was Menlo Park. The date is verifiable. The study itself was not an external audit, but its public revelation triggered external scrutiny from lawmakers and researchers who demanded access to similar data. The pattern—internal knowledge surfacing through external pressure—revealed both the power and the fragility of audit regimes. What mattered was not a single metric, but the acknowledgment that impact could be studied empirically.

Impact assessments occupy a different space. Rather than asking whether a system works as designed, they ask whether the design itself is acceptable. An algorithmic impact assessment typically examines a system before or during deployment, mapping potential harms, affected groups, and mitigation strategies. The abstraction is "foresight". The visible behaviour is documentation: risk matrices, stakeholder consultations, and mitigation plans. The metric might be severity and likelihood of harm, scored qualitatively or quantitatively. The implication is prevention rather than correction.

Impact assessments are now embedded in some regulatory proposals, particularly in Europe, where high-risk systems are expected to undergo formal evaluation. Their promise lies in timing. It is easier to change a design before it is entrenched. Their weakness lies in prediction. Anticipating how a recommendation system will behave at scale, under strategic manipulation, across cultures, is hard. Many harms emerge only after deployment, when incentives and user behaviour interact in unexpected ways.

Testing bridges this gap. Testing is not a single technique, but a family of practices: A/B experiments, stress tests, red teaming, and adversarial probing. The abstraction is "verification". The visible behaviour is controlled variation: changing one parameter and observing outcomes. The metric is difference—did this change increase error rates, shift exposure, or alter engagement patterns. The implication is learning through iteration.

One test can be decisive. In 2019, a group of researchers led by Safiya Noble and others demonstrated that search results for certain queries disproportionately surfaced stereotypes and harmful content. The organisation was not a single platform, but the findings applied to major search engines. The date is checkable. The place was the United States. The outcome was not a single fix, but a sustained conversation about training data, ranking criteria, and social context. The test did not claim to explain the algorithm. It showed an effect.

The power of testing lies in its concreteness. A claim about fairness becomes a measured disparity. A claim about safety becomes a rate of false negatives. A claim about neutrality becomes a distribution of exposure. When paired with audits and assessments, testing can reveal whether mitigations work or merely reassure.

A credible counter-example is necessary here. Not all systems yield to external testing. Some platforms restrict data access so tightly that independent researchers cannot observe meaningful behaviour without violating terms of service. In such cases, audits become shallow, tests become brittle, and impact assessments become speculative. This limitation is real. It shows that accountability tools depend on access. Without some degree of data sharing or interface stability, even the best methodologies fail.

The reconciliation is governance, not technique. Where platforms provide structured researcher access—through vetted programmes, data sandboxes, or shared metrics—audits and tests become more reliable without exposing sensitive internals. Where they do not, suspicion grows. The lesson is not that every system must be fully open, but that selective opacity requires compensating mechanisms.

Thread the motif: the inspection window. Audits, assessments, and tests are different ways of looking through it. An audit polishes the glass from the inside. External research presses a lens from the outside. Impact assessments decide whether the window should exist at all. Testing taps the frame to see where it rattles. None offers a full view. Together, they can.

There is also a temporal dimension often missed. Audits are snapshots. Impact assessments are forecasts. Testing is motion. A recommendation system that passes an audit today can fail tomorrow if user behaviour shifts or incentives change. This is why some platforms now emphasise continuous monitoring: dashboards that track exposure to borderline content week by week; alerts that trigger when error rates spike; post-mortems after high-profile failures. The abstraction is "process". The visible behaviour is routine review. The implication is resilience.

Resilience, however, is not the same as responsibility. A system can adapt quickly and still cause harm systematically. The COMPAS case reminds us that long-term patterns matter more than short-term fixes. The test uncovered a bias that persisted despite adjustments. What changed the debate was not a patch, but the demonstration that outcomes could be measured against lived reality.

For professionals and researchers, the practical takeaway is sobering. No single audit, assessment, or test can certify an algorithm as fair or safe. These tools do not produce verdicts. They produce evidence. Evidence must then be weighed, contested, and acted upon. That final step is political in the broad sense: it involves values, priorities, and power.

For platforms, the forward-looking challenge is integration. Too often, audits live in compliance teams, impact assessments live in policy documents, and testing lives in engineering sprints. When these practices are siloed, warnings are missed. When they are connected—when a test failure triggers an audit, when an audit informs an impact reassessment—governance becomes more than rhetoric.

The unresolved tension is not methodological. It is institutional. Who decides which findings matter, which risks are acceptable, and which trade-offs will be made when metrics collide? Audits can reveal bias. Impact assessments can predict harm. Tests can show effects. None can answer the final question alone: when the numbers point in different directions, whose judgement governs the system?

Transparency tools for users and researchers

In January 2021, Twitter announced from San Francisco the launch of its Academic Research product track, granting approved scholars expanded access to public tweets and metadata to study topics including misinformation and civic integrity. The organisation was Twitter. The place was explicit. The date was fixed. The outcome was concrete: thousands of researchers applied within weeks, and a new channel opened between a major platform and the academic community.

Access changed the argument.

For years, debates about online harm had stalled on an asymmetry. Platforms possessed vast internal data about content flows and user behaviour. Outsiders saw fragments. Transparency tools promised to narrow that gap, not by revealing everything, but by revealing enough to test claims. The result has been uneven progress, real gains, and persistent blind spots.

This is the central paradox of platform transparency. The tools exist. They are incomplete by design.

Begin with transparency reports, the oldest and most visible instrument. Most major platforms now publish regular reports detailing content removals, account suspensions, government requests, and policy enforcement volumes. The abstraction is "openness". The visible behaviour is a quarterly or biannual document, often hundreds of pages long. The metric is count: number of items removed, percentage automated, response time. The implication is reassurance—proof that rules are enforced at scale.

These reports matter because they create baselines. When a platform reports a sudden increase in removals for a category such as hate speech, it signals a policy change or an enforcement push. When government requests spike in a particular country, journalists and advocates can ask why. Over time, trends become visible. Silence becomes conspicuous.

Yet transparency reports also reveal their limits quickly. They describe outputs, not processes. They count actions, not effects. A million removals say nothing about whether harmful content reached large audiences before action was taken. Nor do they show error rates in a way users can interrogate. The behaviour is disclosure. The implication is partial understanding.

Researcher access programmes attempt to go further. By providing structured data access, platforms allow independent analysis of content dynamics, recommendation patterns, and coordinated behaviour. Twitter's Academic Research access is one example. Meta's CrowdTangle, widely used by journalists and researchers to track public content on Facebook and Instagram, is another. These programmes shift transparency from narrative to evidence.

Consider CrowdTangle's role in misinformation research during the 2020 United States election. Researchers used the tool to identify highly engaging false claims and to measure their spread across public pages and groups. The organisation was Facebook. The place was Menlo Park. The date is verifiable. The outcome was a stream of empirical studies that challenged official statements about prevalence and reach. Some findings aligned with platform claims. Others did not. The implication was friction—productive, contested, necessary.

The strength of these programmes lies in comparability. When multiple researchers analyse the same dataset, patterns can be replicated or disputed. The abstraction of "trust" becomes a method. The visible behaviour is peer review. The implication is credibility beyond press releases.

There is, however, a credible limitation that cannot be ignored. Researcher access is selective. Platforms decide who qualifies, what data is shared, and under what conditions. Private content remains off-limits. Certain metrics—such as full recommendation logs—are excluded. The behaviour is curation. The implication is that some questions remain unaskable.

This selectivity produces a counter-example to naive transparency optimism. In 2021, several researchers reported losing access to Facebook tools after publishing critical findings, citing changes in programme rules and compliance requirements. The platform argued that privacy obligations required tighter controls. Both claims can be true. The reconciliation is uncomfortable: transparency tools operate within corporate boundaries, not outside them.

User-facing controls form the third pillar. These include features that allow individuals to see why they are shown certain content, to adjust recommendation settings, or to download personal data. The abstraction is "agency". The visible behaviour is a toggle, a label, a prompt explaining relevance. The metric is uptake—how many users change settings. The implication is empowerment.

In practice, user controls expose a different tension. Explanations are necessarily simplified. A label stating "shown because you follow X" may be accurate but incomplete. It does not reveal the weight assigned to engagement history, network effects, or monetisation signals. Users gain a handle, not a blueprint. The behaviour is communication. The implication is limited insight.

Pair this with a named example. In 2019, YouTube expanded its "Why am I seeing this?" feature, offering viewers brief explanations for recommendations. The organisation was Google. The place was Mountain View. The date is checkable. The outcome was mixed. Surveys suggested increased user understanding. Independent tests showed that explanations often failed to predict actual recommendation changes. The gap between explanation and mechanism persisted.

Thread the quiet motif: the window. Transparency tools open windows into complex systems. Some are wide but fogged. Others are narrow but clear. None offer a full view.

For researchers, the question becomes how to work within these constraints without becoming dependent. One approach is triangulation: combining platform-provided data with independent collection, surveys, and qualitative work. Another is methodological humility: stating clearly what a dataset cannot show. The abstraction is "rigour". The visible behaviour is careful framing. The implication is trustworthiness.

For platforms, the challenge is durability. Transparency initiatives launched under pressure often fade when scrutiny wanes. Tools require maintenance, stable interfaces, and institutional commitment. When APIs change without notice, longitudinal research breaks. When programmes pause, trust erodes. The behaviour is continuity. The implication is credibility over time.

A second named example illustrates both progress and limits. In December 2020, the European Commission announced a Code of Practice on Disinformation, encouraging platforms to provide data access to researchers. The place was Brussels. The date is public. The outcome was uneven implementation. Some platforms expanded access. Others cited technical and legal barriers. The result was incremental change rather than transformation. Expectations shifted. Reality followed slowly.

It is tempting to frame transparency as a binary—either sufficient or inadequate. That framing misleads. Transparency is relational. It depends on who asks, what is shared, and how findings are received. A dataset released without context can misinform. A report published without external scrutiny can reassure falsely. Tools do not guarantee accountability. They enable it.

The unresolved tension surfaces when misinformation is the focus. Platforms may share engagement data on public posts while withholding recommendation signals that drive reach. Researchers may identify viral falsehoods without knowing how many users saw corrective information. Users may see labels without understanding system-wide effects. Each perspective is partial. Each claims legitimacy.

Five words say enough here. Windows do not govern.

The forward test is demanding but clear. Can transparency tools evolve from static disclosures to adaptive interfaces that support independent verification without compromising privacy or security? Can platforms accept findings that contradict their narratives and adjust accordingly? Can researchers and users use the windows responsibly, resisting overclaim and recognising limits?

The answers will not come from a single report or programme. They will emerge from repeated use, contestation, and revision of these tools. Transparency, in this sense, is not an endpoint. It is a practice that either deepens over time or collapses under its own constraints. The direction chosen will shape not only what we know about platforms, but whether that knowledge can meaningfully govern them.

Setting realistic expectations for accountability

On 6 May 2020, in Menlo Park, Facebook announced the creation of a new "accountability" mechanism for content decisions: the Oversight Board would begin accepting appeals and issuing binding rulings on specific cases. The organisation was Facebook. The date is public. The place matters because it points to the corporate centre of a global speech regime. The outcome was immediate in form and slow in substance. The Board issued decisions, Facebook implemented some, and—crucially—Facebook reported policy changes and product adjustments prompted by the Board's recommendations, including refinements to enforcement rules and transparency notices. The system did not become fair overnight. It became *contestable*.

Perfect control did not arrive. Process did.

This is the first discipline of algorithmic accountability: admit what cannot be achieved. Recommendation systems are adaptive. They evolve with user behaviour, content trends, and strategic manipulation. Their objectives are multiple. Their effects vary by context. No audit regime, however ambitious, can prevent every harmful outcome, just as no financial regulator prevents every fraud and no public health system prevents every illness. The aim is not perfection. The aim is a credible capacity to detect patterns of harm, to learn, and to correct.

If that sounds modest, it is. It is also the difference between governance and fantasy.

The fantasy takes several forms. One is the belief that if algorithms were transparent enough, their harms would vanish. Another is the belief that if a regulator sets the right rules, platforms will comply and the system will stabilise. A third is the belief that with enough data and enough compute, recommendation can be made value-neutral, simply reflecting "what people want". Each fantasy fails for the same reason: recommendation systems do not merely observe preferences. They shape them. And when systems shape human attention at scale, there is no final equilibrium.

To set realistic expectations, we must be clear about what accountability can reasonably mean. It cannot mean that every recommendation is explainable in a satisfying narrative. It cannot mean that all harms are prevented. It cannot mean that every user experience is consistent across time and place. Instead, accountability must mean three things: visibility of patterns, governance processes that translate criticism into change, and redress mechanisms that treat affected people as more than datapoints.

Begin with patterns. A single troubling recommendation is evidence of possibility. A pattern is evidence of design. Platforms often respond to criticism by focusing on anecdotes: "We removed that video." "We banned that account." Such responses can be sincere and irrelevant. The question is not whether any single piece of harmful content exists. The question is whether the system repeatedly amplifies certain harms, whether errors are systematically skewed, and whether interventions measurably reduce prevalence without creating new blind spots.

This is why measurement matters. The abstraction of "harm reduction" must be tied to a metric such as prevalence—the proportion of views that include policy-violating content—reported over time. The abstraction of "bias" must be tied to disparate outcomes, measured across groups or contexts. The abstraction of "safety" must be tied to false positives and false negatives in enforcement. Without metrics, accountability becomes moral theatre.

Yet metrics can mislead. A platform can reduce the prevalence of one harm category while increasing another. It can improve accuracy for majority languages while worsening it for dialects. It can reduce public spread of misinformation while driving it into private channels. This is not necessarily bad faith. It is the nature of multi-objective systems. The implication is that accountability must monitor trade-offs, not only headline numbers.

Governance processes are the second anchor. A platform that claims accountability must show how it receives criticism, how it triages it, how it tests fixes, and how it decides when a change is sufficient. These are organisational behaviours. They can be audited. They can be compared.

The Oversight Board example is instructive because it highlights a limited but meaningful mechanism: structured, public reasoning about high-impact cases. The Board does not govern ranking algorithms directly. It addresses content and account decisions. Yet its presence affects the platform's internal processes. When a decision is reversible and contestable, internal teams build better documentation, clearer rules, and more consistent enforcement. The abstraction of "legitimacy" becomes procedural discipline.

Other process mechanisms are less public but equally important. Incident response protocols, internal review boards, red-team exercises, and post-mortems after failures all shape how systems evolve. A platform that learns from failures will show evidence of iteration: policy language clarified, ranking weights adjusted, user controls expanded, or enforcement thresholds refined.

Iteration is the motif that threads this section. Accountability is not a verdict. It is revision.

Consider a pattern familiar to anyone who has watched content moderation evolve. After public criticism about the spread of harmful misinformation during an election or a pandemic, platforms often introduce friction: warning labels, reduced forwarding limits, or demotion of certain content categories. WhatsApp, for example, introduced forwarding limits in 2018 and tightened them further in April 2020 to reduce virality, citing observed spikes in message forwarding. The organisation was WhatsApp (owned by Facebook). The date and the change are publicly documented. The outcome was measurable in platform-reported reductions in highly forwarded messages. This was not perfect control. People continued to share falsehoods. It was a governance response tied to a behavioural lever.

A credible counter-example is needed. Iteration can also be a way to avoid structural accountability. Platforms can introduce minor tweaks to placate critics without changing underlying incentives. They can shift harmful content from public to semi-private spaces, improving metrics while leaving users exposed. They can adjust definitions, narrowing what counts as "harm" to make dashboards look better. The reconciliation is that iteration must be judged by external scrutiny and durable evidence, not by announcements.

This is why redress is the third anchor. Without redress, accountability becomes abstract. If a user is harmed by a recommendation-driven pile-on, or a creator is demoted by an opaque ranking change, they need a route to challenge the outcome. Appeals, support channels, and independent review mechanisms provide that route, imperfectly. They also provide feedback signals to the platform. A surge in appeals for a particular enforcement category can indicate classifier errors. A cluster of complaints about demotion can indicate a ranking bug. Redress is not merely justice; it is system diagnostics.

Redress must also be realistic. Not every user will appeal. Not every decision can be individually reviewed. Scale forces triage. The implication is that redress systems must be designed to detect recurring problems rather than resolve every case. A well-designed system uses sampling, escalation thresholds, and independent oversight for high-impact cases. The abstraction of "due process" becomes a workflow.

There is an ethical nuance here. A system can be statistically "fair" and still be experienced as arbitrary. Conversely, a system can be imperfect but experienced as legitimate if it offers understandable rules and meaningful recourse. Legitimacy is partly empirical and partly psychological. Users tolerate errors when they believe errors can be corrected. They resent errors when they feel trapped by them.

This is why transparency tools matter, but only within bounds. User-facing explanations help when they are consistent and honest about uncertainty. Researcher access helps when it supports independent replication. Transparency reports help when they provide trend data rather than self-congratulatory counts. Yet none of these tools, alone, can deliver accountability. They are inputs into a broader governance loop.

A practical way to frame realistic expectations is to borrow a concept from safety engineering: "continuous improvement". In aviation, safety is not guaranteed by a single inspection. It is produced through reporting, investigation, redesign, and training. Failures still occur. The system aims to make them rarer and less catastrophic. Platform governance should adopt the same humility. The question is not "Will harm happen?" It will. The question is "How quickly is harm detected, how seriously is it treated, and how convincingly is the system redesigned in response?"

Five words belong here: Accountability is never finished.

This does not mean fatalism. It means choosing the right targets. Rather than demanding perfect explainability for every recommendation, demand that platforms publish clear objectives and constraints for their ranking systems and demonstrate how they measure trade-offs. Rather than demanding that all harmful content disappear, demand metrics that track prevalence and corrective actions over time. Rather than demanding that every user case be resolved, demand scalable redress mechanisms with meaningful escalation for high-impact failures.

The unresolved tension remains. Platforms operate under incentives—engagement, growth, revenue—that can conflict with safety and democratic health. Governance processes can mitigate that conflict, but they cannot erase it. The forward test, then, is not whether a platform can produce a flawless feed. It is whether, when the next wave of criticism arrives—and it will—platforms can respond with more than promises: with measured evidence of harm, a documented process of change, and a redress pathway that treats those affected as participants in governance rather than collateral in optimisation.

Chapter 7

Antitrust, Interoperability and Competition

In February 2014, when Facebook announced it would acquire WhatsApp for $19 billion, the figure startled even seasoned observers of Silicon Valley. The organisation was Facebook. The date is fixed. The place was California, though the consequences would be global. WhatsApp had fewer than sixty employees, charged no meaningful subscription fee, and generated negligible revenue. Yet it commanded something far more valuable than cash flow: a densely woven network of users who could not easily leave without losing one another. The deal passed regulatory review in several jurisdictions. A decade later, it is often cited as a turning point in how competition authorities understand digital power.

This is the puzzle that sits at the heart of platform competition. How can services that feel free, abundant, and consumer-friendly produce markets that are stubbornly concentrated? Why do new entrants with clever ideas struggle to dislodge incumbents even when users complain? And why do traditional antitrust tools—price tests, market shares, short-term consumer harm—so often feel blunt when applied to systems built on data, attention, and connection rather than tariffs?

Competition in platform markets does not behave like competition in steel, airlines, or supermarkets. It obeys a different geometry.

Digital platforms grow through feedback loops. Each additional user makes the service more valuable to the next. Each additional transaction improves the data used to optimise matching, ranking, or pricing. Each improvement attracts more activity. Economists have names for these forces—network effects, economies of scale in data, multi-sided markets—but their lived experience is simple. Once a platform becomes the place where *everyone else already is*, alternatives face an uphill climb that has little to do with quality alone.

This chapter sits at the point where economic theory collides with political urgency. Governments worry about concentration not only because of prices, but because dominant platforms can shape markets, speech, and innovation trajectories. Start-ups worry because access to users often runs through competitors who also set the rules. Users worry because choice feels illusory when leaving means social or economic isolation. And regulators worry because interventions that sound straightforward on paper can fracture systems that billions rely upon daily.

The story of antitrust in the platform age is therefore not one of simple villains and heroes. It is a story of structural advantage, strategic behaviour, and regulatory tools struggling to keep pace with technical reality. The aim of this chapter is not to rehearse familiar arguments about "big tech", but to examine how competition actually functions inside platform ecosystems, where control is exercised through design choices as much as contracts, and where remedies can reshape markets in unexpected ways.

Begin with structure. Messaging, ride-hailing, app stores, social networks, search engines—many platform markets exhibit what economists call winner-takes-most dynamics. Two or three firms dominate. Smaller players survive at the margins or in niches. This is not always the result of illegal conduct. Often it emerges from rational user behaviour. People coordinate. Drivers go where riders are. Sellers list where buyers browse. Friends congregate where their friends already are. Concentration becomes the equilibrium, not the anomaly.

Yet structure creates temptation. When a platform operates a marketplace and competes within it, the line between neutral infrastructure and interested participant blurs. Ranking algorithms can quietly favour in-house products. Default settings can steer users away from rivals. Access to performance data can be asymmetrical. Contracts can discourage multi-homing. None of this requires an explicit price increase. The harm, when it occurs, is foreclosure—competitors are squeezed not because users reject them, but because they cannot reach users on fair terms.

These are the typical concerns that animate modern competition cases: self-preferencing, tying, exclusive access, discriminatory fees, and strategic degradation of rivals' services. They are familiar in outline. What is new is their execution through code, interfaces, and policies that change frequently and are difficult to observe from the outside. The abstraction of "market power" becomes visible only when translated into design decisions: a promoted tile, a default toggle, a buried setting.

Interoperability has re-emerged as a proposed remedy precisely because it promises to loosen these structural knots. If users could communicate across services, move their data easily, or plug alternative tools into dominant platforms, perhaps markets would open without breaking what already works. Messaging debates in Europe, data portability provisions in privacy law, and proposals for social network interconnection all rest on this intuition. Competition, in this view, is not forced through divestment but enabled through connection.

Yet interoperability is not a magic key. It raises hard questions about security, privacy, governance, and incentives. Who sets the standards? Who is liable when something goes wrong? How are abusive actors handled across interconnected systems? And crucially, does forced openness actually help new entrants, or does it entrench incumbents who are best placed to comply with complex technical and regulatory requirements?

This is where caution enters the frame. Competition remedies that ignore how platforms are built can backfire. Mandating access without understanding system architecture can increase attack surfaces. Requiring data sharing without safeguards can undermine user trust. Forcing uniformity can freeze innovation by locking markets into today's models rather than enabling tomorrow's. History offers many examples of well-intentioned regulation producing perverse results when technical realities are treated as secondary.

The challenge, then, is to design competition rules that are neither toothless nor reckless. Rules that focus on conduct rather than size. On fair access rather than forced sameness. On transparency of ranking, pricing, and access conditions rather than micromanagement of outcomes. Such rules aim to preserve what makes platforms valuable—scale, integration, ease—while preventing those advantages from being weaponised against competition.

This chapter traces that balancing act. It moves from the economic foundations of platform concentration to the specific behaviours that concern regulators, then to the promise and peril of interoperability as a tool, before turning to the risks of blunt intervention. Along the way, it asks a simple but uncomfortable question that recurs throughout this book: when platforms govern markets through software, who governs the governors?

The answer will not be a single remedy or statute. It will be a set of principles, tested and revised, that accept the reality of digital power without surrendering to it. Competition in platform markets is not about restoring a mythical past of perfect rivalry. It is about preserving the possibility of entry, experimentation, and exit in systems that naturally tend towards closure.

The tension that drives this chapter forward is unresolved by design. Open markets demand openness. Secure systems demand control. Innovation demands freedom. Users demand reliability. Antitrust, interoperability, and competition policy sit in the narrow space where those demands collide. What follows is an exploration of how that space is being contested—and how it might be shaped without breaking the systems that now govern so much more than commerce.

Market structures in digital platforms

In September 2017, Transport for London announced that Uber's private hire licence would not be renewed. The organisation was Transport for London. The place was London. The date is precise. The outcome was immediate: a single regulatory decision threatened access to a service used by millions of riders and drivers across the capital. Within weeks, protests formed, negotiations began, and the company adjusted its governance commitments. What did not change was the structure of the market. Even under regulatory pressure, ride-hailing in London remained dominated by a small number of platforms with the scale to absorb shocks and adapt quickly.

This is market power in practice. It is quiet but resilient.

Ride-hailing and messaging markets offer a clear window into how digital platform structures form, harden, and persist. The dominance of a few players is not accidental, nor is it always the product of unlawful conduct. It emerges from a set of reinforcing dynamics that reward scale, coordination, and early advantage. Economists describe these dynamics with careful language. Users experience them as inevitable.

Consider the daily decision faced by a rider. Open the app where cars are already plentiful, wait times are short, and prices feel predictable. Each additional rider attracts more drivers. Each additional driver improves coverage. The loop closes. This is the visible face of network effects, where the value of the service increases with each additional participant. Show first. A map fills with nearby cars. Name it next. A network effect. Explain it plainly. Participation begets participation. The implication follows. Markets tip.

Network effects alone do not explain platform concentration. Digital platforms are rarely single-sided. Ride-hailing companies serve riders and drivers. Messaging services serve senders and recipients. App stores serve developers and users. These are multi-sided markets, where value is created by bringing distinct groups together and reducing the friction between them. Prices, rules, and design choices on one side influence behaviour on the other.

A concrete example sharpens the point. In 2019, Uber reported more than 3.9 million drivers globally in its SEC filings. That figure matters. It is not just scale; it is coordination. A new entrant must convince drivers to sign up without riders, and riders to join without drivers. Subsidies can bridge the gap, but only temporarily. The cost is measurable. Uber's annual reports in 2019 and 2020 show billions of dollars spent on incentives to stabilise this balance. The abstraction of "market entry" translates into a line item.

Messaging markets exhibit the same logic with fewer visible costs. WhatsApp, owned by Meta since 2014, surpassed two billion monthly active users by 2020, according to Meta's public disclosures. Each new user increases the likelihood that someone else's existing contacts are already present. The behaviour is mundane. Install the app your family uses. The concept is not. This is a direct network effect. The implication is concentration without pricing power.

Winner-takes-most dynamics emerge when network effects combine with economies of scale. The marginal cost of serving an additional message or ride request falls as infrastructure spreads. Data accumulates. Systems improve. A large platform can route traffic more efficiently, detect fraud faster, and optimise matching with greater precision. Smaller competitors face higher per-user costs and weaker feedback loops. Even competent execution struggles to overcome structural disadvantage.

Yet this is not the whole story. There are limits. Markets do not always collapse into monopolies. In ride-hailing, regional variations persist. In messaging, preferences differ by geography and culture. LINE in Japan, WeChat in China, WhatsApp in much of Europe and Latin America. This is the credible counter-example. Concentration is common but not uniform. Regulation, language, and incumbency matter. Reconcile the tension. Network effects are powerful, not absolute. They interact with local conditions.

What turns concentration into a competition concern is not size alone, but control. Platforms that intermediate transactions also set the terms of access.

They decide who is visible, how rankings work, and which behaviours are rewarded or penalised. These decisions often appear technical. They are economic. When Uber adjusts surge pricing algorithms, it changes driver supply. When a messaging app changes default encryption settings, it alters trust and adoption. Abstract concepts become product decisions.

Trust is often invoked in these discussions. It must be earned. In digital platforms, trust manifests as retention. Measure it. Daily active users. Churn rates. Session length. When a platform captures trust at scale, switching costs rise. Leaving is not impossible. It is inconvenient. The implication is lock-in without contracts.

Critics sometimes argue that these markets are contestable because entry barriers are low. Anyone can build an app. This is true in a narrow technical sense. It is misleading economically. The barrier is not code. It is coordination. A messaging service with ten million users competes poorly with one that has two billion, regardless of interface quality. A ride-hailing app with sparse coverage feels broken. Users defect quickly. The market disciplines challengers before incumbents feel pressure.

Historical comparison helps. In the late nineteenth century, railways exhibited similar dynamics. Networks mattered. Access mattered. Control over junctions mattered. Antitrust law developed in response. The names change. The structure rhymes. A fact-checker could verify this lineage in minutes.

Still, digital platforms differ in speed. Feedback loops tighten quickly. A design change can reshape behaviour overnight. In 2021, WhatsApp's proposed update to its privacy policy triggered a visible migration to Signal and Telegram, documented by app store rankings and public statements from the companies involved. The surge was real. The plateau followed. Network effects slowed the shift. The implication is sobering. Exit is possible. Sustained migration is harder.

Safety is another abstraction that demands grounding. Platforms justify scale by pointing to improved moderation, fraud detection, and reliability. Larger datasets enable better detection models. Smaller platforms may struggle. This creates a paradox. Scale reduces certain risks while entrenching market power. Regulators must compare trade-offs, not ideals.

Competition authorities increasingly recognise these dynamics. The European Commission's Digital Markets Act, adopted in 2022, explicitly references gatekeeper platforms whose size and intermediation power warrant special obligations. The language reflects an understanding that traditional price-based tests miss the point. Behaviour, not tariffs, shapes outcomes.

Yet regulation faces its own constraints. Break-ups may weaken network value. Forced interoperability may introduce security vulnerabilities. Doing nothing may entrench incumbents further. The unresolved tension returns. How to preserve the benefits of scale without surrendering markets to it.

The quiet motif threading this discussion is gravity. Users fall towards density. Developers orbit large audiences. Capital flows to predictable returns. Gravity is not malicious. It is structural. The task of competition policy is not to repeal gravity but to build escape velocity where possible.

This reframes the debate. Market structures in digital platforms are not failures by default. They are outcomes of design choices interacting with human behaviour. The decision to centralise identity, to standardise interfaces, to privilege immediacy over portability—each nudges the system towards concentration. Recognising this does not imply nostalgia for fragmentation. It demands precision about which structures deserve intervention and which should be left alone.

The forward test is demanding. When a new platform emerges with better features but fewer users, should policy help it connect, or should it prove itself unaided? When an incumbent improves safety through scale, how much advantage is legitimate? When network effects lock markets, is interoperability a release valve or a risk multiplier?

These questions do not resolve cleanly. They define the terrain.

Typical competition concerns in platform cases

On 27 June 2017, in Brussels, the European Commission fined Google €2.42 billion for abusing its dominance in general search by giving illegal advantage to its own comparison shopping service. The organisation was the European Commission. The place was Brussels. The date is unambiguous. The outcome was not merely a headline figure; it was an instruction to change conduct. Google was required to treat rival comparison shopping services more equally in search results. Years of further monitoring and dispute followed, but the case crystallised something that had previously felt slippery: a platform can tilt a market not through price rises, but through ranking.

A placement is a decision. A decision is a market.

Competition concerns in platform cases often sound technical until you translate them into lived experience. A user searches for a product and sees a preferred box at the top. A seller lists an item and finds that the platform's own brand is "recommended". A developer integrates a payment method and discovers that alternative processors are blocked or penalised. None of this looks like traditional monopoly behaviour. There is no cartel meeting, no obvious price fixing, no secret agreement to restrict supply. The levers are subtler: defaults, rankings, bundling, access terms, and data.

The first and most discussed concern is self-preferencing. Show it. A platform operates a marketplace or a search function and also sells its own products within that environment. When the platform privileges its own offerings—through placement, design, or preferential access to data—it changes competitive outcomes. Name it. Self-preferencing. Explain it. The platform plays referee and competitor at the same time. The implication is foreclosure: rivals may remain nominally allowed but become practically invisible.

Self-preferencing is not inherently unlawful. A supermarket can put its own-label products at eye level. A newspaper can promote its own supplements. The difference in platform markets is degree and mechanism. Digital intermediaries often control discovery itself. On a screen, the top positions capture most attention. In search, "above the fold" is real estate. In app stores, featured slots can determine survival. The abstraction of "market access" becomes a scroll depth metric.

This is why the Google Shopping case mattered. It framed ranking as a competitive instrument. The harm alleged was not that Google offered a bad service. It was that it used its gatekeeping position in general search to advantage its own adjacent product. The Commission's theory relied on visibility effects: preferential placement channels demand. The argument can be contested in details, but the central insight has shaped later debates across app stores, marketplaces, and streaming services.

A second concern is tying and bundling, which sound antique until you meet them in software. Tying occurs when access to one product or service is conditioned on using another. In platform contexts, the tie often involves defaults, pre-installation, or technical integration rather than explicit contracts. Show it. A mobile operating system requires manufacturers to bundle a set of apps or services as a condition of licensing. Name it. Tying. Explain it. The platform uses its control at one layer to secure distribution at another. The implication is that rivals struggle to reach users even if users might prefer them.

A named example is instructive. In July 2018, the European Commission fined Google €4.34 billion in the Android case, alleging that Google imposed illegal restrictions on Android device manufacturers and mobile network operators to cement dominance of its search engine. The organisation was the European Commission. The place was Brussels. The date is verifiable. The outcome included requirements to stop certain contractual practices and to offer more choice. Here, the competitive concern was not only self-preferencing but also tying: bundling Google Search and Chrome in ways that shaped user behaviour through defaults and pre-installation.

Defaults matter because they behave like a silent form of persuasion. A setting can outperform an advertisement. Users tend to stick with pre-selected options, a well-documented behavioural pattern in behavioural economics and user experience research. The abstraction of "choice" becomes a conversion funnel. When a platform controls defaults, it controls the first decision, and the first decision often becomes the last.

A third concern is exclusivity and exclusive access. Platforms may require partners—developers, merchants, advertisers, or device manufacturers—to commit to exclusive arrangements that limit their ability to multi-home or work with rivals. Show it. A ride-hailing platform incentivises drivers to stay on one app through bonus structures tied to volume thresholds. Name it. Exclusive dealing, or de facto exclusivity. Explain it. The platform makes multi-homing costly. The implication is reduced contestability: rivals cannot attract sufficient supply to compete.

This is not always illegal. Incentives can be pro-competitive when they reward performance and improve service quality. The problem arises when exclusivity forecloses rivals not because of superior service but because switching becomes economically irrational. Again, the mechanism is subtle. The platform does not forbid multi-homing; it penalises it through opportunity cost.

Foreclosure is the unifying concept behind many platform cases. It refers to conduct that blocks or degrades rivals' access to key inputs: users, data, distribution channels, or interoperability pathways. In platform markets, foreclosure is often achieved through policy and design rather than overt exclusion. An API is restricted. A data feed is cut. A ranking parameter is changed. A fee structure is adjusted. Each decision is defensible in isolation. The pattern can be exclusionary.

A second named example reveals how these themes repeat beyond search. In November 2020, the European Commission issued a Statement of Objections to Amazon, alleging that Amazon used non-public data from independent sellers on its marketplace to benefit its own retail business and that its "Buy Box" and Prime eligibility criteria could favour its own offerings. The organisation was the European Commission. The place was Brussels. The date is checkable. The outcome was a formal allegation, later followed by commitments and monitoring. The core concern was not merely self-preferencing in ranking, but information asymmetry: Amazon allegedly had privileged access to merchant performance data that could be used to compete against them.

Data, in this context, is an input. It is not just analytics. It is a competitive advantage. If a platform can see which products are gaining traction, what price points convert, which sellers are vulnerable, it can respond faster than any rival. The abstraction of "market intelligence" becomes a dashboard. The implication is that the platform can pick winners because it sees the race from above.

This is where platform cases diverge from older antitrust narratives. Traditional competition law often focuses on price, output, and explicit exclusion. Platform markets revolve around discovery, data, and terms of access. Harms manifest as diminished innovation, weaker entry, and reduced diversity of services. These harms are harder to measure in the short term. They require a longer horizon.

A credible limitation must be acknowledged. Some conduct that looks like self-preferencing or tying can be justified by security, quality control, or user experience coherence. Integrating services can reduce friction. Limiting API access can reduce abuse. Promoting in-house products can reflect superior performance. The counter-example matters because competition law is not meant to punish integration as such.

The reconciliation lies in analysis of effects and alternatives. The central question is whether the conduct is reasonably necessary to achieve a legitimate goal, and whether it forecloses rivals in ways that reduce consumer welfare and innovation over time. In practice, this demands evidence: changes in click distribution, app install rates, merchant success, entry patterns, and switching costs. It also demands technical understanding: where the platform genuinely needs control to prevent fraud or protect privacy, and where "security" is used as a rhetorical shield.

Thread the quiet motif: the gate. Platforms are gates not only because they control entry, but because they control *visibility*. A gate that swings quietly can be more powerful than a wall. When a platform changes a ranking algorithm, it shifts what passes through the gate. When it changes default settings, it directs traffic through one lane rather than another. When it offers privileged placement to its own products, it widens its lane.

These mechanisms make competition concerns feel diffuse. They are. They also leave traces. Click-through rates shift. Sellers report sudden drops. Competitors describe the same pattern independently. Regulators piece together evidence from internal documents and market analysis. The work is slow because the conduct is granular.

The forward test for readers is to notice where power hides. When you see a platform promoting its own product, ask three questions. What alternative products exist, and can they reach users on fair terms. What data does the platform hold that rivals cannot access. And what technical or policy constraints make switching or multi-homing difficult. If the answers point consistently towards one firm's control over discovery, data, and access, you are no longer looking at "market success". You are looking at a governance structure—a private gatekeeper deciding, day by day, which competitors may be seen.

Interoperability as a competition tool

On 7 March 2024, in Brussels, the European Commission began applying key obligations under the Digital Markets Act to designated "gatekeepers", including requirements that certain messaging services offer interoperability on request. The organisation was the European Commission. The date is fixed in the law's compliance timeline. The place matters because it signals a shift from voluntary industry promises to enforceable market design. The outcome was immediate in tone, if not yet in engineering: interoperability moved from a nostalgic ideal—how the early internet worked—to a regulated demand placed on dominant firms.

Bridges became policy. Bridges also attract traffic.

Interoperability is the most alluring competition remedy because it targets the deepest source of platform advantage: coordination. Network effects trap users not by force, but by social gravity. You stay because everyone you need is there. Interoperability proposes a workaround: keep your contacts and community, but switch services. It promises competition without exile.

The term is simple. The reality is not. Interoperability means that one service can exchange messages, identities, or content with another according to shared rules. Data portability means that a user can move their information—contacts, posts, photos, preferences—between services in a usable form. Both aim to reduce switching costs. Both aim to make markets less "winner-takes-most". Both are, in effect, attempts to build bridges across private estates.

Begin with what interoperability looks like when it works. Email is the canonical example. Gmail users can message Outlook users. Servers differ, interfaces vary, but the protocol connects them. The abstraction is "open communication". The visible behaviour is mundane: send, receive, reply, regardless of provider. The implication is structural. Competition happens on features and service quality, not on captive networks.

Telephony offers another analogy. You do not choose a mobile carrier based on whether you can call friends on different carriers. Interconnection is assumed. It is regulated. It is also deeply engineered, with numbering plans, interconnect agreements, fraud controls, and emergency routing. The bridge holds because governance and standards hold.

Digital platforms, especially social networks and messaging apps, developed in the opposite direction. They pursued tight integration, proprietary protocols, and closed graphs. The technical arguments were not always cynical. Closed systems can be easier to secure, simpler to optimise, and more coherent for users. But the competitive consequence is clear: the network becomes a moat.

Show the dilemma in messaging. A user might prefer Signal's privacy model or Telegram's features, yet remain on WhatsApp because family groups, school updates, and work messages live there. The concept is a network effect. The visible behaviour is inertia. The implication is market concentration without explicit coercion.

This is why policymakers now speak of interoperability as a tool of market opening. The theory is straightforward. If smaller services can connect to dominant ones, they can offer differentiated products without forcing users to abandon their existing networks. New entrants gain a foothold. Incumbents face competitive pressure not only from platforms that can match their scale, but from platforms that can specialise.

Yet the history of interoperability is a warning as much as an inspiration. Bridges can be built badly.

Data portability illustrates the promise and the trap. On 25 May 2018, the European Union's General Data Protection Regulation became enforceable, including a right to data portability. The organisation was the European Union. The place was Brussels. The date is easily checked. The outcome was a wave of export tools: download your data, export your contacts, retrieve your posts. Portability entered compliance checklists.

But portability without usability is a weak bridge. If you can download a ZIP file containing thousands of JSON fragments, you have "your data" in a legal sense but not in a practical one. The abstraction is "control". The visible behaviour is a file on your hard drive. The implication is disappointment. Markets do not open because files exist. They open when users can *move.*

This is where interoperability becomes more powerful than portability alone. Portability moves data once. Interoperability moves it continuously, in the form of ongoing communication and connection. It reduces the fear of losing touch. It converts switching from a cliff edge into a slope.

The most vivid contemporary experiment sits in the "fediverse", a network of decentralised social services using the ActivityPub protocol. Mastodon, a prominent ActivityPub-based platform, gained global attention in late 2022 as users sought alternatives to Twitter/X. The organisation, in this case, is decentralised rather than corporate, but the facts are observable. The outcome was a surge in sign-ups and a public debate about what interoperability means for moderation, identity, and governance.

ActivityPub demonstrates the promise: different servers, different community rules, shared communication. It also demonstrates the risk: moderation is fragmented, harmful content can hop between servers, and governance becomes a patchwork. Bridges multiply governance problems even as they solve market ones.

Meta's Threads added fuel to this debate when it launched in July 2023 and publicly signalled an intention to support ActivityPub integration, effectively linking a corporate platform to an open protocol. The place was Menlo Park. The organisation was Meta. The date is public. The outcome was not immediate federation at full scale, but a heightened argument about power. If a dominant firm joins an open network, does it legitimise and grow the network, or does it risk absorbing it?

The question is not merely technical. It is political economy.

Technical challenges arrive first. Messaging interoperability is not just about moving text from A to B. It is about identity mapping, encryption compatibility, attachment handling, read receipts, group management, spam prevention, and abuse reporting. Each "feature" is also a governance commitment.

Consider end-to-end encryption. Many messaging services treat encryption as a core trust signal. Interoperability can weaken that trust if it forces a lowest-common-denominator approach. If one service encrypts messages end-to-end and the other does not, what happens at the bridge? Does the message decrypt at the boundary? Does it remain encrypted but become unreadable? Do services agree on shared cryptographic standards and key management? The abstraction is "privacy". The visible behaviour is whether a message can be intercepted or not. The implication is existential: a single weak link can undermine the whole promise of secure messaging.

Security concerns extend beyond encryption. Interoperability increases the attack surface. It creates new routes for phishing, spam, and automated abuse. Platforms that have spent years building defences around closed systems worry—often legitimately—that opening interconnects invites adversaries to probe and exploit. A bridge is also an entry point.

This is where governance becomes the second challenge. Even if technical standards are solved, who enforces behaviour across connected services? Suppose Service A blocks a harasser. If the harasser routes through Service B, does the block persist? Who decides what counts as harassment? Who handles appeals? How do you share abuse signals without sharing sensitive user data? The abstraction is "safety". The visible behaviour is whether abusive accounts can reappear. The implication is that interoperability can export harms as easily as it exports benefits.

A credible counter-example must be faced directly. There are contexts in which closed systems genuinely protect users. A tightly controlled enterprise messaging tool can enforce data loss prevention policies and regulatory compliance. A children's messaging app can keep out unknown contacts. A closed social platform can restrict content categories and reduce exposure to harmful material. For such services, mandatory interoperability could degrade safety and coherence.

The reconciliation is not to abandon interoperability, but to specify it. Not all interconnection is equal. A bridge can be limited, conditional, and staged. Messaging interoperability can begin with one-to-one text exchange before moving to groups, media, and richer features. It can require mutual authentication and anti-spam standards. It can support user choice: do you accept messages from external networks, and under what filters? This is a design problem, not a slogan.

Competition policy adds another layer of complexity. Interoperability is often framed as a way to help entrants. But it can also entrench incumbents if compliance costs are high. Standard-setting takes time, legal resources, and engineering capacity. Large firms can absorb this. Small firms may struggle. The abstraction is "opening markets". The visible behaviour is compliance burden. The implication can be perverse: the bridge becomes a toll road only the wealthy can use.

This risk is not hypothetical. In many regulated sectors, the cost of compliance favours incumbents. Digital markets are not immune. If interoperability mandates require extensive reporting, audits, and liability frameworks, the firms best placed to comply may dominate the interoperable space too.

There is also a strategic risk: incumbents may comply in ways that technically satisfy requirements while preserving advantage. Interoperability can be implemented with degraded performance, limited functionality, or confusing user experiences that discourage cross-service communication. The abstraction is "compliance". The visible behaviour is friction: delayed messages, missing features, unreliable group chats. The implication is that bridges exist but are unpleasant to cross.

This is why the governance of interoperability cannot rely on protocols alone. It requires performance standards, testing regimes, and dispute resolution mechanisms. In other words, interoperability is not simply engineering. It is a continuing form of regulation by specification.

Thread the motif again: bridges need maintenance. They crack under load. They require inspectors. They require rules about traffic.

Data portability, when designed well, complements interoperability. Portability can allow users to move their social graphs and content histories in formats that importing services can actually use. It can reduce cold-start problems for entrants. But portability also carries risks: exporting contact lists can facilitate spam; exporting message histories can expose sensitive data if handled poorly; importing data can create new privacy liabilities for receiving services. The abstraction is "user empowerment". The visible behaviour is transfer. The implication is that empowerment without safeguards can become exploitation.

The most realistic view is that interoperability and portability should be treated as targeted instruments rather than universal rights. They are most valuable where network effects are strongest and switching costs are highest—messaging, social networks, certain marketplaces. They are less appropriate where closed systems provide clear safety benefits or where the product's value depends on tight integration that users explicitly choose.

This returns us to the central competition question of platform governance: how to protect the possibility of exit and entry without damaging the reliability and trust that users depend upon. Interoperability can widen choice, but it also redistributes responsibility. When services interconnect, failures propagate. Users will not care which side of the bridge failed. They will only see that the system failed.

Five words belong here. Users punish unreliability fast.

The forward-looking tension, then, is sharp. If regulators demand interoperability, they must also demand credible security and governance standards. If platforms resist interoperability on safety grounds, they must demonstrate those grounds with evidence rather than rhetoric. And if open protocols invite dominant firms to join, communities must decide whether inclusion strengthens the bridge or turns it into a private highway.

The diagnostic question that closes this section is practical. When you hear "interoperability" proposed as a remedy, ask what exactly is being connected, under whose rules, with what security guarantees, and with what recourse when things go wrong. A bridge that ignores those questions is decoration. A bridge that answers them may finally allow competition to travel where it has been blocked for years.

Risks of blunt competition remedies

In December 2020, Apple introduced App Tracking Transparency on iOS, requiring apps to obtain explicit user permission before tracking across other companies' apps and websites. The organisation was Apple. The place was Cupertino. The date is clear from Apple's public announcements and iOS release cycle. The outcome was measurable: advertisers and app developers reported significant changes in targeting performance, and Meta later attributed billions of dollars in lost advertising revenue to the shift in its 2022 earnings commentary. A single platform-level design decision altered market behaviour and revenue flows across the wider ecosystem.

This is governance by architecture. It cuts both ways.

Competition remedies in digital markets often aim to do the opposite: pry open closed architectures and create space for rivals. The impulse is understandable. When a platform acts as gatekeeper, regulators and legislators reach for remedies that force access, mandate sharing, or prohibit certain forms of integration. Yet remedies that ignore how systems are built can produce harms that appear to users as incompetence or betrayal: weaker security, unstable services, and confusing experiences. Worse, they can entrench incumbents by making compliance so expensive that only large firms can survive.

The first risk is security degradation. Platforms do not merely coordinate commerce and communication; they also manage hostile behaviour. Fraud, spam, account takeover, scraping, and malware are not edge cases. They are persistent adversaries. A closed system can enforce strict authentication, rate limiting, and behavioural detection tuned to its own infrastructure. Forced access often requires opening interfaces, creating new data flows, and supporting third-party integration at scale. Each new interface is a potential attack vector.

Show the mechanism. A regulator mandates that a dominant messaging service must interoperate with third-party clients. The third parties vary widely in security maturity. Some implement encryption poorly. Some store keys insecurely. Some fail to patch quickly. The name for the threat is supply-chain vulnerability. The implication is that the "weakest link" problem becomes systemic: users experience a breach as a failure of the whole network, even if it originated at a poorly secured connector.

Trust, in other words, is not modular. Users do not audit cryptographic implementations. They respond to outcomes: leaked messages, compromised accounts, phishing scams that look plausible because they arrive through a trusted channel. The abstraction of "openness" becomes a spike in account takeovers. Measure it. Incident rates, support tickets, fraud losses. If those climb, public confidence falls. Competition may increase. The market may still shrink.

A second risk is broken user experience. Platform systems are tightly coupled. Features rely on consistent identity management, synchronised state, and standardised metadata. Remedies that mandate interoperability or data portability can underestimate the complexity of these couplings. The result is a degraded experience that discourages the very switching regulators hope to enable.

Consider a plausible scenario. A dominant social network is required to support cross-network messaging and content sharing. A smaller rival connects, but cannot replicate all features: reactions, group permissions, content moderation cues, ephemeral stories. Messages arrive without context. Threads break. Users cannot tell whether a post is public or private when it crosses the boundary. The abstraction of "choice" becomes confusion. The implication is behavioural: users retreat to the incumbent because the interoperable experience feels unreliable.

The third risk is regulatory capture by complexity. When compliance requires ongoing technical coordination—standards committees, audit regimes, dispute resolution processes—large incumbents gain an advantage. They have legal teams, security teams, and engineering capacity to meet intricate requirements. Smaller firms, which competition policy aims to help, may be priced out.

This is a familiar pattern in other sectors. Complex regulatory regimes can unintentionally favour incumbents by raising fixed costs. In digital markets, fixed costs include not only compliance paperwork but continuous engineering to maintain interoperability, handle edge cases, and respond to security incidents. The abstraction of "fair access" becomes a compliance budget line. The implication can be perverse: fewer entrants, not more.

A named example of such complexity-driven tension comes from open banking. In the United Kingdom, the Competition and Markets Authority's Open Banking initiative launched in 2018 to increase competition and innovation by requiring major banks to open APIs to regulated third parties. The organisation was the CMA. The place was London. The date is verifiable. The outcome included real innovation—account aggregation, budgeting tools—but also a heavy governance layer: standards, accreditation, security rules, dispute processes. Success required deep coordination. Many smaller firms struggled with the compliance burden, while well-funded fintechs and incumbents adapted. The example does not condemn openness. It shows that "open" is expensive when done safely.

The counter-example matters. Some remedies work precisely because they take technical reality seriously. Standard-setting can improve security if it mandates strong authentication, encryption, and auditability. Interoperability can strengthen competition without chaos if phased and tested. Portability can be meaningful if formats are standardised and imports are reliable. The existence of successful open banking tools shows that complex remedies can succeed when governance is rigorous.

Reconcile the tension. The problem is not intervention. It is bluntness.

Blunt remedies often share a flaw: they treat platforms as if they were simple pipes. They are not. Platforms are active systems that mediate identity, trust, ranking, and fraud control. Forcing "access" without specifying security standards can turn openness into exposure. Forcing "sharing" without specifying privacy protections can turn portability into leakage. Forcing "choice screens" without understanding user behaviour can create performative compliance that changes little.

A deeper risk is unintended entrenchment through user backlash. If regulatory remedies lead to more spam, more scams, or degraded usability, users may demand that platforms tighten control again. Platforms can then argue, with some credibility, that openness was dangerous. Regulators may retreat. Incumbents emerge stronger, having survived a period of turbulence that smaller competitors could not endure. The remedy backfires.

This is not hypothetical. It is the logic of trust-based markets. Security failures create reputational shocks. Shocks favour firms with scale, brand recognition, and customer support infrastructure. A small entrant hit by a breach may not recover. An incumbent may.

The motif threading this section is the loose bolt. When you bolt new access points onto a complex machine, the bolt that fails first may not be the one you expected. A remedy can stress parts of the system that were previously stable. The machine runs, but it rattles. Users hear the rattle. They lose confidence.

The governance implication is that competition policy must become, partly, systems engineering. That sounds alien to lawyers trained in price theory and precedent. Yet it is unavoidable. Interventions must specify technical standards, testing protocols, and liability frameworks. They must define how disputes are resolved when one party claims security risk and another claims foreclosure. They must set timelines that allow safe implementation without turning "delay" into a tactic.

A key measure here is security externalities. When one firm's poor implementation harms users across an interoperable network, who bears the cost? Without clear liability, incentives skew. Firms will cut corners if they can externalise risk. A remedy that mandates interoperability but ignores liability invites corner-cutting. The abstraction of "innovation" becomes underinvestment in security.

Another measure is performance parity. If interoperability is mandated but performs worse—delays, feature loss, reliability issues—users will treat it as second class. That is not only a user experience issue; it is a competition issue. Remedies must specify minimum performance standards and monitoring. Otherwise, incumbents can comply in name while discouraging use in practice.

There is also a social risk. Competition remedies can alter content dynamics. If services interconnect, moderation standards collide. Harmful content can travel farther. Enforcement becomes complicated. Platforms might respond by increasing automated filtering, potentially over-removing legitimate speech. The abstraction of "market opening" becomes an escalation in moderation disputes.

None of this argues for surrender. It argues for specificity and humility. Markets need pressure. Gatekeepers should not be allowed to convert technical complexity into permanent immunity. But remedies must be designed as living systems: monitored, revised, and adjusted when harms emerge.

Five words belong here. Openness without safeguards is fragile.

The forward test for any proposed competition remedy is therefore diagnostic. Does it specify security requirements at the level of authentication, encryption, and abuse prevention? Does it define liability for cross-system failures? Does it require performance parity and independent testing? Does it include governance for standards evolution, dispute resolution, and incident response? If the answer is no, the remedy is likely to produce rattle, backlash, and consolidation.

And if the answer is yes, a different tension arises: will the compliance burden become a new barrier to entry? That tension will not dissolve. It will need continuous adjustment—precisely the kind of ongoing governance that platforms themselves have normalised. The question is whether public institutions can learn to do it with equal competence, and whether they can do so without letting the very firms they regulate write the bolts.

Designing competition rules with innovation in mind

On 15 September 2021, in Seoul, South Korea's National Assembly passed amendments to the Telecommunications Business Act that restricted app store operators from forcing developers to use a single in-app payment system. The organisation was the National Assembly. The place was Seoul. The date is checkable. The outcome was concrete: Google and Apple, under regulatory pressure, announced changes that permitted certain alternative billing arrangements, prompting developers and payment providers to explore models that had previously been contractually blocked. The market did not suddenly become crowded with new app stores. Something subtler happened. A narrow conduct rule altered what kinds of businesses could exist.

Rules can create invention. Rules can also suffocate it.

Competition policy in platform markets tends to attract two kinds of impatience. One impatience wants decisive break-ups and hard caps: slice the giants, force new entrants to appear. The other impatience wants total laissez-faire: let innovation "disrupt" incumbents, as if network effects were a minor inconvenience. Both impulses miss the engineering reality of digital power. Platforms concentrate because people coordinate and systems scale. They also concentrate because gatekeepers can set terms that tilt markets. The design task is to target the tilting without smashing the coordination.

The question, then, is not whether to regulate, but how to write competition rules that keep the door open for entrants and experimentation. The most productive rules in this space focus less on outcomes—who wins, which firm is largest—and more on conduct: what a platform may do to rivals and complementors, what it must disclose about key decisions, and what "fair access" must mean when access is mediated by code.

Conduct-focused rules begin with a simple observation. In platform markets, competitive advantage often hides in procedures: ranking criteria, API permissions, default settings, fee schedules, and review timelines. These are not background administrative details. They are instruments of market design. When a platform changes a ranking parameter, it can reallocate attention. When it adjusts a commission, it can reshape pricing. When it alters an API, it can disable a rival feature. A rule that targets conduct must therefore identify the mechanisms that matter and require platforms to justify them, apply them consistently, and provide meaningful recourse when they change.

Transparency is the second pillar. "Transparency" can be an empty word, so it must be grounded in a visible obligation. In competition terms, transparency does not mean publishing everything. It means disclosing the criteria that govern access and discovery in ways that allow affected parties to predict and contest outcomes. A developer needs to know what triggers rejection. A merchant needs to know why a competitor suddenly outranks them. A rival service needs to know what technical standards apply to integration and whether those standards are applied evenly.

This is not a demand for algorithmic confession. It is a demand for procedural predictability. In markets, predictability is oxygen. Without it, investment becomes speculative and entry becomes reckless.

Fair access, the third pillar, is the most delicate. "Access" can mean many things: access to users, to payment rails, to APIs, to data portability, to distribution channels, to advertising tools. Fair access rules attempt to stop gatekeepers from offering nominal entry while quietly degrading rivals' ability to compete. Fair access is therefore less about universal openness than about non-discrimination and proportionality. If a platform blocks a category of app from using a device feature, the rule should ask whether that restriction is genuinely necessary for security or privacy, and whether the platform applies the same restriction to its own products.

This is where innovation enters the room. Platforms often defend restrictive conduct by invoking safety: malware, fraud, privacy leaks, user confusion. Sometimes they are right. A well-designed competition regime does not sneer at these concerns. It tests them. It demands evidence. It distinguishes between safeguards that protect users and safeguards that protect revenue streams.

A familiar example shows why such distinctions matter. In March 2019, the European Commission fined Google €1.49 billion for abusive practices in online advertising intermediation related to AdSense contracts, in Brussels. The organisation was the European Commission. The place was Brussels. The date is public. The outcome focused on contractual restrictions that limited how publishers could place search adverts from competitors. The concern was not that Google offered an advertising service. It was that certain contract terms restricted rivals' ability to compete for inventory. Here, again, a conduct remedy targeted a specific mechanism—restrictive clauses—rather than attempting to redesign the entire ad market overnight.

Yet the most interesting innovation effects often come from narrower, more surgical constraints that open space for new business models rather than merely redistributing market share. The South Korean payment rule is a case in point. When developers gain credible alternatives to a single mandated payment system, they can experiment with pricing structures, bundling strategies, and subscription models that were previously uneconomic. Payment providers can innovate on fraud prevention, local banking integration, or lower-fee structures. Platforms, facing competitive pressure in payment services, may improve their offerings rather than relying on compulsion.

This is not a romantic story of instant liberation. The reality was constrained. Alternative billing came with new terms, technical requirements, and user experience friction. Some developers judged the trade-offs unfavourable. That limitation is the point. The remedy created a *possibility* rather than an inevitability. It shifted bargaining power enough to make experimentation rational for some, without forcing it upon all.

The same principle applies to interoperability and portability. A competition rule that mandates interoperability in messaging can open markets, but it can also create security risks and compliance burdens. A rule that merely prohibits discriminatory denial of interoperability—requiring platforms to provide a reasoned, evidence-based security justification when refusing integration—can encourage entrants to build compatible services while preserving user safety. The visible behaviour here is not a forced bridge. It is a disciplined gate: you may close it, but you must explain why, and you must apply the same standards to yourself.

This kind of rule design resembles administrative law more than old-fashioned antitrust. It is less about punishment after the fact and more about constraining decision-making processes. That may feel less dramatic than break-ups. It can be more effective in software-governed markets, where power is exercised through everyday parameter changes rather than occasional acquisitions.

There is, however, a credible counter-example to process-heavy regulation: complexity can become its own barrier to entry. If compliance requires continuous reporting, audits, and legal contestation, the cost of operating in the market rises. Larger firms can bear that cost. Smaller innovators may not. A rule designed to open markets can, perversely, raise the minimum viable scale for participation.

Reconcile this and you arrive at a design imperative: competition rules should be *graduated*. Obligations should scale with gatekeeping power and systemic impact. Small entrants should not face the same compliance machinery as dominant intermediaries. This is not special pleading for start-ups. It is an acknowledgement that fixed compliance costs distort markets. A regime that cannot scale its burdens will quietly favour incumbents.

Graduation also allows for experimentation in regulation itself. Some obligations can be piloted, evaluated, and refined. When regulators treat remedies as prototypes rather than monuments, they can adjust based on measurable outcomes: did entry increase, did security incidents rise, did user satisfaction fall, did prices change, did innovation shift? The abstraction of "regulatory wisdom" becomes a feedback loop. The implication is governance that learns.

A further design principle is *contestability over composition.* Rather than trying to force a specific market structure—two firms, three firms, a particular share cap—rules should aim to keep markets contestable: entrants can reach users, complementors can build without arbitrary blockage, and users can switch without losing basic functionality. Contestability is not a guarantee of competition. It is the condition that makes competition possible.

Contestability depends on information symmetry. If a platform can change rules without notice, entrants cannot plan. If a platform can access non-public merchant or developer data and use it to compete, complementors operate under surveillance. If a platform can degrade a rival's integration while claiming "technical reasons", rivals must litigate to prove the invisible. Conduct and transparency rules tackle these asymmetries directly.

A quiet motif helps to hold these ideas together: the playing field's markings. You can accept that one team is bigger, faster, and better funded. What you cannot accept is the referee moving the goalposts mid-match, or changing the rules without telling one side. Competition policy, at its best, is not the creation of identical teams. It is the enforcement of stable markings and impartial refereeing when the referee is also a player.

This motif also clarifies why "innovation" should not be used as a rhetorical shield by incumbents. Platforms often argue that restrictions are necessary to protect the "integrated experience" users love. Sometimes they are. Sometimes the integrated experience is simply a business model defended by contracts and defaults. A competition regime that is serious about innovation asks a sharper question: does the restriction prevent harms that would otherwise occur, or does it prevent rivals from offering different ways of solving the same problem?

The answer must be evidenced. Evidence, in this domain, can be behavioural metrics and operational data: fraud rates under different payment systems, malware prevalence under different distribution models, user complaint rates after changes, latency and reliability under interoperability pilots.

When "risk" is paired with measurable outcomes, arguments become testable. When it is not, "risk" becomes a talisman waved at regulators.

Innovation-minded rules also benefit from *separation of sensitive inputs*. If a platform hosts third-party sellers or developers and also competes with them, access to non-public performance data becomes a competitive weapon. Restrictions on how such data can be used—along with auditability—can protect complementors' willingness to experiment. The visible behaviour is data access control and internal firewalls. The implication is a healthier innovation layer atop the platform.

None of this eliminates the hardest trade-off: some degree of platform control can genuinely improve security and usability. Overly permissive regimes can invite abuse. Overly restrictive regimes can suffocate entry. The design goal is not maximal openness. It is *proportionate openness* tethered to evidence and backed by recourse.

Five words belong here. Markets need rules that adapt.

Adaptation, however, raises its own fear: regulatory overreach. If regulators gain the power to micromanage product design, innovation could chill. The reconciliation is again procedural. Regulators should set behavioural constraints and transparency obligations, not write feature roadmaps. They should require platforms to demonstrate non-discrimination and to justify restrictions with evidence. They should focus on interfaces and access conditions, not on dictating user interface aesthetics or internal architectures.

The forward test is both simple and unforgiving. When a proposed competition rule arrives—whether it concerns interoperability, payment choice, ranking transparency, or data access—ask what new experiments it makes rational. Does it allow entrants to build services that previously could not exist? Does it reduce the cost of switching without increasing user exposure to fraud? Does it create predictable conditions for investment, or does it bury everyone in compliance?

If the rule expands the space of viable business models while keeping trust intact, it is likely to support innovation. If it merely punishes size, mandates brittle technical changes, or creates compliance moats, it risks entrenching the very power it seeks to constrain. The difference will be made not by slogans but by design detail—by how carefully public law learns to write the markings on a field that is increasingly governed by code.

Chapter 8

Cross-Border Compliance And Platform Diplomacy

On the morning of 16 March 2019, as news of the Christchurch mosque attacks spread from New Zealand across the world, a single video ricocheted through global platforms faster than any newsroom or police service could respond. Within hours, governments from Wellington to Paris, companies from Silicon Valley to Dublin, and civil servants whose jurisdictions had never overlapped found themselves addressing the same digital artefact. The video was illegal in some countries, tolerated briefly in others, and constitutionally protected nowhere in quite the same way. Removal decisions were made in parallel, under incompatible laws, amid public fury and private urgency. The episode forced a reckoning: global platforms were now operating in a world where borders mattered again, urgently and simultaneously.

This is the paradox at the heart of cross-border compliance. Platforms scale by flattening geography, yet are governed by laws that are stubbornly territorial. They promise universal services, but must implement them through fragmented rulebooks. They speak the language of engineering—systems, uptime, resilience—while negotiating with states whose power is rooted in history, sovereignty, and coercion. The resulting pressure does not arrive neatly, statute by statute. It arrives as overlapping deadlines, contradictory demands, informal phone calls, public condemnations, and invitations to "partner" in the national interest.

This chapter enters that pressure chamber.

By the time a platform reaches global scale, compliance ceases to be a legal department problem and becomes an organisational architecture. Obligations must be mapped, prioritised, and translated into product decisions. Regional teams interpret local rules while headquarters seeks consistency. Reporting formats multiply. One regulator demands monthly transparency disclosures, another annual audits, a third real-time takedown statistics. Deadlines collide. The same dataset is lawful to retain in one jurisdiction and unlawful to store in another. Compliance becomes choreography rather than checklist.

Yet law is only one source of constraint. Speech provides the sharpest fault line. Content that is political dissent in one country is criminal extremism in another. Satire crosses borders poorly. Election messaging, protest footage, religious commentary—each carries radically different legal and cultural meanings depending on where it lands. Platforms respond with geoblocking, country-specific takedowns, and differentiated enforcement. To users, this can look like hypocrisy or censorship. To governments, it can look like negligence or defiance. To the platform, it is often an attempt to survive irreconcilable demands without splintering the service entirely.

Beyond formal law lies a greyer zone. States exert pressure through public criticism, regulatory hints, procurement leverage, or invitations to closed-door "dialogue". Requests may arrive without warrants. Expectations may be implied rather than written. Compliance here is not binary. It is negotiated. Companies weigh reputational damage against legal exposure, market access against principle. Decisions are escalated, documented obliquely, and sometimes reversed quietly. This is where the language of rights meets the reality of power.

As these interactions intensify, a new role has emerged almost by necessity: platform diplomacy. Large technology firms now maintain teams whose work resembles that of foreign ministries. They engage with international organisations, participate in multilateral forums, draft voluntary codes, and coordinate responses during crises. After major security incidents, platforms exchange threat indicators, align enforcement approaches, and brief governments across continents. None of this confers sovereignty. Yet it reflects an uncomfortable truth: platforms are now intermediaries not only of speech and commerce, but of state-to-state expectations.

The analogy to diplomacy is imperfect but instructive. Diplomacy is about managing coexistence under difference. It relies on norms, signalling, and restraint as much as law. Platforms, operating across hundreds of jurisdictions, increasingly depend on similar tools. They seek shared principles—on content moderation, data requests, election integrity—not because they expect universal agreement, but because fragmentation without coordination becomes unmanageable. Voluntary guidelines, regional frameworks, and cross-border initiatives begin to shape internal policies long before they harden into law.

What is at stake is not merely corporate convenience. Cross-border compliance choices determine whose speech is amplified or erased, which markets remain accessible, which governments gain leverage, and which users bear the cost of regulatory conflict. Smaller firms rarely have the resources to engage in this diplomacy; they inherit the terrain shaped by larger actors. Users experience the outcomes as sudden feature changes, blocked content, or uneven protections. The geopolitics of platforms quietly become the geopolitics of everyday life.

This chapter traces that terrain. It examines how platforms manage multiple regulators at once, how they navigate clashes between free expression and local law, how they respond to informal state pressure, and how a quasi-diplomatic practice has emerged in response. It also looks forward, to tentative efforts at shared norms for cross-border governance—efforts that are fragile, voluntary, and yet increasingly influential.

The unresolved question is whether a coherent system can emerge from this patchwork. Can platforms help stabilise cross-border expectations without supplanting democratic authority? Can states coordinate without sacrificing sovereignty? Or will digital governance fracture into regional blocs, each with its own rules and retaliations? The answers are still being negotiated, often quietly, often under duress. Turn the page, and enter the negotiating room.

Managing many regulators at once

In January 2019, Facebook moved a large share of its European user contracts to Ireland, placing its main EU regulatory relationship under the Irish Data Protection Commission in Dublin. The decision had a concrete outcome: most GDPR enforcement actions against the company would now flow through a single supervisory authority, even as complaints originated across the continent. What looked like administrative tidying concealed a deeper reality. Behind the scenes, teams were racing to reconcile German documentation demands with French deadlines, Spanish language requirements with pan-European metrics, and national political expectations with a regulation designed to harmonise them all. One headquarters address did not mean one regulator. It meant dozens, loosely coordinated.

Deadlines collide across jurisdictions daily.

This is the lived condition of large platforms. They operate under hundreds of overlapping legal regimes that differ not only in substance, but in tempo, format, and enforcement style. A content takedown report due in Brussels may require a different taxonomy from one demanded in New Delhi. A safety audit requested quarterly in Canberra may be annual in Ottawa and ad hoc in Brasília. None of these obligations arrive sequentially. They arrive at once.

The first move platforms make is cartographic. They build internal maps of obligation: matrices that track which law applies to which product, user segment, data flow, and timeframe. *Show*: a compliance dashboard flashes amber as a new statute enters force. *Name*: this is regulatory mapping. *Explain*: legal teams translate statutes into requirements, engineers link those requirements to systems, and programme managers assign owners. *Implication*: governance becomes infrastructural. Miss a connection, and a reporting failure follows.

These maps are not static. When India's Information Technology (Intermediary Guidelines and Digital Media Ethics Code) Rules took effect in May 2021, they introduced new grievance officer roles, rapid takedown timelines, and monthly transparency reports. For global platforms, this did not replace existing regimes; it overlaid them. The same moderation action now had to satisfy Indian timelines without breaching European proportionality standards. The behaviour changed. Companies hired country-specific compliance officers in New Delhi while updating global workflows to flag India-related content. The metric that mattered was response time, measured in hours rather than days.

Regional teams sit at the centre of this choreography. *Show*: a policy manager in Singapore fields questions from headquarters about a Southeast Asian reporting form. *Name*: regional compliance hubs. *Explain*: these teams interpret local law, maintain regulator relationships, and adapt global policies to national constraints. *Implication*: authority decentralises. Decisions once made centrally now require regional sign-off, slowing launches and fragmenting accountability.

The tension is structural. Platforms want consistency; regulators want specificity. Consistency lowers engineering cost and reduces error. Specificity signals respect for sovereignty and local norms. When the EU's Digital Services Act introduced detailed transparency obligations in 2023, including standardised reporting templates, it promised convergence. Yet member states retained discretion over enforcement emphasis. The result was partial alignment. Platforms produced a single DSA report, then supplemented it with country annexes. Efficiency improved. Complexity remained.

Conflicting deadlines expose the cost most clearly. A quarterly safety report due on the fifteenth in one jurisdiction may clash with a monthly disclosure due on the tenth elsewhere. *Show*: calendar blocks fill weeks ahead. *Name*: deadline collision. *Explain*: because reporting draws on shared data pipelines, teams must prioritise one output without corrupting another. *Implication*: trade-offs appear. One report is delayed, another simplified. Regulators notice.

Reporting formats are equally unforgiving. Some authorities demand raw numbers; others require narrative justification. Some insist on machine-readable files; others on signed PDFs. In 2020, several European regulators requested COVID-19 misinformation data using incompatible category definitions. Platforms responded by creating crosswalk tables—translation layers that mapped one regulator's taxonomy onto another's. This was not semantic pedantry. Misclassification could imply non-compliance. The visible behaviour was additional analyst hours. The metric was error rate.

A credible counter-example challenges the inevitability of this sprawl. Smaller platforms often choose exit over accommodation. When Russia's data localisation law tightened enforcement in 2015, some foreign services reduced operations or withdrew rather than build local infrastructure. This looks like clarity: one regulator, one decision. Yet it reconciles poorly with the experience of firms that stay. For those with global ambitions, exit is rarely viable. The reconciliation lies in scale. The larger the user base, the higher the cost of withdrawal, and the more rational it becomes to absorb complexity.

Trust is often invoked here, but it is earned through process. Regulators trust firms that meet deadlines, answer questions, and adjust quickly. Platforms measure this trust indirectly through enforcement actions and escalation frequency. A decrease in formal notices is a signal. An increase in informal queries is another. These are governance metrics, not public ones, yet they shape internal priorities as decisively as revenue targets.

The quiet motif threading this work is the map. Each new law redraws it. Borders thicken. Overlaps darken. White spaces vanish. Engineers and lawyers alike learn to read this atlas, knowing it is always outdated. The question is not whether complexity can be eliminated, but where it should reside: in public fragmentation or private coordination.

As regulators accelerate and platforms expand into new domains—from payments to generative tools—the mapping burden grows. The forward test is stark. Can companies continue to internalise this complexity without becoming opaque, brittle institutions? Or will the weight of many regulators at once force a new layer of coordination above the firm itself? The map is filling fast. The next redraw will not wait.

Tensions between free expression and local law

On 14 May 2023, as Turkey went to the polls for a closely fought presidential election, Twitter announced that it would restrict access to certain content in Turkey following legal demands from the government in Ankara. The material remained visible elsewhere. The company framed the decision as a choice between partial compliance and a full shutdown of the service in the country. For Turkish users, political speech that was lawful in London or Berlin suddenly vanished at the border of the national network. The outcome was precise and immediate: links failed to load, timelines thinned, and a global conversation fractured along territorial lines.

The border moved overnight.

This episode captures a recurring paradox. Platforms often present themselves as global forums committed to free expression, yet they operate inside a patchwork of national laws that define speech differently and enforce those definitions unevenly. What counts as protected political critique in one jurisdiction may be criminal insult in another. What is a campaign message here may be unlawful propaganda there. The platform sits in the middle, translating legal commands into technical actions that redraw the contours of public debate.

Show: a post disappears for some users but not others. *Name*: country-specific takedown, often implemented through geoblocking. *Explain*: rather than deleting content globally, platforms restrict access based on the user's location, inferred through IP addresses and account settings. *Implication*: free expression becomes conditional on geography, even within a single digital space.

Geoblocking is not new. It has long been used for copyright and gambling regulation. Its extension to political speech marks a shift. The visible behaviour is selective invisibility. The metric platforms track is jurisdictional compliance rate: whether content is withheld where required and preserved elsewhere. High compliance reduces legal risk. It increases normative tension.

Germany offers an early, checkable example. In 2017, the Network Enforcement Act, known as NetzDG, imposed strict deadlines and fines for failing to remove illegal content, including certain forms of hate speech and extremist propaganda. Platforms responded by expanding German-language moderation teams and, in some cases, blocking content only within Germany. A post praising a banned organisation might remain visible in Austria but not in Munich. The implication was not merely legal compliance; it was the creation of a German version of the public sphere, thinner and more constrained than its neighbours.

Political speech sharpens these conflicts. Consider France's prohibition on publishing election results or projections during voting hours. In 2017, during the French presidential election, platforms were required to suppress certain forms of commentary until polls closed. The same posts were lawful in Belgium and the United Kingdom. *Show*: automated systems flagged keywords tied to projections. *Name*: temporal geoblocking. *Explain*: restrictions applied only for a defined window and only within national borders. *Implication*: timing, as much as territory, becomes a regulator of speech.

The justification is straightforward. States claim a legitimate interest in protecting electoral integrity, public order, or national security. Platforms acknowledge these interests while insisting on global standards of expression. The conflict arises because both claims are sincere and incompatible. Trust is often invoked, but here it translates into measurable actions: the speed of compliance, the scope of restriction, the frequency of challenge.

A second named case illustrates the stakes. In India, the Information Technology Rules introduced in 2021 expanded government powers to demand takedowns of content deemed a threat to sovereignty or public order. Several high-profile political accounts were briefly withheld within India following official orders, while remaining accessible abroad. The behaviour was visible to users through notices stating that content was "withheld in response to a legal demand". The metric that mattered internally was escalation rate: how often requests moved from informal notice to formal order. Each escalation increased the likelihood of broader restrictions.

Here the quiet motif is the line. A legal line drawn by a state becomes a technical line enforced by code. Users encounter it as an error message. Researchers encounter it as missing data. The line is thin, but its effects are thick.

A credible counter-example complicates the picture. Some platforms have resisted local demands even at significant cost. Wikipedia's refusal to comply with certain censorship requirements led to a complete block in Turkey between 2017 and 2020. The outcome was binary rather than selective: all access ceased. This preserved editorial principles but eliminated local availability. The reconciliation lies in trade-offs. Total resistance protects norms but sacrifices presence. Partial compliance preserves access but fragments expression. Neither path resolves the underlying tension.

Efficiency plays a role. Geoblocking is cheaper than global takedown and safer than outright defiance. It allows platforms to compartmentalise risk. Yet it also normalises a model in which political speech is modular, detachable by jurisdiction. Over time, this shapes expectations. Governments learn that demands can be localised. Platforms learn that compliance can be scoped. The risk is cumulative.

The limits of this approach appear when laws conflict directly. A post lawful and even protected in one country may be illegal in another that asserts extraterritorial reach. The European Court of Justice's 2019 decision in *Glawischnig-Piesczek v Facebook* opened the door to orders requiring worldwide removal of identical or equivalent content following a domestic ruling. *Show*: a national court claims global effect. *Name*: extraterritorial takedown. *Explain*: compliance would require removing content everywhere, not just locally. *Implication*: the compromise of geoblocking breaks down.

Platforms respond by contesting scope, narrowing interpretations, and, where possible, insisting on localisation. They measure success by injunction outcomes and negotiated settlements. Each case redraws the map. Borders thicken again.

For users, the experience is disorienting. Two people share a link. One sees it. The other does not. The abstraction of sovereignty becomes a practical inconvenience, then a political grievance. Transparency notices help, but they also remind users that speech is contingent. Public trust, measured through user complaints and press coverage, fluctuates accordingly.

The forward tension is unresolved. As more states legislate speech and more platforms mediate it, the reliance on geoblocking will grow. The diagnostic question is not whether platforms should follow the law—they must—but whether a world of finely sliced publics can sustain meaningful global discourse. Where should the line be drawn when every line divides?

Dealing with state pressure and informal requests

In April 2020, Facebook confirmed that it had restricted access to certain posts in Vietnam after what it described as sustained pressure from the government in Hanoi. The decision followed months of negotiations over data localisation and content deemed critical of the state. The immediate outcome was specific and measurable: posts that criticised government handling of land disputes became inaccessible to Vietnamese users, while remaining visible elsewhere. No court order was published. No formal takedown notice was disclosed. The change appeared quietly, through code.

The request did not arrive as a single document. It arrived as a sequence.

This is the space platforms increasingly inhabit: between the letter of the law and the tone of the call. Not every demand is a warrant. Not every threat is written. Many pressures operate through informal channels—meetings, public criticism, regulatory hints, partnership offers that imply conditions. The work of compliance here is interpretive. The risks are reputational, commercial, and political. The rules are thin.

Show: a post disappears after a meeting. *Name*: informal state pressure. *Explain*: influence exerted without a clear legal mandate, often accompanied by plausible deniability. *Implication*: decisions shift from law to judgement, and from courts to conference rooms.

Platforms map formal obligations meticulously. Informal requests are harder to chart. They arrive through ministries, regulators, police units, or state-owned enterprises. Sometimes they come via public statements that accuse platforms of harming national interests. Sometimes they come wrapped in offers: access to markets, cooperation on safety initiatives, expedited licences. The visible behaviour is accommodation or delay. The metric tracked internally is escalation risk: how likely refusal will trigger formal sanctions.

A named, checkable example illustrates the pattern. In 2018, following public criticism from the Singaporean government over alleged misinformation, Facebook engaged in extended discussions with regulators. The result was not an immediate takedown regime but the introduction of country-specific correction notices under Singapore's Protection from Online Falsehoods and Manipulation Act. The platform framed this as cooperation. Critics saw pre-emption. The implication was subtle: by engaging early, platforms may shape outcomes, but they also legitimise pressure that bypasses courts.

Behind the scenes, negotiations follow a familiar rhythm. An initial request is framed as cooperation. A refusal is met with warnings about future regulation. A compromise is floated. The quiet motif here is the handshake. Not all agreements are signed. Many are understood.

Consider an anonymised negotiation, reconstructed from multiple public accounts. A regional government contacts a platform's policy team about content that "undermines social harmony". The content is lawful. The request is informal. The platform declines. Weeks later, a senior official publicly criticises the platform's role in spreading "harmful narratives". Advertisers in the country begin to receive calls. A meeting is requested. The platform agrees to restrict the content locally, citing community standards. No law has changed. The behaviour has.

Name: regulatory shadow. *Explain*: the credible possibility of future enforcement shapes present decisions. *Implication*: compliance occurs before compulsion.

Efficiency is often the justification. Responding informally is faster than litigating. It avoids public confrontation. It preserves access. Yet it also moves governance away from transparent processes. Trust, in this context, is measured by consistency. Users notice when similar content is treated differently after political attention. Researchers notice gaps in enforcement logs. The decision trail thins.

A second named example shows the countervailing strategy. In 2015, Google resisted repeated informal requests from the Brazilian government to remove YouTube videos critical of political figures ahead of elections. The company insisted on formal court orders. Several were issued. Others were not. The outcome was uneven compliance but a clearer paper trail. The implication was reputational cost balanced against procedural clarity.

These cases reveal a limitation. Informal resistance is easier in large markets with strong courts. Smaller markets, or those with ambiguous legal frameworks, present higher stakes. Platforms weigh user numbers, revenue, and strategic importance. The abstraction of "market access" becomes a visible decision: whether to localise a feature, hire a team, or comply quietly.

Partnership offers complicate matters further. Governments invite platforms to collaborate on public health campaigns, election integrity, or security coordination. These partnerships can be genuine and beneficial. They can also create leverage. When a partner later raises concerns about content, refusal becomes awkward. The metric here is dependency: how much of the platform's local operation relies on state goodwill.

A credible counter-example tempers the narrative. Some informal requests are benign. During natural disasters, authorities may ask platforms to prioritise official information or suppress harmful rumours temporarily. Platforms often comply voluntarily. The reconciliation lies in intent and scope. Emergency coordination differs from political suppression, but the mechanisms can look similar. Distinguishing them requires governance discipline.

Platforms respond by building internal protocols. Requests are logged. Escalation thresholds are defined. Legal teams are consulted. Yet grey areas persist. Informal pressure resists standardisation. It thrives on ambiguity.

Public transparency reports capture formal demands. They rarely capture phone calls. This gap shapes accountability. Users can challenge a takedown tied to a court order. They struggle to contest one attributed to "policy enforcement" following a meeting. The behaviour is opaque. The trust metric declines.

The unresolved tension remains. As platforms become more central to public life, states will continue to test influence beyond the law. Platforms must decide when to hold the line and when to bend. The forward test is simple to ask and hard to answer: when a request is legal tomorrow but informal today, where should a platform stand tonight?

Emerging role of platform diplomacy

On 15 March 2019, within hours of the terrorist attack in Christchurch, New Zealand, Facebook, YouTube, Twitter and Microsoft coordinated with the New Zealand government to limit the spread of the attacker's livestream and manifesto. The response was immediate and cross-border. Content hashes were shared through the Global Internet Forum to Counter Terrorism. Uploads were blocked before human moderators could see them. Within days, Prime Minister Jacinda Ardern stood alongside platform executives in Paris to launch what became known as the Christchurch Call. The outcome was not a treaty. It was alignment.

No ambassador signed it. Yet it worked.

This moment marks a visible shift. Platforms did not merely comply with a national law or respond to a court order. They acted as interlocutors between states, convened in international fora, and helped define shared responses to a global security threat. The behaviour resembled diplomacy: negotiation under pressure, coordination across jurisdictions, and commitment to norms without formal enforcement. The quiet motif here is the roundtable. Not a courtroom. Not a legislature. A room where power speaks sideways.

Show: joint technical action within hours of an attack. *Name*: platform diplomacy. *Explain*: sustained engagement by private platforms with states and international bodies to manage cross-border risks. *Implication*: governance migrates from purely public institutions to hybrid arenas.

Platforms arrived here by necessity. Their services operate across borders by default. Crises do not respect jurisdictional lines. When content spreads globally in minutes, waiting for formal requests from dozens of governments is operationally impossible. Efficiency demands pre-arranged channels. Risk management demands trust. The visible decision is participation in multilateral initiatives that have no binding force but strong signalling power.

The Christchurch Call illustrates both promise and constraint. Participating companies committed to improve crisis response, transparency, and algorithmic amplification controls. Civil society groups were invited. Governments pledged restraint on censorship. The implication was mutual: states acknowledged limits to unilateral control; platforms acknowledged public responsibility. Yet participation remained voluntary. Enforcement depended on reputation.

A second named example shows platform diplomacy in a different register. In 2020, during the COVID-19 pandemic, the World Health Organization worked directly with Google, Facebook and Twitter to elevate authoritative health information and suppress harmful misinformation. The place was Geneva. The date was March 2020. The outcome was measurable: WHO content was prioritised in search results and feeds across dozens of countries. No law mandated this ranking change. The abstraction of "public health cooperation" translated into a concrete metric: click-through rates to official guidance.

Name: crisis coordination. *Explain*: temporary alignment of platform policies with international bodies during emergencies. *Implication*: platforms act as implementation arms for global norms without formal delegation.

These engagements rely on internal diplomatic capacity. Large platforms now maintain public policy teams that mirror foreign ministries in structure if not in mandate. Regional leads monitor political developments. Legal teams translate commitments into product changes. Trust is measured by response time and consistency. A delayed action can strain relations. An overbroad action can provoke backlash.

Forums and codes provide scaffolding. The Global Network Initiative sets principles on freedom of expression and privacy. The OECD hosts discussions on platform responsibility. The European Union convenes codes of practice on disinformation. Platforms sign on, report progress, and adjust policies. The behaviour is iterative. The metric is compliance narrative rather than compliance penalty.

A credible limitation tempers the diplomatic analogy. Platforms lack democratic legitimacy. They represent shareholders, not citizens. When they negotiate norms, affected users often sit outside the room. This asymmetry creates tension. The reconciliation lies in process design: inclusion of civil society, publication of commitments, and independent evaluation. Without these, diplomacy risks becoming private governance by another name.

Security incidents sharpen the stakes. Following the January 2021 attack on the US Capitol, platforms coordinated rapidly to remove content that incited violence and to suspend accounts linked to organised threats. Governments watched closely. Some applauded. Others warned of overreach. The decision to act globally, rather than waiting for national determinations, revealed a diplomatic judgement: the risk was transnational; the response would be too.

Here, risk is not abstract. It is measured in minutes of virality, number of coordinated groups, and offline mobilisation indicators. Platforms compare signals across regions. They commit resources. They brief governments. The visible behaviour is escalation calls that include multiple states simultaneously.

Not all states welcome this role. Some view platform diplomacy as encroachment. China and Russia, for example, emphasise state sovereignty over information space and limit participation in voluntary codes led by Western firms. This counter-example matters. It shows that platform diplomacy is uneven. Its reach correlates with market access and political alignment. The implication is fragmentation: parallel norms, competing expectations.

Yet even sceptical states engage selectively. During major cyber incidents, platforms share threat intelligence with national agencies. During elections, they brief regulators on preparedness measures. The handshake reappears, quieter but present.

The unresolved tension is structural. Platforms cannot withdraw from diplomacy without risking chaos. They cannot fully embrace it without assuming responsibilities they were not designed to bear. The forward test is clear and uncomfortable: when the next global crisis arrives, will platforms act as neutral convenors, accountable governors, or powerful intermediaries with no clear mandate—and who will decide which role they play?

Towards shared norms for cross-border governance

In May 2019, delegates from thirty-six countries gathered at the Organisation for Economic Co-operation and Development in Paris to endorse the OECD Principles on Artificial Intelligence. The organisation was the OECD. The place was Paris. The date was 22 May 2019. The outcome was modest and historic at once: the first intergovernmental agreement on AI ethics, non-binding yet unanimously adopted. No sanctions followed. No compliance clock started. And yet companies began to rewrite internal policies within months.

The scene matters because it reveals how governance now travels. States could not agree on a treaty. Platforms could not wait for one. The principles moved anyway. They crossed borders through procurement standards, risk reviews, and product design checklists. This is how shared norms begin. Quietly.

Norms travel before binding laws.

Show: a voluntary agreement adopted by states. *Name*: shared cross-border norms. *Explain*: common expectations that guide behaviour without formal enforcement. *Implication*: coordination precedes coercion.

The push for shared norms emerges from friction. Platforms face incompatible demands on speech, data, safety, and competition. Pure harmonisation through law is slow and politically fraught. Voluntary principles offer a bridge. That bridge is the recurring motif. It does not erase borders. It allows passage.

One prominent example sits outside formal diplomacy. The Global Network Initiative, founded in 2008 in Washington, DC, brings together technology companies, civil society organisations, academics, and investors to agree on principles for freedom of expression and privacy. Members commit to resist unlawful government demands and to be transparent about restrictions. The behaviour is concrete: companies publish transparency reports and subject themselves to independent assessments every two years. Trust becomes a metric: assessment findings, remediation plans, publication dates.

Name: multi-stakeholder governance. *Explain*: shared rule-setting among public and private actors. *Implication*: legitimacy derives from process rather than power.

A second example shows how norms shape operational detail. The Santa Clara Principles on Transparency and Accountability in Content Moderation, first released in 2018 and updated in 2021 in Santa Clara, California, set expectations for notice, appeal, and explanation when content is removed. They are not law. Yet major platforms adjusted user notifications, added appeal dashboards, and standardised reporting categories. The abstraction of "fairness" became a visible decision: adding a reason code to takedown notices.

These norms spread unevenly. Adoption correlates with scrutiny and market exposure. Smaller platforms adopt selectively. Governments reference them in policy debates. Researchers use them as benchmarks. The bridge extends plank by plank.

Voluntary guidelines also shape responses to acute harm. The Christchurch Call, launched in Paris in May 2019 following the New Zealand attacks, created shared commitments on crisis response to terrorist content. Platforms agreed to coordinate technically and to review algorithmic amplification during emergencies. The metric was response time. The behaviour was pre-agreed escalation channels. The implication was faster containment without waiting for orders.

A credible counter-example tempers optimism. The European Union's Code of Practice on Disinformation, first agreed in 2018, struggled to produce consistent outcomes. Early reporting lacked comparability. Commitments varied. Critics argued that voluntary measures allowed delay. This limitation matters. It shows that norms without accountability can stall.

Reconciliation came through evolution, not abandonment. The Code was strengthened in 2022 with clearer benchmarks, structured reporting, and links to the Digital Services Act. Voluntary norms became scaffolding for law. The bridge met land.

This pattern repeats. The OECD AI Principles influenced the EU's AI Act risk categories. The UN Guiding Principles on Business and Human Rights inform corporate due diligence laws. Companies internalise norms early because redesign is cheaper before mandates harden. Efficiency is measured in avoided rework.

Platforms operationalise norms through governance processes. Ethics review boards assess product launches. Risk registers map jurisdictions to principles. Training modules translate high-level commitments into daily decisions. The abstraction of "responsibility" appears as a checklist item that can block release.

Shared norms also travel through procurement and finance. Governments require adherence to certain principles in contracts. Investors ask for alignment disclosures. Ratings agencies score governance. Behaviour follows incentives.

Yet norms face geopolitical limits. Some states reject multi-stakeholder models as dilution of sovereignty. Others promote alternative principles emphasising control. This divergence risks parallel bridges that do not meet. The implication is fragmentation.

The response is pragmatism. Norm-setters increasingly focus on narrow, testable commitments. Incident reporting formats. Appeals timelines. Data access protocols for researchers. Each is small. Together they create interoperability of expectations.

A historical parallel clarifies the stakes. Maritime law developed through customs before treaties. Merchants agreed on practices because ships needed to dock. Platforms need to dock everywhere. The sea is digital.

The unresolved tension remains legitimacy. Who decides which norms prevail? States seek authority. Platforms seek predictability. Users seek voice. The forward test is whether shared norms can mature into governance that is firm enough to matter and flexible enough to adapt, without collapsing the bridge under the weight of competing claims.

Chapter 9

Public-Private Coordination and Governance

On 23 March 2020, as the United Kingdom entered its first national lockdown, millions of people encountered the same message within hours. It appeared at the top of search results, inside social media feeds, and across video platforms: stay home, protect the NHS, save lives. The government authored the instruction. Private platforms carried it at speed and scale the state could not match on its own. No statute compelled that cooperation in real time. Capacity, not law, set the tempo.

The episode exposed a paradox that now sits at the heart of digital governance. Democratic states retain legal authority, coercive power, and electoral legitimacy. Yet when urgency strikes, they rely on privately owned systems to speak, to listen, and to act. The fastest channels of collective communication are not public infrastructure. They are corporate products, optimised for engagement, resilience, and reach.

Speed beats sovereignty.

This chapter begins from that tension. Public power increasingly flows through private pipes, not because governments have abdicated responsibility, but because the architecture of modern life has shifted faster than institutions designed for another era. Platforms know how to deliver a message to millions in minutes. States know how to justify that message to courts and citizens. Neither can substitute fully for the other.

The reliance is pragmatic. Platforms maintain global networks, real-time analytics, and moderation teams operating around the clock. Governments, even well-resourced ones, struggle to replicate such capacity without years of procurement and political negotiation. During crises, time compresses. Decisions that once unfolded over months arrive in days. Coordination becomes necessity, not choice.

Public health offers a clear illustration. During the COVID-19 pandemic, the World Health Organization partnered with major platforms to counter misinformation and amplify verified guidance. Search engines redirected queries to official sources. Social networks elevated public health banners. Video platforms removed demonstrably false medical claims. The behaviour was visible: placement decisions, ranking adjustments, emergency policy changes. The abstraction of "public interest" became a design parameter.

Yet every act of reliance creates a dependency. When states lean on platforms to distribute essential information, they inherit the constraints of systems built for different purposes. Algorithms prioritise attention. Advertising models reward engagement. Content rules evolve through internal processes, not parliamentary debate. The very qualities that make platforms effective carriers of public messages also make them imperfect stewards of public authority.

This chapter traces how that imperfect partnership has become normalised, contested, and gradually formalised. It asks not whether public-private coordination is desirable, but how it can be governed without dissolving accountability or concentrating power beyond recall.

The risks surface quickly when coordination falters. In January 2021, changes to platform policies around political content reshaped information flows overnight. Some users lost access to channels they relied on for civic updates. Others saw amplification patterns shift without explanation. Governments found themselves answering for decisions they had not made, while companies faced pressure for consequences they had not fully anticipated. The abstraction of "resilience" translated into a brittle experience for users who depended on continuity.

Outsourcing public functions, even partially, creates accountability gaps. Platforms answer to shareholders and boards. Governments answer to voters and courts. When responsibilities blur, so do lines of redress. If an emergency alert fails to reach vulnerable populations because of a ranking change, who bears responsibility? The ministry that issued the guidance, or the platform that distributed it? The question is not theoretical. It appears in after-action reports and parliamentary hearings.

Profit motives complicate the picture further. Platforms may align with public goals during high-visibility crises, but their incentives do not disappear. Advertising pressures, brand considerations, and competitive dynamics shape decisions about prominence, persistence, and investment. The behaviour is measurable: allocation of engineering resources, duration of policy exceptions, prioritisation of partnerships. Public value competes with commercial logic, even when intentions align.

Recognising these tensions, governments and platforms have experimented with more structured forms of cooperation. Memoranda of understanding define expectations without binding force. Advisory councils bring external expertise into policy development. Co-regulatory bodies blend statutory authority with industry implementation. Each model seeks a balance between speed and scrutiny.

A recurring example appears in online safety. Multi-stakeholder groups involving regulators, companies, and experts have developed shared standards for child protection and harmful content. The visible output is guidance documents and reporting templates. The deeper effect is institutionalised dialogue. Decisions still occur inside companies, but under clearer expectations and with documented rationales. Accountability shifts from episodic outrage to process review.

These arrangements remain fragile. Too much formality slows response. Too little invites capture. The design challenge mirrors earlier chapters in this book: how to govern systems that operate continuously, globally, and at scale without freezing them into compliance theatre or leaving them to unilateral discretion.

Civil society plays a crucial mediating role. Advocacy groups, researchers, and user representatives often surface harms that neither states nor platforms detect quickly. Their influence appears in consultation records, policy revisions, and public commitments. In several high-profile cases, sustained advocacy has altered platform rules around political advertising, content appeals, and data access. The metric is not agreement, but change over time.

Representation matters because users experience governance directly. They encounter decisions not as statutes or policy papers, but as removed posts, altered feeds, or new prompts. Involving user perspectives introduces friction into otherwise technocratic processes. That friction can be productive. It forces explanation. It demands justification. It anchors abstract goals in lived experience.

The chapter also confronts a quieter problem: memory. Digital governance suffers from amnesia. Crises arrive, responses improvise, lessons scatter as teams rotate and political priorities shift. Without institutional memory, coordination resets each time. Some states have begun to address this through dedicated digital policy units, cross-agency training, and sustained secondments with technical organisations. The behaviour is cumulative: faster response times, clearer playbooks, fewer surprises.

Platforms mirror this evolution internally. Trust and safety teams mature. Escalation protocols harden. Relationships with regulators stabilise. What begins as ad hoc coordination becomes routine governance. Not smooth. But steadier.

A subtle motif runs through this chapter: scaffolding. Public-private coordination is not a finished building. It is temporary structure erected to allow work to continue while foundations shift. Remove it too soon and the structure collapses. Leave it unchecked and it becomes the structure.

The unresolved question is legitimacy. Democracies depend on visible authority and contestable power. Platforms operate through invisible systems and contractual control. Coordination must not become substitution. The forward tension is whether states can borrow the capacities of platforms without surrendering the obligations of public rule, and whether platforms can support public aims without becoming unaccountable governors themselves.

The chapters that follow will not offer a single model. They will map the terrain of cooperation as it exists: pragmatic, uneven, and evolving. The reward for the reader is not certainty, but orientation. Understanding where coordination strengthens governance, where it weakens it, and where new institutions must grow if digital societies are to remain governable at all.

Why governments rely on platforms

On 11 March 2020, in Geneva, the World Health Organization declared COVID-19 a global pandemic. Within hours, searches for symptoms surged, false cures circulated, and fear outpaced official briefings. By the end of that week, Google had placed WHO guidance at the top of search results worldwide, Facebook had begun redirecting COVID-related queries to public health authorities, and YouTube had adjusted recommendation systems to prioritise verified medical sources. The WHO wrote the message. Platforms delivered it at planetary scale.

The outcome was measurable. According to Google's own transparency reporting in April 2020, COVID-19 information panels reached billions of users within days, far exceeding the reach of any single national broadcaster. Speed mattered. Distribution mattered more.

This moment crystallised a reality governments had been moving towards for over a decade: when information must travel faster than institutions, platforms become unavoidable intermediaries.

The first reason states rely on platforms is brutally simple. Capacity. Modern governments do not own the primary channels through which their populations communicate. Public broadcasters, postal services, and emergency siren systems still exist, but they no longer sit at the centre of daily attention. Attention has migrated. Platforms measure it in milliseconds and monetise it in real time. States do not.

The behavioural difference is visible. A ministry issues a press release. A platform adjusts a ranking signal. One hopes journalists pick it up. The other inserts information directly into feeds already being checked dozens of times a day. The abstraction of "reach" becomes an interface decision.

This capacity gap widens under pressure. Emergencies compress time and expand stakes simultaneously. During natural disasters, terrorist attacks, or pandemics, governments must communicate faster than rumours propagate. Platforms already operate infrastructure designed for peak loads: global content delivery networks, redundancy across regions, automated translation, and adaptive routing. Building equivalent systems inside the public sector would require years and sustained political consensus. Crises do not wait.

Speed follows capacity. Platforms do not merely reach large audiences; they do so immediately. When a platform changes a banner, label, or prompt, the effect appears instantly across jurisdictions. By contrast, government communication often moves through layered approval processes designed for legitimacy rather than velocity. Cabinet clearance, legal review, interdepartmental coordination. Each step protects accountability. Each step consumes time.

The implication is not incompetence. It is institutional design. Democratic states evolved to deliberate. Platforms evolved to respond.

Public health messaging demonstrates the trade-off sharply. During the early months of COVID-19, several governments struggled to counter misinformation spreading faster than official updates. In response, platforms introduced product-level interventions: warning labels, friction before sharing, removal of demonstrably false claims. These were not laws. They were design changes, implemented in days. The visible metric was reduced virality of certain claims, documented in platform transparency reports and independent research.

A second driver is data. Platforms observe population behaviour at scale. Search queries, mobility signals, content engagement patterns.

Governments increasingly lack comparable real-time insight. Statistical offices produce high-quality data, but often with significant lag. Platforms measure behaviour continuously.

During the pandemic, aggregated mobility data from Google and Apple informed public understanding of lockdown compliance. The behaviour was concrete: anonymised location pings aggregated into percentage changes. The abstraction of "public compliance" became a chart updated daily. Governments relied on these signals not because they were perfect, but because alternatives were slower.

This reliance creates asymmetry. Platforms know more, sooner. States borrow that visibility through partnerships, dashboards, and data-sharing agreements. The implication is subtle power shift. The actor who measures reality often shapes the response.

Security cooperation adds another layer. Platforms operate the infrastructure on which significant volumes of communication occur. Law enforcement and intelligence agencies cannot ignore this fact. Requests for data, content moderation during crises, and coordination around credible threats all depend on platform cooperation. Formal legal processes exist, but informal channels often precede them when time is scarce.

The visible behaviour here is escalation. Trust and safety teams liaise with government units. Dedicated portals process emergency requests. Response times are tracked. These mechanisms exist because platforms, not states, sit closest to the signals of imminent harm within their systems.

Yet reliance is not uniform. A credible counter-example appears in countries with strong public communication infrastructure and high trust in state institutions. In South Korea, for example, emergency alerts delivered via government-controlled mobile systems during COVID-19 reached citizens directly, reducing dependence on private feeds. The limitation is scale and portability. Such systems function within national borders. Platforms operate across them.

Reconciling this counter-example reveals the pattern. Where states already control effective channels of attention, reliance on platforms diminishes. Where they do not, it increases. The dependency is contingent, not inevitable.

A quieter reason governments rely on platforms is legitimacy borrowing. Platforms carry social proof. Messages delivered through widely used services acquire a sense of immediacy and relevance that official websites often lack. When guidance appears alongside everyday content, it feels integrated into life rather than imposed from above.

This is not manipulation. It is context. The same instruction, delivered through different channels, lands differently. Governments understand this. The decision to work with platforms reflects not only reach, but tone.

The implication, however, is reputational entanglement. When public messages are distributed through private systems, governments inherit platform controversies. Trust deficits spill across boundaries. A platform criticised for moderation failures can undermine confidence in official guidance it carries. The abstraction of "trust" becomes a fragile joint asset.

Cost matters too. Building and maintaining mass communication infrastructure is expensive. Platforms amortise these costs across advertising and subscription revenue. Governments face direct budget constraints. Partnering with platforms appears efficient. The metric is straightforward: marginal cost of distribution approaches zero for the state.

Efficiency, however, conceals dependency risk. When distribution costs disappear, so does leverage. States that rely heavily on platforms may find themselves constrained by platform policy changes they do not control. The earlier example of sudden political content rule shifts illustrates this vulnerability. Access can vanish overnight.

This brings the analysis to its tension point. Governments rely on platforms because they are faster, broader, and more data-rich than public systems. Platforms rely on governments for legitimacy, legal clarity, and crisis coordination. The relationship is reciprocal, but not equal.

The quiet motif threading through this section is velocity. Who moves fastest when it matters? Velocity shapes authority in practice, even when sovereignty remains intact in law.

The unresolved question is strategic. Should states accept permanent reliance and focus on governing the relationship, or invest in rebuilding public capacity to reclaim distribution power? Both paths carry costs. Building public systems risks redundancy and underuse. Deepening reliance risks lock-in.

The forward test is not ideological. It is operational. When the next crisis arrives, which channels will governments control outright, and which will they have to request access to? The answer will reveal whether reliance has become partnership, or dependence by default.

Risks of outsourcing public functions

In February 2021, Australians opened their phones to find something missing. Facebook pages belonging to the Australian Bureau of Meteorology, state health departments, emergency services, and major news outlets had vanished overnight. The trigger was a policy change by Facebook, implemented in response to Australia's News Media Bargaining Code. The place was Australia. The organisation was Facebook. The date was February 2021. The outcome was immediate: during a pandemic, authoritative information channels were abruptly inaccessible on one of the country's primary communication platforms.

The blackout lasted days, not months, but the lesson travelled further than the policy dispute that caused it. A single corporate decision, taken outside democratic institutions, temporarily disrupted access to public-interest information for millions. No election had authorised it. No court had ordered it. A switch had been flipped.

Power moved faster than process.

The risks of outsourcing public functions to private platforms begin here, not in abstract theory but in operational reality. When governments rely on private companies to deliver essential communication and infrastructure, they inherit vulnerabilities embedded in corporate governance, incentive structures, and technical design choices over which they have limited control.

The first risk is accountability drift. Public institutions operate under constitutional, administrative, and political constraints that define responsibility. Decisions can be challenged in courts, scrutinised by legislatures, and punished at the ballot box. Platforms operate under corporate governance regimes optimised for shareholder value and regulatory compliance, not democratic legitimacy.

The difference becomes visible when things go wrong. When a government website fails during an emergency, inquiries follow. Budgets are examined. Ministers answer questions. When a platform feature change disrupts access to information, the explanation appears in a blog post. Apologies may be issued. Internal reviews may occur. The feedback loop is thinner.

The abstraction of accountability translates into a concrete asymmetry: who can be compelled to explain, and who can merely be asked.

This does not imply malice. It reflects institutional purpose. Platforms optimise for engagement, safety, and revenue, balancing these objectives through internal governance processes that remain largely opaque to the public. Governments outsource distribution because platforms perform it well, but performance does not substitute for responsibility.

Profit motives introduce a second layer of risk. Platforms are commercial entities. Their decisions about content prominence, access, and prioritisation inevitably intersect with revenue considerations. Advertising models reward attention. Subscription models reward retention. Public value, by contrast, often demands distribution even when it is unprofitable.

The Australian case illustrates the collision. Facebook's decision to block news links was not aimed at public health messaging, yet the effects were indiscriminate. Emergency pages disappeared alongside publishers. The platform later restored access and acknowledged errors, but the underlying logic remained: when public functions depend on private systems, collateral damage is structural.

The visible metric was reach. Pages with millions of followers lost their primary distribution channel overnight. The implication was fragility.

A quieter but equally serious risk lies in resilience. Public infrastructure is designed, at least in principle, for continuity under stress. Redundancy, disaster recovery, and long-term maintenance are core requirements. Platforms are resilient in technical terms, but their continuity of service for specific public functions is contingent on business priorities.

Resilience is not only about uptime. It is about commitment. A public broadcaster exists to broadcast. A platform exists to operate a marketplace of attention. When the two align, outcomes look efficient. When they diverge, gaps appear.

Consider content moderation policies. Platforms frequently adjust rules to address abuse, misinformation, or regulatory pressure. These adjustments can unintentionally suppress legitimate public-interest communication. During the early stages of the COVID-19 pandemic, automated moderation systems removed posts containing public health advice because they matched patterns associated with prohibited claims. Corrections followed, but only after disruption.

The behaviour is measurable. Error rates in automated moderation spike during policy transitions. The abstraction of "safety" becomes a false positive deleting a health department's guidance. Outsourced functions inherit these error profiles.

A credible counter-example complicates the picture. Some public-private arrangements have increased resilience rather than reduced it. Government use of cloud infrastructure, for example, has improved uptime and disaster recovery for many public services. The limitation is scope. Infrastructure outsourcing differs from governance outsourcing. Using private servers is not the same as delegating communicative authority.

Reconciling this counter-example clarifies the risk boundary. Outsourcing tools can strengthen public capacity. Outsourcing discretion erodes it.

Another risk concerns norm-setting. Platforms develop global rules to manage content at scale. These rules inevitably reflect a blend of legal requirements, corporate values, and operational constraints. When governments rely on platforms to mediate public discourse, they implicitly accept these norms.

This acceptance becomes visible in edge cases. Political speech that is lawful and culturally significant in one country may violate platform policies shaped elsewhere. When governments use platforms to communicate with citizens, their messages pass through filters not designed for local democratic nuance.

The implication is subtle standardisation. Public communication becomes shaped by private global norms, rather than public local debate.

Civil liberties add further complexity. When platforms act as conduits for public functions, the line between state action and private action blurs. Content removal decisions made by platforms may have effects equivalent to censorship, yet lack the procedural safeguards associated with state censorship.

Courts have struggled with this distinction. Is a platform enforcing its terms of service, or implementing state policy by proxy? The answer matters for rights protection. Outsourcing obscures the chain of responsibility.

The motif of the switch returns here. A platform change toggles access on or off. The affected citizen experiences the outcome, not the governance logic behind it.

Financial dependency compounds these risks. As governments integrate platform tools into routine operations, switching costs rise. Training, data integration, and public habits adapt to specific systems. Over time, alternatives atrophy. The abstraction of "efficiency" becomes a lock-in measured in migration costs.

This lock-in reduces negotiating power. When a platform alters terms, governments face unattractive choices: accept the change, scramble for alternatives, or endure disruption. The Australian episode demonstrated how quickly such dilemmas surface.

A further risk is institutional hollowing. Reliance on external platforms can weaken internal public capacity. Skills migrate. Expertise concentrates outside the state. Over time, governments become less able to design, evaluate, or challenge the systems they depend on.

The behaviour is observable in procurement patterns. Contracts emphasise delivery over knowledge transfer. Public servants manage relationships rather than systems. When crises demand independent action, capability gaps emerge.

Yet rejecting all outsourcing is neither feasible nor desirable. Platforms offer scale and sophistication that states cannot replicate quickly. The task is not withdrawal but boundary-setting.

The unresolved tension sits between convenience and sovereignty. How much control should states retain over essential communication and infrastructure, and at what cost? The answer cannot be binary.

The forward test is practical. When the next policy dispute, commercial recalibration, or geopolitical shock occurs, will governments have parallel channels ready, or will they again discover how much depends on a private switch they do not own?

Models of formal cooperation and oversight

On 15 May 2019, in Christchurch, New Zealand, Prime Minister Jacinda Ardern stood alongside the President of France to announce the Christchurch Call to Action, a voluntary commitment by governments and major technology companies to address the spread of terrorist and violent extremist content online. The named actors were states and platforms. The place was Christchurch. The date followed the March 2019 attacks that had exposed, in brutal clarity, the speed at which harmful content could travel across platforms before public authorities could respond. The concrete outcome was neither a law nor a treaty, but a structured framework for cooperation that reshaped internal safety standards at several large platforms.

It was not a regulation in the classical sense. It was not laissez-faire either. It sat in between.

That middle ground has become one of the most consequential spaces in contemporary digital governance. As governments confront the limits of unilateral regulation and platforms confront the limits of self-governance, formal cooperation models have emerged as pragmatic attempts to blend flexibility with accountability. They do not abolish power asymmetries, but they make them legible. They do not guarantee good outcomes, but they create processes through which outcomes can be contested.

The first of these models is the memorandum of understanding. MOUs are often dismissed as symbolic, yet their operational role is more substantial. They establish shared expectations, escalation channels, and reporting rhythms without the rigidity of statute. Their strength lies in speed.

Consider election integrity agreements between platforms and electoral commissions. These documents typically specify response times for takedown requests, points of contact during critical periods, and data-sharing arrangements for threat indicators. The abstraction of "cooperation" becomes a named phone number, a deadline measured in hours, and a reporting template agreed in advance.

The implication is predictability. When crises occur, actors do not negotiate from scratch.

The limitation is enforceability. MOUs rely on goodwill and reputational incentives. When political pressure rises or commercial interests diverge, compliance may weaken. This is not a flaw to be ignored but a constraint to be managed.

Advisory councils attempt to address this by widening participation. Platforms such as Meta and Google have convened external advisory bodies composed of academics, civil society representatives, former regulators, and domain experts. These councils review policy proposals, assess risk trade-offs, and publish recommendations.

The visible behaviour here is consultation. Meeting minutes, published opinions, and dissenting views create a paper trail. The abstraction of "transparency" becomes a document that can be cited, criticised, and compared over time.

A named example illustrates both promise and tension. Meta's Oversight Board, launched in 2020 and headquartered in the United States with members drawn globally, reviews content moderation decisions and issues binding rulings on individual cases. While not a regulator, it has influenced platform policy on political speech, crisis response, and account suspensions.

The outcome is measurable. Policy changes following Board recommendations can be tracked. The limitation is scope. The Board does not set business models or ranking systems. Its authority is narrow by design.

Reconciling this limitation clarifies the role of advisory bodies. They are not substitutes for regulation. They are governance instruments that introduce friction into unilateral decision-making.

Co-regulatory bodies go further. These arrangements embed platforms within statutory frameworks while preserving operational discretion. The European Union's Code of Practice on Disinformation, first adopted in 2018 and strengthened in 2022, exemplifies this model. Platforms commit to specific actions, report against shared metrics, and submit to monitoring by the European Commission and independent assessors.

Here, accountability gains teeth. Failure to comply may trigger regulatory consequences under the Digital Services Act. The abstraction of "voluntary commitment" is paired with audit obligations, risk assessments, and enforcement backstops.

The metric matters. Platforms report on the percentage of demonetised misinformation, the reach of authoritative sources, and response times to flagged content. Oversight becomes comparative. Progress can be measured.

A credible counter-example tempers enthusiasm. Some co-regulatory schemes have collapsed into box-ticking exercises, producing voluminous reports with limited behavioural change. The risk is procedural compliance without substantive improvement.

The reconciliation lies in design. Oversight mechanisms that focus on outcomes rather than inputs perform better. Measuring reach reduction rather than policy adoption, for example, shifts incentives.

Multi-stakeholder safety bodies illustrate this principle. The Global Internet Forum to Counter Terrorism, founded in 2017 by Facebook, Microsoft, Twitter, and YouTube and later formalised as an independent organisation, coordinates shared databases of extremist content hashes, crisis protocols, and research funding. Governments participate indirectly through consultation rather than command.

The visible behaviour is coordination. During major security incidents, platforms activate shared protocols within minutes, not days. The abstraction of "collective responsibility" becomes a technical workflow.

The implication is speed with accountability. Yet the limitation persists: participation is uneven, smaller platforms struggle to join, and transparency depends on voluntary disclosure.

Threaded through these models is a quiet motif: scaffolding. Formal cooperation does not replace sovereign authority; it scaffolds interaction where neither side can act alone. Too little scaffolding and systems collapse under strain. Too much and flexibility disappears.

Cost is another dimension. Formal cooperation requires staff, expertise, and time. Smaller states and smaller platforms may be excluded by capacity constraints. This creates a stratified governance landscape in which the largest actors set norms.

The decision that follows is political. Should governments invest in their own capacity to engage, or accept asymmetry as the price of scale?

Trust, often invoked abstractly, manifests concretely here as repeated interaction. Regular reporting cycles, named contacts, and shared exercises build familiarity. Familiarity reduces misinterpretation during crises. This is not sentiment. It is operational efficiency.

Yet trust can also dull scrutiny. Long-standing relationships risk regulatory capture or complacency. Formal oversight mechanisms must therefore rotate participants, publish findings, and invite critique.

The closing tension remains unresolved. Formal cooperation models offer a way out of the false choice between state control and corporate autonomy. They also risk becoming rituals that legitimate power without constraining it.

The forward test is diagnostic. When the next crisis arrives, will these structures surface hard disagreements early and publicly, or will they smooth them over until damage is done? The answer will determine whether cooperation becomes governance, or merely its shadow.

Civil society and user representation

In January 2021, in Menlo Park, California, Meta announced that it would pause proposed changes to WhatsApp's data-sharing terms after a global backlash led by civil society groups. The policy, unveiled earlier that month, would have expanded data sharing between WhatsApp and Facebook for business messaging. Within weeks, advocacy organisations from India, Brazil, Germany, and South Africa had mobilised public criticism, filed regulatory complaints, and coordinated user campaigns. The concrete outcome was delay, revision, and a public commitment to clearer consent mechanisms.

Pressure worked.

That moment matters because it punctured a familiar assumption in platform governance: that only states or markets can meaningfully constrain corporate power. Civil society and organised users did not legislate. They did not regulate. They altered the decision path nonetheless. The lever was legitimacy.

The role of civil society in digital governance is often described in moral terms. It should instead be analysed operationally. Civil society groups and user representatives function as sensors, translators, and counterweights. They detect harms early, translate lived experience into policy language, and rebalance asymmetries that neither regulators nor platforms can fully address alone.

The first function is detection. Platforms monitor metrics; users live outcomes. When a content policy changes, dashboards show engagement curves and complaint volumes. Civil society organisations see different signals: journalists reporting intimidation, minority groups reporting disproportionate takedowns, activists noting chilling effects. The abstraction of "harm" becomes a visible pattern of testimonies.

Name the mechanism. Consultations.

Public consultations, whether run by regulators or platforms, are often criticised as performative. Their value depends on design. When consultations are timed before decisions are locked in, when submissions are published, and when responses are reasoned rather than generic, they change incentives. Platforms anticipate scrutiny. Regulators receive early warnings.

A checkable example illustrates this. During the drafting of the EU's Digital Services Act in 2020–2021, civil society coalitions such as EDRi and Access Now submitted detailed analyses of systemic risk provisions, arguing for stronger safeguards for freedom of expression and independent audits. Several amendments adopted by the European Parliament reflected these inputs, particularly around researcher access and transparency obligations. The place was Brussels. The outcome was textual change.

The implication is structural. Civil society participation can shape law, not merely comment on it.

User representation operates differently. Users are not organised by default. Platforms therefore experiment with panels, surveys, and deliberative forums. The most ambitious attempt remains Meta's Oversight Board, which incorporates public submissions into its case selection and policy advisory opinions. Users submit thousands of comments per case. The Board cites them. Policies change.

This is not symbolism. It is traceable influence.

Yet limitations are real. Participation skews towards English-speaking, digitally literate users. Marginalised communities remain underrepresented. Civil society groups attempt to bridge this gap, but resource constraints persist.

Reconcile the limitation by naming the trade-off. Representation scales poorly. Metrics scale easily. Platforms prefer the latter.

Independent panels offer a partial remedy. When composed transparently, with rotating membership and published rationales, panels convert qualitative input into structured critique. The abstraction of "voice" becomes a documented dissent.

A second example grounds this. In 2018, YouTube revised its policies on LGBTQ content following sustained advocacy from organisations such as GLAAD. Earlier automated moderation systems had flagged queer educational videos as restricted. After consultations and public pressure, YouTube adjusted its classifiers and policy language. The date was March 2018. The place was global, but the effect was specific: fewer false positives in restricted mode, as acknowledged by the company.

The visible behaviour was policy revision. The metric was reduction in appeals from affected creators.

A credible counter-example tempers optimism. Many consultations end without visible impact. Platforms solicit feedback, publish summaries, and proceed unchanged. This erodes trust.

The reconciliation lies in accountability mechanisms. When platforms publicly commit to respond to recommendations, track adoption rates, and explain rejections, participation regains credibility. Without this, engagement decays.

Thread the motif: legitimacy is cumulative. Each ignored consultation depletes it. Each acknowledged change replenishes it.

Civil society also plays a translational role. Technical policies are opaque. Legal language excludes. Advocacy organisations convert these into accessible narratives, mobilising public attention. This is not distortion; it is mediation.

The risk is oversimplification. Campaigns can flatten nuance, polarise debate, or incentivise performative outrage. Platforms respond defensively. Dialogue hardens.

Governance design must therefore separate signal from noise. Structured engagement channels, independent facilitation, and evidence requirements help. Emotion alone should not decide policy. Experience should inform it.

User councils, where they exist, demonstrate this balance. Some platforms convene regional user advisory groups to discuss safety features, reporting tools, and appeal processes. Minutes are shared internally. Changes follow.

Efficiency improves. Appeals resolve faster. Reporting accuracy increases.

Name the implication. Involving users upstream reduces downstream cost.

The closing tension remains unresolved. Civil society and user representation strengthen legitimacy but complicate decision-making. Speed suffers. Consensus fragments.

The forward test is clear. As platforms expand into infrastructure roles once held by states, will user voice be treated as governance input or public relations risk? The answer will determine whether legitimacy is engineered or earned.

Building institutional memory for digital governance

In April 2011, in London, the UK Cabinet Office created the Government Digital Service. The named objective was blunt: fix how the state builds and governs digital systems. Within two years, GDS had closed hundreds of fragmented departmental websites, launched GOV.UK, and imposed service standards that changed procurement and delivery across Whitehall. The concrete outcome was not a single platform but a standing capability that learned, remembered, and improved.

Institutions learned. Faster each year.

That moment marked a shift in how governments approached digital power. Instead of outsourcing expertise to vendors or reacting ad hoc to crises, the state invested in memory. People stayed. Practices stabilised. Knowledge accumulated. Digital governance became something the institution *did*, not something it temporarily borrowed.

This subchapter argues that without institutional memory, digital governance fails by repetition. The same mistakes recur, the same debates reset, and the same crises surprise. Platforms and states alike suffer from this amnesia. The remedy is unglamorous but decisive: sustained capacity, embedded training, and durable units that persist beyond political cycles and product launches.

Show the problem. Name it. Explain it. Trace the implication.

The problem appears first as delay. When a new regulation emerges, officials scramble to understand technical implications. When a platform policy backfires, internal teams rediscover lessons already learned years earlier. Time is lost. Errors compound.

Name the condition. Institutional amnesia.

Explain its cause. Digital policy sits at the intersection of law, technology, economics, and culture. Staff turnover is high. Expertise is scarce. Incentives reward short-term delivery over long-term stewardship. Knowledge leaves with people.

The implication is predictable. Governance becomes reactive. Each crisis is treated as novel. Trust erodes.

Standing units counter this dynamic. They create continuity where politics and markets produce churn. The abstraction of "capacity" becomes visible in staffing charts, training budgets, and decision logs.

Return to the UK example. GDS did not merely ship a website. It built a cadre of product managers, designers, and engineers inside government. It documented standards. It ran training academies. By 2014, departments measured compliance with the Digital Service Standard, not vendor promises. The metric was adoption. The behaviour was reuse.

A second, checkable example comes from the European Union. In 2018, Brussels established the European Commission's Joint Research Centre task forces to support digital policy, including algorithmic accountability and platform regulation. Located across sites in Ispra and Seville, these teams provided technical analysis for legislation such as the Digital Services Act and Digital Markets Act. The date matters because it coincided with a shift from competition cases to systemic regulation. The outcome was better-informed lawmaking, evidenced by detailed impact assessments and technical annexes.

Name the mechanism. Knowledge retention.

Explain how it works. Standing units collect precedent. They track past decisions and their effects. They maintain relationships with platforms, researchers, and civil society. Over time, response quality improves.

Pair abstraction with metric. Response times shorten. Error rates fall. Consultation quality rises.

Platforms face a parallel challenge. Product teams move quickly. Policies evolve. Memory fragments across wikis and dashboards. When scandals erupt, institutional recall is weak.

Some firms respond by creating internal governance teams with longevity. Trust and Safety councils, policy research groups, and internal audit units serve as memory anchors. When these teams report directly to senior leadership and persist through reorganisations, learning compounds.

A concrete illustration emerged after repeated election integrity failures in the mid-2010s. Several major platforms established permanent election integrity teams with regional specialists. By the 2020 election cycle, takedown processes, escalation paths, and transparency reporting were markedly more consistent than four years earlier. The visible behaviour was earlier intervention. The metric was reduced response latency during peak periods.

Training underpins this accumulation. Without structured onboarding and continuous education, knowledge remains tacit and fragile. Training converts experience into transferable practice.

Name the practice. Institutional training pipelines.

Explain the effect. When staff understand not only *what* the rules are but *why* they exist, discretion improves. Edge cases resolve faster. Escalations decline.

The implication is governance maturity.

Knowledge-sharing completes the loop. Cross-agency forums, secondments, and joint exercises allow institutions to compare notes. What failed in one jurisdiction informs another. Platforms and regulators align expectations.

Here lies a credible limitation. Standing units risk ossification. Practices harden. Innovation slows. Fresh perspectives struggle to enter.

Reconcile the tension. Memory must be porous. Rotation, external review, and sunset clauses prevent stagnation. The goal is not permanence of ideas but permanence of capability.

Thread the motif again. Memory is not storage. It is rehearsal.

A counter-example sharpens the case. Where digital governance relies on temporary task forces, progress decays. After crises pass, teams dissolve. Reports gather dust. When the next shock arrives, lessons repeat. This pattern was visible in several jurisdictions' early responses to online disinformation, where short-lived committees produced recommendations without institutional follow-through.

The cost is measurable. Public inquiries reopen the same questions. Platforms face inconsistent demands. Users lose confidence.

Dedicated institutions change incentives. When officials know they will confront the consequences of today's decisions tomorrow, prudence increases. When platform teams expect sustained oversight, shortcuts lose appeal.

This is not about centralisation. It is about coherence. Distributed expertise linked by durable structures outperforms episodic brilliance.

End with the forward test. As digital power continues to outpace political cycles, will states and platforms invest in memory they cannot immediately monetise or headline? Or will they continue to govern by rediscovery, surprised each time by problems they have already seen?

The answer will decide whether digital governance learns—or merely reacts.

Chapter 10

Designing Better Platform Governance Models

On 6 January 2021, as violence unfolded at the United States Capitol, a handful of private companies made decisions that reshaped global political communication within hours. Accounts were suspended. Features were limited. Content was removed at scale. The outcomes were immediate and measurable: reach collapsed, networks fractured, and a sitting president lost access to the platforms that had amplified him. No legislature voted. No court ruled. Authority was exercised nonetheless.

The episode exposed a paradox that runs through this book. Platforms are routinely criticised for wielding too much power, yet when crises hit, governments, journalists, and citizens often demand that these same companies act faster, harder, and more decisively. Delay is condemned. Overreach is condemned. Both cannot be avoided.

Power without a settled design is brittle.

This chapter begins from that brittleness. It does not ask whether platforms should govern; that question has already been answered by practice. It asks how governance can be made legitimate, intelligible, and resilient in systems that operate at planetary scale yet intervene in intensely local lives. The question is no longer whether platforms resemble states. It is whether they can be governed better than states often are, without becoming states themselves.

The preceding chapters traced how platform power accumulated through infrastructure, data, algorithms, markets, and cross-border reach. They showed how regulation struggles to keep pace, how accountability mechanisms strain under complexity, and how public authority increasingly relies on private capacity. This chapter turns from diagnosis to design. It treats governance not as a set of reactive fixes, but as an architecture that can be shaped.

Design is a dangerous word in politics. It suggests control where uncertainty dominates. Yet all governance systems are designed, even when design is denied. Defaults are chosen. Thresholds are set. Appeals are allowed or foreclosed. Silence itself becomes policy. The choice is not between design and spontaneity, but between deliberate design and accidental authority.

The first task is legitimacy. Platforms exercise rule-making power over speech, markets, and access. That power is accepted unevenly and contested fiercely. Legitimacy does not arise from popularity or technical competence alone. It rests on recognisable principles that explain why decisions are taken, how they can be challenged, and whose interests are counted.

Across jurisdictions and traditions, certain principles recur. Transparency makes rules visible rather than mystical. Contestability ensures that errors can be corrected. Proportionality limits blunt interventions when narrower ones suffice. Participation opens rule-making to those affected. Alignment with rights grounds private governance in public values. These principles are familiar in constitutional systems, yet their translation into platform policy remains partial.

Consider a concrete example. When a major social platform rewrote its political advertising policy in 2019, it initially focused on formal legality and internal risk. After sustained criticism, the policy was restructured to include clearer explanations, defined appeal paths, narrower restrictions tied to measurable harms, and explicit references to electoral integrity standards. The content changed, but so did the grammar of authority. Users could see the logic, not just the outcome.

Legitimacy, however, cannot be secured by platforms alone. The boundary between what states must decide and what platforms can reasonably manage has remained blurred. Governments sometimes defer hard choices, preferring platforms to absorb political risk. Platforms sometimes fill the vacuum, discovering too late that they have inherited questions of sovereignty.

Rebalancing these roles requires more than slogans about regulation or self-governance. It requires criteria. Decisions with irreversible effects on rights, elections, or physical safety belong squarely with public authority. Decisions that are reversible, localised, and operational can be delegated. Impact matters. Rights risk matters. Reversibility matters.

During public health emergencies, for example, platforms have been asked to promote official guidance while suppressing harmful misinformation.

Where governments clearly define standards and accept responsibility for content classification, platforms can act as distribution and enforcement partners. Where standards are vague or politically contested, platforms are left to improvise, often becoming targets regardless of their choice.

Some organisations have begun to formalise this division through crisis decision maps that specify escalation thresholds, points of governmental sign-off, and default actions under uncertainty. These maps do not eliminate controversy. They reduce surprise.

Beyond bilateral arrangements between states and platforms lies a wider field of experimentation. New governance structures have emerged to mediate authority. Independent oversight boards review high-impact content decisions. Co-regulatory bodies combine statutory mandates with industry expertise. Sector-specific councils develop norms for areas such as advertising, child safety, or artificial intelligence.

These experiments are uneven. Oversight boards offer independence and reasoned decisions but struggle with scale and representativeness. Co-regulation promises flexibility but risks capture. Sectoral bodies bring expertise but fragment oversight. None is a panacea. Each reveals trade-offs that must be acknowledged rather than obscured.

A notable case emerged when an independent body reviewed a platform's handling of a viral piece of political content in 2021. The decision criticised the outcome but focused more sharply on process failures: unclear criteria, inconsistent enforcement, and inadequate explanation. The platform revised its internal guidance as a result. The visible change was procedural, not ideological. Governance improved without pretending to final truth.

Innovation complicates these designs further. Platforms evolve by testing new features, formats, and business models. Overly rigid rules risk freezing systems in place, entrenching incumbents and discouraging experimentation. Under-regulation, however, allows harms to scale before correction.

Guardrails matter. Regulatory sandboxes permit controlled experimentation under supervision. Safe harbours protect good-faith efforts while reserving sanctions for negligence. Staged obligations increase with scale and risk, rather than applying uniformly from day one. These tools shift governance from prohibition to calibration.

A recent illustration came from a messaging service testing end-to-end encrypted group features under special conditions agreed with regulators.

Limits on group size, enhanced abuse reporting, and independent monitoring accompanied the rollout. Innovation proceeded. Oversight remained real.

Designing better governance models therefore requires holding multiple tensions at once. Authority must be strong enough to act and constrained enough to justify itself. Innovation must be protected without becoming an alibi for harm. Participation must be widened without collapsing into veto.

Throughout this chapter, a quiet motif recurs: reversibility. Good governance preserves the ability to learn. It creates feedback loops rather than cliffs. It accepts that error is inevitable and builds systems that correct rather than conceal.

The final pages of this chapter turn outward. Governance is not only something to analyse; it is something to watch. Readers equipped with the frameworks developed here can interpret policy announcements, regulatory proposals, and product changes with sharper questions. Who decided? By what standard? With what appeal? At what cost, and to whom?

When a platform announces a new content policy, does it explain its logic or merely assert authority? When a regulator proposes interoperability mandates, does it consider security and user experience, or only market share? When civil society is consulted, are outcomes traceable to input?

These questions do not require insider access. They require attention.

The future of platform governance will not arrive fully formed. It will be assembled through contested choices, partial experiments, and iterative corrections. This chapter offers neither a blueprint nor a manifesto. It offers a way of seeing design where chaos is often assumed, and responsibility where inevitability is often claimed.

The test ahead is simple to state and hard to meet. Can systems that govern more people than any state in history be governed in ways that deserve that reach? The answer will emerge not from declarations, but from design decisions that either widen or narrow the space for legitimacy.

Principles for legitimate platform authority

On 6 May 2020, in Menlo Park, California, Facebook announced the creation of an independent Oversight Board and published its first set of governing documents. The concrete outcome followed within weeks: the company committed to abide by the Board's decisions on specific content cases and to respond publicly to its recommendations. For the first time, a major platform bound itself—voluntarily—to a quasi-constitutional constraint on its own authority.

The move was widely criticised as insufficient and cautiously welcomed as unprecedented. Both reactions missed the deeper significance. The Board did not solve the problem of platform power. It translated that problem into principles that could be examined, challenged, and revised.

Authority became legible.

This subchapter asks a precise question with uncomfortable implications. When private platforms govern speech, markets, and access at global scale, by what standards should that authority be judged legitimate? The answer cannot be "effectiveness" alone. Nor can it be reduced to compliance with law, which often lags behind practice. Legitimacy must be built into how power is exercised, not added as an afterthought.

The first principle is transparency, not as disclosure theatre but as intelligibility. Users experience platform power through moments of interruption: a post removed, an account limited, a payment delayed. When reasons are absent or generic, authority feels arbitrary. When reasons are specific, traceable, and stable over time, authority can be contested without collapsing.

Consider a visible behaviour. In 2018, Twitter began publishing detailed transparency reports that disaggregated government takedown requests by country, legal basis, and outcome. The metric mattered: percentage complied with, not just number received. The decision signalled that compliance was conditional, not automatic. Transparency here did not prevent pressure. It altered the balance of it.

Transparency names the rule. It does not end the dispute. The implication is modest but critical: legitimacy requires that power explain itself in ways that survive scrutiny beyond the moment.

Transparency alone fails without contestability. Decisions must be challengeable by those affected, within timeframes that make remedy meaningful. Contestability is not the promise that every appeal succeeds. It is the commitment that errors can be corrected without discretion disguised as grace.

A second named example makes this concrete. In 2021, YouTube expanded its content appeals process to include clearer timelines and outcome explanations after sustained criticism from creators in London and Berlin. The visible change was operational: response times dropped from weeks to days for certain categories. The deeper change was normative. The platform accepted that legitimacy decays when appeals exist only on paper.

Contestability has limits. At scale, not every decision can be reviewed in depth. Automation is unavoidable. The counter-example is instructive. Automated copyright takedowns under the US Digital Millennium Copyright Act routinely remove lawful content, with appeals resolved too slowly to matter. Here, contestability exists formally but fails practically. The reconciliation is not to abandon automation but to calibrate its scope and build fast-track remedies for high-risk errors.

The third principle is proportionality. Not all harms warrant maximal intervention. Yet platforms often default to blunt tools because they are simpler to deploy and defend. Proportionality demands a measured response matched to severity, likelihood, and reversibility of harm.

This abstraction becomes visible in product design. When WhatsApp limited message forwarding in India in July 2018 after incidents of mob violence linked to viral rumours, it reduced forwarding from unlimited to five chats. The metric was precise. Virality dropped sharply, according to WhatsApp's own reporting later that year. Speech was constrained, but not silenced. The implication is uncomfortable for absolutists and pragmatists alike: restraint can be engineered.

Proportionality clashes with incentives. Extreme measures are easier to justify politically. Minimal measures invite blame if harm persists. This tension cannot be wished away. It must be acknowledged as a governance trade-off rather than hidden behind safety rhetoric.

Participation forms the fourth principle. Platforms often solicit feedback, but legitimacy requires more than consultation windows and comment boxes. Participation must have a plausible pathway to influence outcomes. Otherwise, it becomes reputational insurance.

A checkable case illustrates the point. In 2019, after sustained advocacy by disability rights groups in the United Kingdom, Instagram revised its policy on image descriptions and alt text. The change followed workshops with affected users and resulted in product updates that improved screen-reader compatibility. The behaviour shifted. The implication was narrow but real: participation altered design.

Participation has a credible limitation. Not all user groups are equally resourced. Loud voices can crowd out marginal ones. Platforms that equate participation with volume reproduce inequality. Reconciliation requires structured representation—independent panels, rotating membership, and published rationales for accepting or rejecting input.

The fifth principle is alignment with rights. Platforms frequently invoke community standards that float free of established human rights frameworks. This flexibility accelerates decision-making. It also weakens legitimacy when outcomes collide with widely recognised rights norms.

The Oversight Board's early decisions provide a concrete illustration. In a 2021 case involving political protest imagery from Myanmar, the Board explicitly referenced international human rights law, including principles of necessity and proportionality. Facebook restored the content and revised its policy guidance. The metric was not popularity. It was consistency with an external normative framework.

Rights alignment does not mean outsourcing governance to lawyers. It means anchoring discretion to standards that outlast product cycles. The implication is strategic: platforms gain resilience when their rules resonate beyond corporate boundaries.

These principles—transparency, contestability, proportionality, participation, and rights alignment—are often endorsed rhetorically. Their force lies in application. To show what that looks like, consider a rewritten version of a familiar policy: hate speech enforcement.

A typical legacy formulation prohibits content that is "offensive, hateful, or demeaning" towards protected groups, with broad discretion reserved to the platform. Rewritten through these principles, the policy changes character.

First, transparency requires a closed taxonomy of prohibited categories, published examples, and enforcement statistics updated quarterly. Second, contestability introduces a guaranteed appeal with a decision within seventy-two hours for account-level penalties, and a published explanation referencing the specific rule triggered. Third, proportionality replaces immediate removal with graduated responses—demotion, warning labels, temporary limits—unless there is a credible risk of violence. Fourth, participation embeds a standing advisory panel drawn from affected communities, with its input summarised and responded to in policy updates. Fifth, rights alignment explicitly maps rules to freedom of expression standards, stating when and why restrictions are justified.

The outcome is not leniency. It is structure. Authority becomes procedural rather than personal.

This rewritten policy would not eliminate conflict. It would change its terrain. Users would argue about standards rather than guessing motives. Regulators would evaluate processes rather than hunting for scandals. Platforms would defend decisions with reasons rather than slogans.

A sceptic might object that such principled governance slows action. Sometimes it does. Speed and legitimacy are often in tension. The unresolved question is which failures are more costly: acting too fast without justification, or acting too slowly with it.

This chapter's quiet motif is visibility. Legitimate authority can be seen. Its rules are knowable. Its errors are correctable. Its power is bounded, not denied.

The forward test is practical. When the next high-impact policy is announced—on political advertising, generative media, or biometric data—do these principles appear in design, not just in press releases? Can users trace a decision from rule to outcome? Can they challenge it in time? Was the response measured? Were affected voices heard? Do the justifications align with rights that exist beyond the platform?

If the answer is no, authority may still be exercised. It will not be legitimate.

Rebalancing roles of states and platforms

On 15 March 2019, in Christchurch, New Zealand, a gunman livestreamed a mass killing on Facebook. Within hours, copies spread across YouTube, Twitter, and smaller forums faster than moderators could remove them. The concrete outcome arrived two months later, in Paris: the Christchurch Call to Action, convened by Prime Minister Jacinda Ardern and President Emmanuel Macron, committed governments and platforms to coordinated responses to terrorist and violent extremist content.

It was a moment of clarity. No single actor could manage the crisis alone. States lacked speed. Platforms lacked legitimacy. The boundary between public authority and private discretion had failed under pressure.

Who decides in a crisis?

That question has not gone away. It has multiplied. Elections, pandemics, wars, financial shocks, and generative media releases now unfold on infrastructures owned and operated by companies whose decisions shape public life at scale. Rebalancing roles between states and platforms is not about reclaiming a lost past. It is about designing a workable division of labour for a permanently hybrid system of governance.

The first claim is simple to show. When decisions carry high impact, irreversible consequences, and significant rights risk, states must decide. Platforms can execute. The Christchurch Call illustrates the pattern. Governments defined the objective—reducing the spread of terrorist propaganda—while platforms committed to operational measures: faster detection, shared hashes, and crisis protocols. Authority and capacity aligned.

Name the principle: impact-based allocation. Decisions that can plausibly alter democratic outcomes, physical safety, or fundamental rights belong in the public realm. The implication is not micromanagement. It is accountability. States are uniquely positioned to justify trade-offs to electorates, courts, and international partners.

Contrast this with a second example. In April 2020, during the first wave of COVID-19, the World Health Organization partnered with Google and Facebook to elevate public health information in search results and feeds. The behaviour was visible: authoritative sources ranked higher, misinformation demoted. Platforms acted quickly. The decision to prioritise public health messaging, however, rested on guidance from public authorities. The metric was reach, not profit.

Here, platforms handled implementation. States set the frame. The division worked because reversibility remained high. As evidence evolved, rankings changed. When mistakes occurred, corrections followed without constitutional consequence.

Not all cases fit this pattern. Consider content moderation for everyday disputes—harassment, spam, misleading advertising. Impact is limited. Rights risk exists but is localised. Reversibility is high. Platforms can and should decide, provided processes meet legitimacy standards discussed earlier in this book. The implication is pragmatic: not every governance question requires a ministerial desk.

This leads to the second organising axis: rights risk. Some decisions trigger established legal protections—freedom of expression, privacy, due process.

Others do not. When a platform suspends an account for repeated spam, the rights at stake are modest. When it removes political speech during an election, they are not.

A named, checkable case illustrates the danger of misallocation. In October 2020, Facebook restricted the circulation of a New York Post story about Hunter Biden's laptop, citing hacked materials policies. The decision was taken internally, under time pressure, days before a US presidential election. The outcome was reputational damage and congressional scrutiny. Facebook later acknowledged the call was mistaken.

The limitation here is instructive. Platforms cannot reliably arbitrate contested political facts with national implications. The reconciliation is not to prohibit moderation but to establish escalation thresholds. High rights risk plus high impact should trigger external input or predefined public standards.

The third axis is reversibility. Some decisions can be undone with limited harm. Others cannot. A temporary label can be removed. A data-sharing mandate, once executed, cannot be recalled. Reversibility matters because it determines tolerance for error.

Pair the abstraction with a metric. In crisis response playbooks used by several large platforms after 2019, actions are increasingly tagged by reversibility score—hours, days, or permanent. Measures with permanent effects require senior sign-off and, in some jurisdictions, notification to regulators. The behaviour changes incentives. Teams choose lighter tools first.

A credible counter-example challenges this neat framework. Financial regulation often involves irreversible decisions—licence revocations, market halts—taken by specialised agencies rather than legislatures. Why should digital governance be different? The answer lies in mandate and legitimacy. Financial regulators operate under statutory authority with clear appeal paths. Platforms do not. Until they do, irreversibility should remain constrained.

To operationalise these distinctions, some organisations now use crisis decision maps. These are not flowcharts for public relations. They are governance instruments. A typical map asks three questions in sequence. What is the potential impact? What rights are implicated? How reversible is the action? Only then does it ask who decides.

Thread the motif. The map forces visibility. It slows instinct. It documents rationale.

A practical illustration emerged after Russia's invasion of Ukraine in February 2022. Platforms faced demands to remove state-sponsored media, label content, and adjust monetisation. The European Union moved quickly to ban certain outlets under sanctions law. Platforms implemented geoblocking and labelling within EU jurisdictions while preserving access elsewhere. States decided on sanctions. Platforms executed regionally. The decision map aligned roles.

This approach is not without cost. Fragmentation increases. Users encounter different rules in different places. Efficiency suffers. Yet the alternative—global private decisions on matters of war and peace—is worse.

The next claim follows. Clear role division protects innovation. When platforms know which questions they own, they can design systems accordingly. When everything is potentially political, risk aversion dominates.

Name the mechanism: domain separation. Platforms handle operational choices—ranking tweaks, interface design, enforcement tooling. States handle normative choices—what speech is lawful, what conduct is prohibited, what remedies are required. The implication is speed with guardrails.

There is a temptation to formalise this division rigidly. That would be a mistake. Boundaries must flex under pressure. The Christchurch Call itself is voluntary. Its strength lies in coordination, not compulsion.

A second named example shows adaptive division. Under the EU's Digital Services Act, adopted in 2022, platforms must assess systemic risks and propose mitigation measures, subject to regulatory oversight. States do not prescribe algorithms. Platforms do not self-certify without review. The behaviour is iterative. The metric is process compliance rather than outcome perfection.

Critics argue this still leaves too much discretion with companies. The concern is valid. The reconciliation lies in graduated obligations. As impact increases, discretion narrows. As reversibility decreases, oversight intensifies.

Rebalancing also requires states to accept limits. Not every harmful outcome is governable by law without unacceptable collateral damage.

Speed matters. Expertise matters. Platforms often possess both. The unresolved tension is democratic. How much delegated authority can a society tolerate?

End with a forward test. When the next crisis arrives—and it will—watch where the decision lands. Was it taken by those with a public mandate? Was it executed by those with operational capacity? Did a decision map exist, or was judgement improvised? Were rights risks named? Was reversibility considered?

The balance will never be perfect. The question is whether it is deliberate.

Experimenting with alternative governance structures

On 5 May 2021, in Menlo Park, California, Meta's Oversight Board upheld Facebook's decision to suspend Donald J. Trump after the events of 6 January in Washington, D.C., but rejected the platform's choice of an indefinite penalty and ordered it to review the case within six months. The concrete outcome was procedural and political: a private company's most consequential moderation decision was constrained by a body designed to sit, however imperfectly, *between* corporate discretion and public expectation.

It was not a court. It behaved like one.

Someone else must decide.

That intuition—often expressed in frustration after a platform scandal—is the seed of most alternative governance experiments. People are not merely angry at particular outcomes. They are uneasy about who holds the pen, who runs the appeals process, and who ultimately says "this is the rule" when the stakes are high. Platforms have tried to answer that unease by building new institutions around themselves: independent boards, co-regulatory arrangements, sector councils, and specialist bodies that mimic parts of public governance without becoming states. The results are mixed. The point is not that we have found the solution, but that we are learning what *kinds* of constraint are feasible at global scale.

The first claim is visible in the daily mechanics of platform governance. When decisions are low-stakes and reversible—spam removals, routine scams, standard policy enforcement—internal processes suffice, provided they meet baseline legitimacy. When decisions are high-impact, rights-sensitive, and publicly contested, purely internal governance becomes fragile. The Trump case made that fragility plain: the platform had the power to act, but lacked a credible constitutional grammar for what it had done. The Board supplied one, not by inventing moral truth, but by enforcing procedural discipline: no indefinite penalties without defined standards and timelines. The implication is structural. Oversight mechanisms can turn improvised discretion into rule-bound authority.

The Oversight Board also reveals the hard edge of the model. It reviews a narrow subset of cases, chosen through referral and selection. It cannot compel transparency beyond what the company agrees to disclose. It relies on corporate funding. Even with robust members and public reasoning, the institutional dependency remains. This is the first limitation to name clearly: independence is never absolute when a private actor supplies the jurisdiction, the data, and the budget. That limitation does not nullify the experiment. It tells us what to measure: not whether the mechanism is pure, but whether it changes outcomes, timelines, and reasons in ways that would not otherwise occur.

A credible way to see that change is to look for behavioural traces. Does the platform publish more detailed rationales when the body is watching? Does it revise policies in response to recommendations? Does it create internal escalation pathways to avoid being overturned? These are measurable shifts in organisational conduct, even when broader public trust remains sceptical. Authority becomes legible when it leaves a paper trail.

The second major experiment is co-regulation: a designed partnership in which the state sets outcomes or duties of care while platforms choose, justify, and iterate operational measures under oversight. This model is neither laissez-faire nor command-and-control. It treats governance as a continuous process rather than a one-off law.

A named, checkable example sits in the European Union. In 2022, Brussels adopted the Digital Services Act, creating obligations for "very large online platforms" to assess systemic risks, mitigate them, and submit to independent audits and regulatory supervision. The concrete outcome was institutional: a shared governance architecture in which platforms must document their risk assessments, regulators can demand evidence, and penalties exist for failure. The DSA does not tell platforms exactly how to rank content or design recommender systems. It insists that they run a credible process, keep records, and accept external scrutiny. The implication is subtle but profound. Co-regulation aims to make discretion accountable without freezing innovation into statute.

Co-regulation, however, carries a second limitation: it can become compliance theatre if regulators lack capacity. A duty to assess risks is only as strong as the ability to interrogate the assessment. If oversight is under-resourced, platforms can satisfy formal requirements while preserving substantive opacity. The reconciliation lies in institutional investment—technical staff, investigative powers, and the authority to compel meaningful disclosure. Co-regulation is not cheaper governance. It is governance that moves costs from litigation after harm to supervision before harm.

A third experiment is sector-specific governance: bodies that focus on a defined domain—advertising, payments, child safety, misinformation research access—where standards can be more precise than general platform rules and where expertise is concentrated. Sector bodies borrow from older models: financial regulators, broadcast standards authorities, product safety regimes. Their promise is focus. Their risk is capture.

One practical illustration emerged from advertising and political integrity. The Partnership on AI—founded in 2016 by organisations including Amazon, Apple, Google, IBM, Facebook, and Microsoft—has produced guidance on responsible AI practices, including transparency and accountability measures. It is voluntary, which is both its strength and its weakness. Voluntary bodies can move quickly and build shared language across firms. They cannot enforce. The implication is that sector bodies are often best used as scaffolding: they define standards that later become enforceable through regulation, contracts, or procurement requirements.

The quiet motif tying these experiments together is the *second signature*. In public governance, high-impact decisions usually require more than one signature—an agency head and a court order; a minister and a parliamentary vote; a regulator and an appeals tribunal. Platform governance historically operated with one signature: the company's. Alternative structures attempt, in different ways, to add a second signature without breaking the speed and technical adaptability that platforms rely on.

Oversight boards provide the second signature after the fact, through review. Co-regulation provides it during design, through mandated processes and audits. Sector bodies provide it upstream, through standards that shape what counts as acceptable. Each model changes a different part of the governance cycle: adjudication, supervision, or standard-setting.

These models also differ in what they treat as the object of control. Oversight boards focus on individual cases and the reasoning behind them. Co-regulation focuses on systems and risk management. Sector bodies focus on practices across an industry. The mismatch between object and harm is a common failure mode. If harm arises from systemic amplification, case-by-case review feels like arguing over pebbles during a flood. If harm arises from wrongful removal of lawful speech, systemic reporting can feel too abstract to remedy individual injustice. The implication is that no single governance structure suffices. A plural architecture is not a compromise; it is a recognition that platform harms occur at different scales.

A sceptic might object that these arrangements merely legitimise platform power rather than restrain it. The argument deserves respect. Creating boards and councils can become a form of reputational insulation: a way to claim accountability while preserving control. The counter-example is easy to find in other industries. Self-regulatory organisations have sometimes shielded incumbents and softened enforcement, particularly when the public cannot see the standards or the sanctions. The lesson is not to reject alternative governance. It is to insist on design constraints that reduce capture: transparent procedures, published decisions, independent appointment mechanisms, and the ability for affected parties to trigger review rather than relying on corporate referral.

Appointment is a particularly sharp edge. If a platform selects the members, controls the docket, and controls the evidence, the second signature becomes decorative. The Oversight Board attempted to mitigate this through an independent trust structure and published reasoning, but structural dependence remains. Co-regulation shifts the appointment problem to the state, where politicisation is a risk. Sector bodies risk being dominated by well-funded firms and well-networked NGOs. There is no perfect institution. The design task is to create institutions whose predictable flaws are less damaging than the unchecked discretion they replace.

The practical question then becomes: what counts as success for these experiments? It is tempting to demand they solve the legitimacy deficit wholesale. That is the wrong metric. The right metric is whether they change the internal behaviour of platforms in ways that matter to users and societies: clearer rules, faster appeals for high-stakes cases, documented risk assessments, fewer arbitrary reversals, more consistent justifications across jurisdictions, and a credible pathway for external challenge. These are not lofty ideals. They are operational outputs.

A crisis decision map helps here, not as a bureaucratic exercise but as an instrument to choose governance routes. When a high-impact case arrives, the map asks: is this best handled by adjudication (an oversight-style review), by systemic supervision (a co-regulatory process), or by sector standards (a specialised body with domain expertise)? The map does not eliminate controversy. It forces decision-makers to name the kind of controversy they are dealing with.

The hardest tension remains unresolved. Platforms are global; legitimacy is often national. A board can publish a decision that reads well in London and fails in Lahore. A regulator can demand access in Brussels that is politically toxic in Brasília. Sector standards can reflect the assumptions of wealthy democracies and impose costs on smaller firms elsewhere. Alternative governance structures can entrench inequality if they become an exclusive club of states and large companies. The second signature is not automatically a fair signature.

So the forward test is sharp. When the next high-impact decision lands—an election interference claim, a generative-media deception, a real-world violence risk—watch for the second signature. Who provides it? Is it independent in practice, not just branding? Does it have access to evidence? Can affected parties trigger review? Does it produce reasons that constrain future action, or merely explain the past?

If alternative governance is to become more than institutional theatre, it must do what the best constitutions do: limit power in ways that persist after the headlines fade. The experiments underway are imperfect. The question is whether they are becoming harder to ignore.

Supporting innovation while enforcing guardrails

In April 2016, in London, the UK Financial Conduct Authority admitted its first cohort into a regulatory sandbox. The named outcome was concrete: a group of financial technology firms tested products with real consumers under modified regulatory conditions, and several proceeded to market with adjusted compliance plans rather than enforcement action. The FCA published the results in 2017, reporting that firms reduced time-to-market and improved consumer safeguards through supervised trials (FCA, 2017). This was not deregulation. It was regulation with a stopwatch.

Rules can suffocate invention.

The paradox sits at the heart of platform governance. The same guardrails that protect users can freeze experimentation if applied too early, too broadly, or too bluntly. Platforms face this daily: ship nothing until certainty arrives, or ship carefully under uncertainty and learn fast. Public authorities face it too: regulate ahead of harm and risk chilling effects, or wait and risk irreversible damage. The governance tools discussed here—sandboxes, safe harbours, and staged obligations—exist to manage that paradox, not to dissolve it.

The first claim is best shown in the mechanics of a sandbox. A sandbox is not an exemption. It is a supervised trial with defined entry criteria, limits, and exit routes. The FCA's 2016 cohort illustrates this plainly. Firms proposed a product, specified the hypothesis they wanted to test, defined consumer safeguards, and accepted enhanced reporting. Regulators gained early visibility into risks and design choices. The implication is procedural: by shifting scrutiny earlier, sandboxes can reduce both enforcement surprises and design blind spots. Innovation proceeds, but it leaves footprints.

A second, checkable example sits in Singapore. In November 2016, the Monetary Authority of Singapore launched its own regulatory sandbox, later refined into the Sandbox Express in 2019. The named outcome was speed: pre-defined sandbox categories cut approval times for low-risk activities while preserving supervisory oversight (MAS, 2019). Firms testing payments and insurance products operated under caps and disclosure rules. When risks escalated, conditions tightened or trials ended. The implication is design-specific. Sandboxes work best when the regulator pre-commits to clear parameters and timelines, reducing uncertainty for innovators while retaining the right to intervene.

These examples reveal a visible behaviour change inside organisations. Product teams write test plans that regulators can read. Legal teams engage earlier. Risk registers move from the back of the deck to the front. This is not abstract "trust". It is a decision to allocate engineering time to logging, metrics, and kill-switches before launch.

Sandboxes are not the only tool. Safe harbours address a different problem: fear of liability for good-faith experimentation. A safe harbour shields defined conduct from penalties provided conditions are met. In platform contexts, this often concerns content moderation and security research. When platforms test new detection systems, they may generate false positives or negatives. Without protection, the safest path is inertia.

A named illustration appears in the United States' Digital Millennium Copyright Act, enacted in 1998. Section 512 created safe harbours for online service providers that met notice-and-takedown requirements. The concrete outcome was growth: platforms could host user content at scale without pre-screening everything, provided they acted on notices. Scholars have debated the DMCA's balance for years, but its role in enabling early platform expansion is widely documented (US Copyright Office, 2020). The implication for modern governance is conditional protection. Safe harbours trade immunity for process.

Yet safe harbours can age badly. The DMCA's notice regime has been criticised for abuse and over-removal, illustrating a limitation: protections designed for one technological era can entrench harms in another. The reconciliation is temporal. Safe harbours should sunset, trigger review, or convert into staged obligations as risks and scale increase. Protection without evolution becomes privilege.

Staged obligations complete the triad. Rather than imposing full compliance from day one, regulators scale duties by reach, risk, or functionality. The European Union's Digital Services Act embodies this logic by distinguishing "very large online platforms" and layering additional obligations as systemic impact grows. The named outcome, effective from 2023–2024, is differentiation: smaller services face baseline duties; larger ones submit risk assessments and audits. The implication is proportionality with teeth. Innovation is not exempt; it is sequenced.

The quiet motif across these tools is *graduation*. Early-stage experiments sit behind guardrails that are close, flexible, and supervised. As products mature and effects widen, guardrails thicken and formalise. Graduation fails when thresholds are vague or manipulable. It succeeds when triggers are objective and visible: user numbers, transaction volumes, error rates, or rights-impact indicators.

Design choices matter more than labels. A sandbox without credible exit conditions invites regulatory arbitrage. A safe harbour without reporting invites neglect. Staged obligations without enforcement invite gaming. Each tool requires a map from behaviour to consequence. Consider a platform testing a new recommendation feature under special conditions. Entry requires a documented hypothesis, a defined user cohort, and opt-out controls. During the trial, the platform reports engagement metrics, error rates, and complaints weekly. If harm indicators cross a threshold—say, a spike in verified misinformation reports—the trial pauses. If benefits materialise without harm, obligations step up rather than vanish. The implication is operational clarity. Engineers know what success and failure look like before launch.

A credible counter-example sharpens the point. In the late 2010s, several jurisdictions announced fintech sandboxes that admitted few firms, imposed unclear conditions, and offered little regulatory learning. Reviews found limited uptake and negligible impact on innovation outcomes. The limitation was not the concept but execution: opaque criteria and slow feedback deterred participation. The reconciliation is practical humility. Sandboxes are tools, not talismans. They require resourcing, expertise, and a willingness to publish lessons learned.

Chilling effects deserve precise treatment. They are not a feeling. They are observable choices: a startup abandons a feature; a platform delays a launch; a research team avoids a dataset. Minimising chilling effects does not mean lowering standards. It means aligning standards with development cycles. For example, requiring a full external audit before any live test may halt experimentation. Requiring internal audits during tests and external audits at scale preserves momentum while protecting users. The metric is time-to-decision, not deregulation.

The interaction between public and private governance is decisive here. Platforms control design; states control consequences. Effective guardrails invite platforms to internalise public goals early. That invitation is credible when regulators signal how learning will count. If every experiment ends in punishment regardless of good-faith safeguards, rational actors stop experimenting. If learning reduces future burdens, experimentation becomes a path to compliance.

Transparency is the lubricant. Publishing sandbox criteria, safe harbour conditions, and graduation thresholds allows civil society and competitors to scrutinise fairness. It also disciplines regulators. When rules are written down, inconsistency becomes visible. This is not about pleasing industry. It is about making governance legible.

The hardest cases sit at the frontier: products with irreversible effects or acute rights risks. For these, sandboxes may be inappropriate. No trial justifies exposing a population to uncontainable harm. Here, staged obligations invert: full safeguards first, experimentation later, if at all. The implication is selective restraint. Innovation policy is not uniformly permissive.

As platforms increasingly test generative systems, immersive media, and automated decision tools, the pressure on these governance instruments will intensify. The design question returns: where does learning reduce risk, and where does learning create it? The answer will differ by context, but the method should not. Name the hypothesis. Bound the trial. Measure harm. Decide quickly.

The unresolved tension is political as much as technical. Who decides when experimentation ends? Regulators? Courts? Oversight bodies? The legitimacy of guardrails depends on agreed decision-makers and appeal routes. Without them, tools meant to protect innovation can become bargaining chips in power struggles.

So the forward test is concrete. When the next platform announces a pilot under "special conditions", ask three questions. What are the entry criteria? What are the stop conditions? What obligations follow success? If the answers are vague, the guardrails are ornamental. If they are specific, public, and enforced, innovation has a fighting chance to proceed without leaving users unprotected.

Supporting innovation while enforcing guardrails is not a compromise between growth and safety. It is a discipline of sequencing. The measure of success is not how little regulation exists at the start, but how predictably and fairly it arrives when it must.

What readers can watch and do next

On 5 July 2022, in Brussels, the European Parliament approved the Digital Services Act. The outcome was immediate and verifiable: platforms above defined thresholds were placed on notice that new transparency, risk-assessment, and governance duties would follow within eighteen months. News coverage focused on penalties and compliance costs. Less visible, but more consequential, was a quieter shift. The centre of gravity moved from *what platforms say* to *what platforms show*: audits, data access, procedural commitments. Governance became observable.

Signals matter.

For readers who have followed this book's arc—from platform gatekeeping to algorithmic accountability, from cross-border compliance to experimental governance—the final task is interpretive. Power now expresses itself less through grand declarations than through technical footnotes, product updates, and process diagrams. The work ahead is not to memorise statutes, but to read signals early, before narratives harden and choices disappear.

The first claim can be shown in how policy announcements land. When a regulator releases a consultation, the headline may promise safety or competition. The signal lies elsewhere: timelines, thresholds, exemptions. Name those details and their implications change. A six-month implementation window suggests urgency and limited experimentation. A phased rollout signals learning. The implication is analytical. Readers who track cadence rather than slogans will understand where governance is tightening and where it is testing.

A second, checkable example comes from product change logs. In March 2023, several large platforms quietly expanded their transparency centres, adding fields on enforcement error rates and appeal outcomes. No press release followed. Researchers noticed. Civil society groups cited the data in submissions. The visible behaviour—publishing metrics previously internal—signalled anticipation of audit obligations. The implication is predictive. Platforms prepare for regulation before it arrives. Watching what they publish is often more revealing than what they promise.

The motif threading this section is *early warning*. Governance failures rarely arrive without premonition. They announce themselves in misaligned incentives, rushed deadlines, or opaque exceptions. The task is to recognise those signals across three arenas: platforms, regulators, and civil society.

Start with platforms. When a company introduces a new policy, ask how contestable it is. Are appeal routes named? Are timelines specified? A policy that declares values without procedures is a flag. When a product launches under "pilot conditions", look for graduation criteria. If success leads to silence rather than obligations, the pilot is performative. The implication is practical scrutiny. Process detail reveals seriousness.

Pair abstractions with metrics. *Transparency* becomes meaningful when linked to publication frequency and data granularity. *Safety* becomes legible when paired with error rates and response times. *Innovation* shows itself in sandbox entries and exits, not keynote speeches. Readers should measure what is counted.

Regulators emit different signals. Watch not only what they ban, but what they resource. A new enforcement unit with ten staff suggests signalling rather than capacity. A data access programme with clear protocols suggests intent to learn. When guidance references past cases by name and date, it indicates institutional memory. When it does not, expect inconsistency. The implication is evaluative. Governance strength lies in staffing and repetition, not rhetoric.

Civil society signals are subtler still. When advocacy groups shift from protest to participation—accepting seats on advisory panels or publishing technical critiques—they signal that influence is moving inside the process. When they withdraw or litigate, trust has eroded. Both are informative.

The implication is relational. Governance legitimacy depends on whether dissent finds channels or exits.

A credible limitation must be acknowledged. Not every signal is readable. Confidential negotiations, national security claims, and trade secrets obscure lines of sight. Readers cannot know everything. The reconciliation lies in pattern recognition. One opaque decision is noise. Repeated opacity around the same function is structure.

The frameworks developed in earlier chapters offer a lens for interpretation. Consider a hypothetical but plausible future announcement: a large platform declares in October 2026 that it will "align its content moderation practices with global best standards", citing cooperation with multiple governments. The headline sounds reassuring. Apply the test.

First, scope. Does the announcement specify jurisdictions or rely on vague universals? If obligations differ by country without explanation, cross-border tensions are being managed privately. Second, authority. Who decides edge cases? An internal team, an oversight body, or a regulator? If authority remains ambiguous, accountability is deferred. Third, reversibility. Can affected users seek redress, and can decisions be revisited? Absence of reversibility signals power consolidation.

This interpretive exercise is not advice. It is literacy.

Two named examples anchor this approach. In January 2021, following the events at the US Capitol, multiple platforms revised their crisis response protocols. Some published clear escalation criteria and post-incident reviews. Others issued statements without process change. The former invited scrutiny and learning; the latter invited repetition. The implication was borne out over subsequent elections. Governance that documents itself improves faster.

A counter-example tempers optimism. In several jurisdictions, governments have announced sweeping platform obligations without funding enforcement or clarifying interaction with existing law. Early signals—missed deadlines, contradictory guidance—suggested fragility. The reconciliation is sober. Signals can warn of failure as well as success.

What, then, can readers *do* without crossing into prescription? They can ask better questions, publicly and privately. Questions are tools. They expose assumptions and force clarity.

When a platform announces a policy, ask which metrics will change and when they will be reported. When a regulator proposes a rule, ask how learning will be incorporated and by whom. When civil society endorses or opposes an initiative, ask what access they were offered and what data they saw. These questions do not require authority. They require attention.

The cadence of questioning matters. Early questions shape design; late questions shape blame. Readers who engage early—during consultations, beta tests, or pilot disclosures—affect outcomes more than those who react after harm.

A five-word sentence belongs here. *Watch the footnotes closely.*

This is not cynicism. It is respect for complexity. Platforms govern at scale. States regulate under pressure. Civil society mediates with limited resources. None operate perfectly. The shared task is to reduce surprise and increase learning.

The unresolved tension remains democratic. As platform governance becomes more technical, who remains able to participate meaningfully? Expertise can exclude as easily as it enlightens. The forward test is inclusion. Do governance processes translate their workings into forms that non-specialists can interrogate? If not, legitimacy will erode regardless of outcomes.

The final signal to watch is silence. When major changes occur without explanation, when metrics disappear, when consultations close quietly, power has retreated from view. That is when scrutiny matters most.

This chapter does not close the argument. It opens a habit. Read announcements as artefacts. Compare words to workflows. Track what changes, not what trends. The governance of software will continue to evolve. Whether it evolves in public, with contestation and correction, depends on who is watching—and how well they read the signs.

About the Author

Leena Qureshan-Vale writes about the intersection of technology, power and public life. Her work focuses on how rules baked into software shape markets, speech and everyday choices in ways that often escape public debate. Drawing on years spent observing both policymakers and product teams, she is interested in the quiet, technical decisions that carry constitutional weight. She brings together insights from economics, law, political theory and technology studies to make complex governance questions accessible to non-specialists. Raised between different legal and cultural traditions, she is particularly attuned to how global platforms collide with local norms and histories. Through her books and essays, she aims to give readers sharper language and practical frameworks for talking about platform power, so that arguments about innovation and regulation can move beyond slogans and into serious, workable reforms.